Families Coping
with Mental Illness

Families Coping

with **Mental Illness**

Stories from the US and Japan

Yuko Kawanishi

Routledge
Taylor & Francis Group
New York   London

Published in 2006 by
Routledge
Taylor & Francis Group
270 Madison Avenue
New York, NY 10016

Published in Great Britain by
Routledge
Taylor & Francis Group
2 Park Square
Milton Park, Abingdon
Oxon OX14 4RN

© 2006 by Taylor & Francis Group, LLC
Routledge is an imprint of Taylor & Francis Group

Printed in the United States of America on acid-free paper
10 9 8 7 6 5 4 3 2 1

International Standard Book Number-10: 0-415-95201-8 (Hardcover)
International Standard Book Number-13: 978-0-415-95201-9 (Hardcover)
Library of Congress Card Number 2005017053

Library of Congress Cataloging-in-Publication Data

Kawanishi, Yuko, 1957-
    Families coping with mental illness : stories in the U.S. and Japan / Yuko Kawanishi.
        p. cm.
    Includes bibliographical references and index.
    ISBN 0-415-95201-8 (hardbound)
    1. Mentally ill--United States--Family relationships--Case studies. 2. Mentally ill--Japan--Family relationships--Case studies. 3. Families of the mentally ill--United States--Case studies. 4. Families of the mentally ill--Japan--Case studies. I. Title.

RC455.4.F3K385 2005
362.2--dc22   2005017053

Taylor & Francis Group
is the Academic Division of Informa plc.

Visit the Taylor & Francis Web site at
http://www.taylorandfrancis.com

and the Routledge Web site at
http://www.routledge-ny.com

For my father

Contents

Acknowledgments

My deepest gratitude goes to all those American and Japanese families with mentally ill family members who participated in the interviews that form the basis for this book. Over the years I have been engaged in research for this book and other projects, I have necessarily dealt with deeply private information — the health records of family members as well as the participants' innermost thoughts and emotions. Although the participants and I, as a social science researcher, had reached agreement prior to the interviews with regard to confidentiality and respect for their right to refuse to answer certain questions, it was always nerve racking when the interview began. I would try, of course, to make the interviewees feel comfortable and safe enough to disclose their personal lives to me as an outsider. Many participants in this study had suffered from the burden of a family member's mental illness for a number of years, a situation many of them found hard, even close to impossible, to discuss. However, despite my initial concern, most of the people who agreed to be interviewed were candid and willing to be a part of this study. Interview sessions tended to be intense, and many tears were shed by the participants as they recalled their painful past and present. However, some participants from the United States and Japan were kind enough to say to me after the interviews that they had told me things they had never told even their closest friends, or that my questions inspired a lot of deep reflection about their own lives. All of the interview sessions were moving. It was a little frustrating when some individuals had difficulty expressing themselves in as articulate a manner as I had hoped. However, by the end of the session, I was always touched by their stories of how they had been coping with their loved ones' mental illnesses. In short, there was not a single case that did not deeply impress me and did not teach me something of value. I hope that as a result this book will convey much of what touched me so deeply. This book is for all those courageous and resilient individuals who took part, as much as it is for mental health professionals and others who are interested in the issue of the effects of mental illness on a patient's close family members.

I am extremely grateful to the people of Routledge who found the telling of these stories to be worthwhile. Thanks to Dr. George Zimmar, Dana Bliss, Lori Fredrickson, and Patricia Connolly for all their help and support.

A number of people helped me find participants and set up the interview sessions. In the United States, I am greatly indebted to the staff of Step Up on Second in Santa Monica, California, which provides excellent programs for psychiatric patients and their families. In particular, I would like to thank Ms. Susan Dempsay, who was executive director at the time. Not only did she introduce me to many other key people in the mental health community, but I learned a great deal from her experience and insight. Mr. Mitsuyo Akiyoshi of the Mental Health Association in Los Angeles County also assisted me early on. In Japan, the help and information I received from all staff members of Zankaren (National Federation of Families of the Mentally Ill) was invaluable. Mr. Akio Takayama, director of several family support groups in Tokyo, also enabled me to contact many other family groups and members.

I was able to pursue this research as a result of a grant from the Social Science Research Council in New York, and I am very grateful for their assistance.

Of course, without the support and encouragement of many of my close friends, I would not have been able to complete this project. Masahiro Togo was a lifesaver when I needed a proofreader for the initial draft of the manuscript before contacting the publisher. John Clammer was my advisor and moral support in the process of contacting a publisher. My dearest friends in Los Angeles, Harumi Ziegler, Takiko Morimoto, Noriko Kohashi, and Per Jogi, have all helped me to this day by providing logistical and emotional support that has enabled me to keep my life organized as I travel back and forth between Japan and the United States. And I thank all the other people who have directly and indirectly given me support all these years and enabled me to reach this stage of my life.

Introduction

This book is about the resilience of the human mind in the face of tragedy, and to illuminate this extraordinary strength, it uses personal and subjective accounts of how people experience and survive the difficulty of trying to help a mentally ill family member. The purpose of this book is to describe mental illness from the standpoint of family experience. Despite clinical and political progress in openly debating issues relating to mental disorders, attention is still focused mainly on the patient's treatment, and mental health professionals tend to relegate family members to adjunctive roles or sometimes even regard them as barriers to recovery.[1] One of the unique features of mental illness is that, unlike physical illness (which centers on the patient's bodily experience), mental illness is often expressed in the context of the patient's interactions with the environment and other human beings through language use, attitudes, and behaviors that range from eccentric to bizarre.[2] Therefore, mental illness is seldom a solely individual experience, but rather a phenomenon that extends beyond the sick person and involves others both in his or her close circle and beyond in the outside world of neighborhood, work, and school. The patient's symptoms can become the indirect, but very personal, experiences of those who interact with him or her. The mentally ill patient's significant others are most likely to be affected by the illness itself, and, in a way, this makes mental illness a contagious disease.

Patients' family members also suffer from the social stigma attached to mental disorders. The usual expectations of and understanding from society in the case of physical illness do not apply to mental illness. Usually, being seriously ill physically means that the person is temporarily exempt from social duties and obligations and is expected to focus on making a recovery. The sick person is not held responsible for the condition.[3] Together with medical treatment, the patient and the family can ask for and receive sympathy and understanding from those in their personal circle. In other words, society is supportive of the patient being taken care of both physically and emotionally. The patient is enabled to recover from the illness not only through medical treatment, but also through this crucial psychological support from his or her environment. However, due to a general lack of knowledge about mental illness, mentally ill patients and their families are often seen by the society as somehow responsible for the problem, and are also shunned out of fear. Despite the advances in medical technology that have produced biological evidence for mental illness, misconceptions about the cause of serious mental disorders still persist, not only in society but also among some mental health professionals. There is still a risk, even in the 21st century, that families will be implicitly blamed for the patient's illness. At a time when anxious family members need emotional support more than anything, they must often fight a lonely battle. The people who would normally come to the support of a family in distress keep their distance. Being the family of a mentally ill person clearly poses a double structure of suffering: they are not only victims of an illness that has worsened or destroyed their relationship with the patient, but also are victims of social stigma, prejudice, and misconceptions. The extreme social stress associated with mental illness sometimes causes people to postpone seeking necessary help for a family member. Thus the distress of the family in this situation can be complicated by and even hazardous to their own mental health.

This social and "contagious" nature of mental disorders, and the persistent social stigma that involves not only the patient but also the family, makes discussions that only focus on a patient-centered perspective seriously inadequate in understanding the entire picture of mental illness issues in our society. Unless attention is focused on the whole family's suffering and pain, and the effects of a family member's mental illness on the survival of both the mentally ill individual and on the family as a system, then only a part of the reality of mental illness has been addressed.

Most importantly, the book aims to describe exactly what family members have to struggle with and how they cope with this tragedy. Once a loved one has been hit with a serious mental disorder, the lives of those who love him or her will never be the same. Their lives will be shaken and often drastically changed by the event. There are times when they cannot help but feel that they are at the mercy of various external cultural and social forces, such as expectations about the role of families that in practical terms may seem impractical in the face of the onset of mental illness, and prejudice against mental illness. Nevertheless, human beings have a unique capacity to adapt, and we discover or create meanings out of the most dire life circumstances. In the face of major challenges, we take actions that lead not only to the improvement of the given circumstance but also to profound personal growth.

Another important aspect of families' experiences is social. Because the burden on families of the mentally ill often goes beyond a single family's capacity, appropriate intervention by social and administrative agencies as well as clinical professionals is also deemed crucial. Thus, whether the families like it or not, direct involvement with the social structure will be a critically needed and inescapable aspect of their lives. I hope this book will also suggest ways in which society can better assist and care for the mentally ill.

I conducted the research for this book in two countries, Japan and the United States. I felt that it would be interesting to look at the differences between these two societies. Both are highly advanced postindustrial societies at the same technological level and with similar economic, political, and educational systems. Family structures in the two societies are also similar: the majority of the population want to believe they belong to the middle class although the reality may be somewhat different, and the populations of both countries typically have nuclear families. However, having noted these similarities, at a more crucial level the two countries are quite different in culture, social values, norms, and family gender roles. It is these differences that affect the way in which each society and its families handle mental illness. Ironically, within the discussion about social policies on mental illness, the contrasting realities are being questioned in both Japan and the United States with regard to the issue of institutionalization.

Approximately 5 million people or 2.8% of adults are estimated to suffer from severe mental illness (including schizophrenia, manic depression, and major depression) in the United States,[4] and 2.2 million of these patients are reported to have schizophrenia.[5] According to a World Health Organization (WHO) study, about 1% of the populations across ten countries are affected by schizophrenia.[6] The substantial prevalence of mental illness is, not surprisingly, similar in Japan: 2.04 million people, or one in 60, are estimated to have serious mental illness including schizophrenia and other types of illness.[7] However, the circumstances surrounding the patients are quite different.

For example, in the United States, the deinstitutionalization process began in the 1960s. This was partly due to developments in pharmacology in the 1950s. In the 1970s, the issue of patients' rights became a major civil rights issue and this has since made it difficult to involuntarily hospitalize the mentally ill. Thus, the role of the primary caretaker was shifted from the institution to the family and community-based services. However, families were far from being prepared to accommodate the patient's life at home.[8] In fact, according to Torrey, the other side of this reality is that almost 90% of the people who would have been in hospitals 45 years ago are not in hospitals today.[9] Many of them manage to live successfully if medication and aftercare services are appropriately provided. However, it is also true that many of them have been left untreated outside the hospital and become homeless or end up in prison. It is estimated that as many as 135,000 people with schizophrenia are living in jails and prisons in the United States.[10] While various grassroots efforts to create support networks have been organized in response to the evolving situation, this move has resulted in increased stress on many families (increased physical, emotional, and financial burdens), and the institutional assistance to these families is considered inadequate.[11] The hasty and ill-prepared push for deinstitutionalization without establishing necessary resources in the communities has ended up building "a cradle for catastrophe."[12]

In Japan, on the other hand, hospitalization is still dominant. Outpatient treatment for the mentally ill has not been well developed.[13] Another outstanding characteristic of the Japanese psychiatric system is lengthy hospitalization. Today it is estimated that 330,000 people are hospitalized and more than half of them have been in the hospital for five years or longer. Furthermore, for 72,000 of them there is no medical reason for hospitalization. In other words, their conditions can be managed with medication and supportive therapy. This situation is referred to as "social hospitalization" because, although they are well enough to leave the hospital, there is a lack of facilities where the formerly institutionalized can live in a supportive environment in the community. The reason for this situation is twofold. The community is unwilling to accommodate the presence of the mentally ill, and mental hospitals in Japan, which are mostly private, need to keep their patients. The 1988 mental health law was intended to improve this situation and created programs and more intermediate facilities for mentally ill patients who have been discharged from psychiatric hospitals. However, the situation basically remains unchanged, leaving more than 70,000 individuals who do not require hospitalization to remain institutionalized.[14]

In Japan, families have been regarded culturally and traditionally as caretakers for the chronically disabled, and their role as guardians is stipulated as a legal duty in the current Japanese Mental Health Law and the Civil Code.[15] Japanese families try to care for their sick family members as long as possible by themselves because they fear that hospitalization may be regarded as abandonment of their responsibilities.[16] Keeping the patient at home also guarantees that the mental illness will remain a family secret.

However, because families often cannot perceive the symptoms and illness objectively, and because they are too close to the patient, they become even more confused.[17] When they finally realize how seriously ill their relatives are, they are too burned out to provide adequate care. At this point, out of a combination of guilt and a strong fear of stigmatization, families will intentionally choose a hospital far from where they live.[18]

The two-way political discourse (criticism of deinstitutionalization vs. criticism of institutionalization) seen both in the United States and Japan is just one obvious difference in the milieu of the mentally ill and their families. But other differences in sociocultural background may affect families' experiences more significantly. Are there differences and similarities in perceived stress and coping mechanisms in the United States and Japan? Are there social, structural, or cultural factors that explain the differences and similarities? We are all products of our time and culture as well as our position in society. We normally try to tailor our behaviors to conform to society's established standards and to fulfill the various expectations attached to our social roles. There is no question but that we are very much controlled by the social and structural factors that surround us. Even in psychiatric settings, it has been reported that patients from different ethnic groups sometimes express their symptoms according to the frame of reference unique to their culture. This leads to the problem of misdiagnosis if the clinician is not well trained in understanding various cultural nuances. Furthermore, certain groups of psychiatric symptoms are defined as "culture-bound syndromes"; *koro* and *amok* are examples of such illnesses in Southeast Asia.[19] If the influence of culture can be so powerful, it seems reasonable to anticipate that there will be substantial differences in families' behaviors relating to the given illness that originate from social, structural, and cultural factors.

Family dynamics is another important and complicating factor. While the family of a mentally ill patient tends to be seen as one unit, each family member's experience can differ from that of other family members depending on relative position within the family structure. There are as many realities of family life as the number of people who share the experience. How does being the parent, sibling, or spouse of a mentally ill person affect the individual's perception of a set of events? If there are so many kinds of perceptions at work in a family, how does the family manage to survive as a system?

Ultimately, the core of my investigation lies in the question: How do people survive and cope with the tragedy of mental illness? All the people I interviewed struggled with the reality for a long time, ranging from five years to several decades, during which time they made enormous adjustments. To me they were all courageous survivors with incredible perseverance. I wanted to find out what inner and outer personal qualities had enabled them to survive. In other words, I wished to explore what went *well* for these people, rather than what went wrong, which tends to be the central part of the research on many social problems. How do they come out of the position of a vulnerable victim and keep themselves from feeling defeated again by various burdens and constraints? I wanted to find out what had kept them going and what the source of their strength was in the face of this atypical, socially stigmatized tragedy.

The book is based on the data collected through in-depth, face-to-face, open-ended interviews with 26 Japanese and 24 Americans with a family member who suffered from a severe, chronic mental illness, from a variety of socioeconomic backgrounds. American participants were primarily of European American descent, including several Jewish families and one Hispanic family. There was only one African-American participant, who was the husband of a patient. The ages of these individuals ranged from the early 40s to the early 80s. Their only commonality was that they had a family member with serious mental illness. They were recruited through self-help and support groups, as well as via personal introductions. From the United States, 11 mothers, 5 fathers, 6 siblings, and 2 spouses, and from Japan, 11 mothers, 6 fathers, 3 spouses, 5 siblings, and 1 daughter were interviewed. The most common diagnosis was schizophrenia: 19 cases in the United States, and 22 cases in Japan. Other diagnoses included manic depression (three in the United States and one in Japan), depression associated with drug addiction, and a combination of several mental or brain disorders such as borderline personality and epilepsy. Therefore, stories presented in this book are skewed toward the experiences of families of patients with schizophrenia. Although the families' socioeconomic backgrounds vary somewhat, they may also be limited to families with relatively high standards of living: several parents from the United States and Japan were quite wealthy. Many families of the mentally ill in both countries would find it difficult if not impossible to create an adequate environment for their sick relatives. All the interviewees had some resources in that they were part of support networks and had the time to participate in this study. Furthermore, the accounts are also strictly based on families' understandings of the psychiatric diagnosis made regarding the patient, whether it was a child, a sibling, or a spouse. Their doctors may have given them a more specific psychiatric label for their loved ones' conditions than they were able to report. Two Japanese mothers were very reluctant to disclose the real diagnosis during the interviews and only told me how they personally understood the disease. But they were fully aware that their sons had a severe mental illness and were willing to be interviewed. After trying to clarify the situation several times, I did not press them further to establish the accuracy of the diagnosis. In fact, it was not crucially important for this study because the focus was on families' perceptions of their situation and how they were coping with their version of reality.

The main research locations were the greater Los Angeles area and Tokyo, both of them being metropolitan areas with easy access to information on relevant groups and organizations. The interviews were conducted at the interviewees' homes, my apartment in Los Angeles, or other places of their choice, including hospitals and support group offices. The in-depth, qualitative interviews were for the most part of two to three hours' duration. This study focused on the feelings, perceptions, and subjective meanings created by the individuals through personal experiences and events. Therefore, it was considered pertinent to let the voices of family members in distress and their personal stories speak for themselves as much as possible. In order to grasp the larger context of the issues beyond the individual experiences, I also undertook ethnographic observations at various support groups, hospital meetings, clinics, psychoeducational programs, and halfway houses. In addition, I met with key personnel in community mental health services in the two cities on opposite sides of the Pacific. However, the voices of families in distress were so powerful that the way they present the story of each individual in their own words is more eloquent than any theoretical presentation could be.

Although all the chapters deal with the process of family members' adjustments to mental illness, chapter 1 first looks at the various implications of mental illness and its effect on families' present and future lives. Some sociological perspectives are also introduced to help better understand and analyze their situations, which otherwise seem totally chaotic on the surface. Chapter 2 describes how the families' struggles with mental illness began, and in chapter 3, their emotional responses to different stages are discussed, from perceiving initial signs of illness, to hearing the psychiatric diagnosis for the first time, and dealing with hospitalization of their loved ones. These chapters are mainly about the consequences of mental illness within the family. Although most family members were devastated by the onset of mental illness, the individual responses vary, depending upon family background, the way in which the illness developed (whether sudden onset or more gradually over time), and the person's position in the family, whether a parent, sibling, or spouse of the patient.

Chapters 4 and 5 take a further look at family members' responses and focus on the relationships at home. What happens to the major dyad in the family, such as husband and wife, or parent and well children and other relatives? The accounts of not only individual struggles, but also the struggle by the family as a whole, present to us how profound the ramifications of this tragedy are in every aspect of the home.

Chapters 6 and 7 describe another adjustment process: the cognitive and perceptual adjustment. While family members are mainly "reacting to" the various new problems in the beginning, after a while they begin to closely study their sick family member's condition, in order to try to understand the illness and to slowly regain control of reality and of their lives. These are important steps in the process of changing from victims to taking an active role. Realization of the nature of mental illness leads not only to better understanding, but also to acceptance and sympathy for the patient. In addition, how these families cope with the persistent social stigma (which mainly stems from ignorance and misunderstanding) is discussed as well.

Chapters 8 and 9 discuss the ways in which families cope with their daily stress. Here the family members are no longer reacting to the tragedy but are "proactively" adopting various strategies for coping and survival, including taking action, seeking outside help, changing their perspective about their situation, or creating various meanings from their experiences. The richness and resilience of the human mind in reinterpreting their plight as something from which they can draw positive meanings is both impressive and very moving. Finally, in chapter 10, the sources of their strength for all those years of living with the mental illness of their loved one are closely examined, and ultimately, the inner mechanism by means of which human beings survive a seemingly unmanageable life tragedy is discussed. This is, above all, the central theme of this book.

All the names of the individuals used in the text have been changed to ensure the anonymity of the participants. Insignificant changes have been made to their backgrounds to conceal their identities, which was a serious concern for some participants.

Notes

1. A. Hatfield, "Family as Caregivers: Historical Perspective," in *Families of the Mentally Ill: Coping and Adaptation*, ed. A. B. Hatfield and H. P. Lefley (New York: Guilford Press, 1987), 3–29.
2. T. Takizawa, *Kokoro no yamai to kazoku no kokoro* (Mental Illness and the Psychology of the Family) (Tokyo: Chuo Hoki, 1993).
3. L. G. Weiss and L. E. Lonnquist, *Sociology of Health, Healing, and Illness* (Saddle River, NJ: Prentice–Hall, 1994), 133.
4. NAMI California Website http://www.namicalifornia.org/
5. E. F. Torrey, *Surviving Schizophrenia* (New York: Quill, 2001), 8.
6. K. T. Mueser and S. R. McGurk, "Schizophrenia,"*Lancet* 363 (2004): 263–72.
7. Yuichiro Ito, Director of "Harakara no Ie" Welfare Association, lecture at Tokyo Health Center, February 6, 2004.
8. K. G. Terkelson, "A Historical Perspective on Family-Provider Relationships," in *Families as Allies inTreatment of the Mentally Ill: New Directions for Mental Health Professional*, ed. H. P. Lefley and D. L. Johnson (Washington, D.C.: American Psychiatric Press, 1990), 9–21.
9. Torrey, *Surviving Schizophreniar*, 20.
10. Ibid., 8.

11. W. Doll, "Family Coping With the Mentally Ill: An Unanticipated Problem of Deinstitutionalization," *Hospital and Community Psychiatry* 27, no. 3 (1976): 183–85.

12. Torrey, *Surviving Schizophrenia*, 19–24.

13. I. Oshima and K. Nakai, "The Japanese Mental Health System and Family Movement: History, Present Status, and Research Findings," in *Innovations in Japanese Mental Health Services*, ed. James M. Mandiberg (San Francisco: Jossey-Bass, 1993), 13–23.

14. Yuichiro Ito, Lecture, February 6, 2004.

15. Oshima and Nakai, "The Japanese Mental Health System."

16. Takizawa, *Kokoro no yamai to kazoku no kokoro.*

17. Ibid.

18. Ibid.

19. American Psychiatric Association, *Diagnostic and Statistical Manual of Mental Disorders*, 4th ed. rev. *(*DSM-IV-TR*)* (Washington D.C.: American Psychiatric Association, 2000), xxxiii.

PART I
Overview

CHAPTER 1

Mental Illness in the Family: What Does It Mean?

"This couldn't be happening to my family!" said 52-year-old Ken Morris.

"Well, at that point, I knew he was terribly sick. I just had no idea what the problem was. This couldn't be happening to my family. It just couldn't." Ken was a successful real estate broker, living comfortably in Los Angeles with his wife and his 20-year-old twin children, Charles and Lucy, who were both in college. Ken had always been proud of being a high achiever. The Morris family goal was to "achieve everything we put our mind to." From the beginning, he and his wife had taught their children the importance of setting goals and working successfully toward them.

"This" meant schizophrenia, which had begun to afflict Charles, now 27, seven years earlier. It hit Ken and his whole family like a thunderbolt, without warning. Until then, Charles had been not only a normal, healthy college sophomore, but also, in his father's words, "quite the little superstar." Charles had won a national paddle tennis championship at age ten, he went on to become a football and volleyball star, and his efforts had helped to secure a prestigious award for his school. He was a popular champion and his future looked bright. He was a proud son who lived up perfectly to his father's expectation — to "do the best you can possibly do" — in whatever he set his mind to. The signs of impending tragedy were elusive at first, but soon they grew too conspicuous to ignore.

Seven years ago, Charles returned home from college one weekend, and Ken and his wife discovered him wandering around, disoriented, in the front yard of the house. They did not think too much about it then. But two weeks later, Lucy, who was attending another university in the same area, called home, saying that when they had shared a ride back to school her brother was very upset about something unimportant and had cried most of the way back. "So, basically, that was the first time we really felt that there was something wrong," Ken recalls.

Ken and his wife immediately contacted the college psychological counseling office and made an appointment for their son. The counselor said that their son was depressed and suicidal, so they took him out of school immediately. They thought something was definitely wrong with Charles, but that it would pass once he came back home to stay with his parents. Neither Ken nor anyone else in the family had the slightest idea that this would develop into something far more serious. They thought it was only a phase. Perhaps Charles was finding college harder than they had expected. But six months had passed already since Charles dropped out of school, and a sense of uncertainty started to torment Ken. He began to search for information that could give him some understanding of his son's situation.

> I hoped that maybe after a six-month period, maybe after a semester at home, this problem would pass. I thought perhaps he was simply depressed about something. I felt it might be the school ... his grades were suffering and he was sleeping all the time....

But Charles continued to be disoriented at home. He slept a lot and could not concentrate on anything. Ken gave his son some easy physical tasks, but the tasks were never completed. If Charles was supposed to paint a wall, after he finished painting, he would make marks on the new paint and ruin it. Ken and his wife discussed what to do, but they came to no conclusion.

> It just wasn't working out. You know, it just wasn't working out.... I felt extremely frustrated because our family members have been very high achievers in everything. When somebody can't achieve, it's usually because he doesn't want to. I felt very anxious. I felt very bad. I was trying to understand and help him, and yet, I didn't understand what was going on. Was it because he was having those rebellious teenage years? Or was it because he was sick? Or ... I just didn't know. And the doctors weren't helping me.

The situation continued to deteriorate. Charles became increasingly paranoid, antagonistic, and delusional, claiming his best friend across the street was stealing from him. He locked himself in his room because he feared that people were going to harm him. He ran away from home and lived on the street for several days. Eight months after Charles came home from college, Ken finally went to a psychiatric hospital with his son, who clung to him, afraid of being hurt by strangers. The hospital admitted Charles immediately.

When the doctor said "I think it is schizophrenia," the reason that was supposed to explain his son's behavior at last, Ken's reaction was utter denial. Now, he looked for reasons why he should not believe the diagnosis.

> That made me feel "I don't trust this doctor." This is a severe illness and how could he possibly know just by looking at my son? There's no way. So I don't trust this guy at all. I also don't trust him because I saw his name on twenty different charts in the hospital.

Ken realized that obviously many patients were assigned to the doctor and immediately thought to himself that this man was getting paid $175 per patient each day, and there was no way he could accurately figure out his son so quickly. He did not trust the doctor's diagnosis. His denial simply reflected his long-held perception on this illness: schizophrenia, in his mind, was just too devastating for anyone to accept. He remembers well how he felt.

> Because there are dire consequences. Even consequences that I didn't understand at the time. If my son had schizophrenia, his chance of holding political office was nil.... I'm saying the consequences for my son were severe. And I was very afraid for him. That's why I did not want to accept the consequences.... He probably could not become a policeman. He probably could not hold down a job. He probably could not go back to school. He probably would not give me grandchildren. I mean, there's just all these things. It's huge.

The process of acceptance did not come easily. Ken's quest for more information continued. He searched for a better diagnosis to convince himself the first doctor was wrong. He went to a mental health education group for parents and siblings, talked to one of his own relatives who was a psychologist, and kept changing doctors. "I spent a lot of money," he said, only to feel he was not getting anywhere. He finally found a doctor who agreed to keep Charles under close observation for six weeks. Then Ken asked the ultimate question, "Doctor, do you have a book that you could give to me to explain what my son is going through?" The doctor handed him a book: it was about schizophrenia.

> So schizophrenia keeps coming up and coming up and coming up, you know, so I had to start to accept it. And then I finally asked, "Well, how do you know he's got schizophrenia?" And they tell me about *DSM-IV.* And they say, "Well, look. There are two pages and there are fourteen different symptoms. And if your son has ten of the fourteen symptoms, he's got schizophrenia." And I said, "Well, are you sure about that?" And the doctor said, "Let's talk about this...."

On the other side of the Pacific, Yoko Tomita, a 43-year-old city office worker in Tokyo, was struggling all by herself with the nightmare that was her new reality.

> Every day I thought to myself this must be a dream. When I go home, I will see my healthy, normal husband waiting for me like before. Everything we went through would be a dream. With this expectation and wish, I would open the front door. But....

Yoko recalls how she used to live during those early days: giving herself a fantasy to cling to, an escape from the otherwise too harsh reality. "Except for that, I was completely thrown into everyday survival."

Yoko and her husband, Eiji, met for the first time at art school in Tokyo. Eiji was 20 and Yoko 21: They were both studying fine arts and oil painting. It did not take long for these two passionate, aspiring artists to fall madly in love with each other. They soon started living together. When the financial support sent by their parents was no longer enough for the high tuition, both dropped out of school and began working to support themselves. It was by no means an easy time, but Yoko recalls it as if those bittersweet days were the happiest of their lives. Besides, she was very much in love, and against the odds, was very committed to the relationship.

> We quarreled all the time. I knew he was an extremely sensitive man. That's what I found attractive about him. At a supermarket, he would get upset when I picked up something and did not return it to the same place. He was also fussy about the way I talked. (I used to talk with little consideration for others'

feelings.) I was the kind of person who didn't care about such things. So it was a big culture shock for me. But his attitude was consistent. He didn't discriminate people because of status or ranks, he always treated everyone the same. I really respected him. No matter how much we argued, I never thought of breaking up.

Six years after they first met, despite strong opposition from her parents, they married. "In retrospect, it was like a fever. I had such a special feeling toward him," Yoko laughs, with a blushing, innocent girlish smile. He took a job at a book-binding company for five years, and then at that point decided to concentrate on painting. She began to work at a social welfare office as a bookkeeper and supported his artistic activity.

Around 1988, Yoko noticed Eiji absorbed in washing his hands, talking to himself. It made her feel strange. He would purposelessly wander around the apartment, wadding up tissue paper and dropping it in the trash can. Then he started to insist that he had AIDS, "so separate my laundry from yours," looking extremely intense and exhausted. Yoko would tease and laugh at him at first saying that he was like a raccoon. But she soon realized that this was not a joke. She finally turned to the local public mental health center.

At work, Yoko became increasingly isolated. The pressure at home intensified, making it difficult for her to take care of her husband and keep up with her work at the same time. She asked for a different job with fewer deadlines. Some of her colleagues who said that they would help out and fill in for her never really did anything for her, and she took it as a personal betrayal. The stress brought her close to the edge. Losing control, she shouted in the busy office, "I cannot quit working! Why can't you give me a job I can do?" No one truly cared. She was completely alone. At least that was what she felt.

During many doctor visits, she had always believed that her husband's problem was depression. When she was finally told in March 1989 that her husband in fact had schizophrenia, she was completely at a loss. It was the kind of shock greater than she had ever experienced. *Utsu-byoo* (depression) was one thing, but schizophrenia was something fundamentally different in her mind: it was "insanity." The books in which she desperately searched for information only confused her even more. Having worked at the social welfare office for some years, she perceived that schizophrenia was in a separate category from other mental illnesses. Her own ignorance made Yoko feel shattered and hopeless. On the other hand, she remembers how surprised she was by her own sense of commitment to this relationship.

> Soon after my husband was diagnosed as having schizophrenia, my mother came to see me. She asked, "So what are you going to do?" I didn't understand what she meant. She meant was I going to get a divorce or stay married. When she asked me, I was surprised to realize that I hadn't even dreamed of leaving him. I was just so confused then. I just wanted to do something about each moment. I never thought about my future. But I was really surprised by my own feelings, too.

The serious illness of a family member is always one of the most catastrophic events in life. It can threaten the family's sense of stability with a myriad of difficulties and drastically affect family members' psychological, social, and financial situations. It changes each family member's relationship with the sick person in both the present and for the rest of his or her life. It radically forces a new situation on the family, ruthlessly requiring everyone involved to make significant adjustment whether they want to or not.

However, when the illness is a mental disorder, the ramifications are especially profound and pervasive. Mental illness has a strikingly unique nature in that it is most keenly perceived through the patient's interactions with others and at the same time it deeply affects the state of the mind of other people who are not sick. This makes mental illness similar to a contagious disease. If one family member becomes mentally ill, no one else in the home can completely escape its influence.

In addition to the social and contagious nature of mental disorders, the chronic nature of its impact is a crucial element in shaping the family's experience. The acute distress brought to the family by the onset and diagnosis of mental illness does not completely disappear. It remains as a chronic strain. The problem may become less noticeable in cases where medication and perhaps supportive therapy can stabilize the patient, enabling him to lead a pretty normal life. Nonetheless, it is often the case that while a mental illness can be *managed,* it cannot be *cured* — it is a permanent presence in the patient's life and that of his or her family. For example, medication may have side effects that the patient finds intolerable, so he tries reducing the dose, only to have the symptoms of the illness return. A new medication will take some time to work fully, and in some cases the patient will not be able to tolerate it. Problems with medication may cause a previously stabilized patient to lose his job, and once more become a financial burden to the family. All of these uncertainties, which continue throughout the patient's lifetime, cause incomparable levels of anxiety.

The impact of the chronic strain to human well-being cannot be overstated. Studies of the effects of stress have shown that chronic strain is a powerful predictor of depressive disorders and various health problems.[1] While the acute life event can invite more attention and support from others and is likely to lead to effective intervention, the chronically stressful situation can foster unhealthy inertia, often escaping necessary scrutiny and, therefore, chances for resolution. The daily stress of dealing with a mental disorder can be experienced by patients' families in various ways, including "role strain," which makes it impossible for them to fulfill their normally expected social roles and instead forces them to play an unwanted role as caretaker, often out of obligation.

Yoko Tomita remembers the moment when she realized that it would be she who would have to take charge of their household as well as protect her husband.

> I was so distraught over what happened to my husband that I was overwhelmed by my own anger and sorrow. But one day I heard him crying in a worn-out voice, washing his hands, and telling (singing to) himself "Don't cry, don't cry...." He was extremely distressed about his condition, but was trying to encourage himself. I just felt so sorry for him and I was determined to be strong.

Yoko decided that she would become the head of the household and make all the decisions for their future. In a society where this was traditionally the husband's role, she found her own situation even more isolated. She thoroughly researched the welfare system, classified her husband as her dependent, and obtained financial services for him, including a disability benefit. She managed to buy a small condominium, as well as mortgage insurance, just in case she died first, so that he would have a place to live. Suddenly all the financial burdens for now and the future were on her frail shoulders.

> I'm not his parent, but I find myself taking that role in many ways. Several years ago when his condition was stabilized, and I finally started to understand this illness, I began worrying about his future. What if I get sick? What would happen to him? He has no contact with his parents and cannot turn to them for help. Of course, it would be out of the question that he would turn to my family. I fear he would be completely alone. The prospect is extremely worrying.

When she has time to worry about herself, "it's about my health," she says. "Since he became ill, I cannot afford to get sick. If I have a fever, he gets sick, too. When I think about this, even my fever goes down. But if I continue to live like this too long, I worry that I may one day break down."

One of the strains caused by mental disorder is that its intrinsically social nature tends to make objective symptom assessment and diagnosis tricky and confusing to most people. This brings us to the simple reality that people just don't understand mental illness. If they have some knowledge about mental illness, it may be incorrect or tainted with stereotypes. Furthermore, it is difficult to use physical evidence to prove the existence of mental pathologies. The usual process of perceiving the onset of illness is assessment of symptoms, followed by interpretation of those symptoms as abnormal and indicative of disease. Availability of an animal model also makes it easier to clearly identify the pathogen involved. However, in the case of schizophrenia, for example, it does not exhibit a lesion in the brain that is common to all patients, and there is considerable variance in its clinical features.[2] Although there have been major advances in technology, such as brain imaging, in detecting physiological changes that often accompany the development of schizophrenia, no decisive measures have been discovered to specifically point out the presence of a particular illness. This quality of mental disorders makes the decision to seek help more complex. The reality is that most people do not have any idea of where and when to seek help. In the meantime, they feel bewildered due to lack of information about mental illness. Dealing with the psychiatric system, which is unfamiliar to most people, throws families in general into an ocean of overwhelming uncertainty. Even when assessment and diagnosis are made accurately, the lack of consensus with regard to the etiology causes some psychiatric professionals to make extremely hurtful comments to the families. Although the evidence of the biological roots of mental disorders has been established for some time within the medical community, and any rational specialist knows the absurdity of old theories such as "bad families" or "bad mothers" causing psychotic illness, these ideas still persist, even among professionals in mental health–related fields. Researchers at the National Alliance for the Mentally Ill (NAMI), who work in clinical settings, report that they witness "the regularity with which families of the chronically mentally ill are still being represented as pathogenic," noting that this attitude is communicated in many formal and informal ways.[3] There is no doubt at all that these inaccurate perceptions are an added strain on the families of the mentally ill.

When Yoko Tomita contacted the mental health section of the municipal health center for the first time, she was implicitly blamed for her husband's condition. The center's staff member, who was not a medical doctor, was clearly unqualified to diagnose severe mental illnesses. This staff member as well as her husband's relatives told her that it might well be her fault. Her husband was, after all, a grown-up married man, with no regular job, just staying at home. It was Yoko who enabled him to live a life under these conditions. Their view was that Yoko must have become his mother, rather than his wife, spoiled him, and allowed him to avoid taking up his responsibilities as a mature man.

> Well, I did not completely disagree with them, either. But he and I went to art school together. I knew how hard it was for a painter to be financially independent. I knew it would not easily lead to financial success. So I had accepted it. There were times when I envied others, but my conclusion was always that I had to be patient. But then, I also wondered if I was really responsible for his mental state. I just feared that our life was collapsing. I was extremely confused…. Then the confusion turned into anger, but I did not know where to place my anger. I felt like cursing at God.

If misconceptions about the cause of mental illness are implicitly expressed toward family members, social stigma attached to the illness itself is sometimes more explicitly and cruelly targeted. The persistent social stigma accounts for the magnitude of the shock for families when a child, sibling, or spouse is diagnosed as being mentally ill.

"I don't hide my son's illness, but when I meet new people I don't throw it at them immediately, because I have found in the past that when I did that, I was shunned…. It's because I became a leper, you know," says Linda Katz, a fragile-looking, petite woman of 72. Her son, Rick, has lived with schizophrenia since the late 1960s. He had just turned 20 and was starting his third year of college. Soon after the first sign of abnormality hit him, her son's disease gained speed like "a snowball going downhill on a mountain, gathering size and momentum." It was an era when there was even less understanding of psychiatric problems than there is today, and and the U.S. mental health support system was much less adequate than it is today. It was almost ten years before Rick was sent to a psychiatrist, when Linda finally realized that her son needed to be hospitalized. She and her husband continued to support their son. After her husband, who had been her greatest support, died, Linda continued to take care of her son alone. She never married again. Now, she goes to see Rick twice a week at the board and care home where he lives. Linda knows what the stigma is like. Being a widow and living alone, she tries to participate in senior groups in her area.

There's always a nice woman I can sit and chat with. Once during a trip, on a vacation by myself, I spoke of Rick to a woman who had been buzzing cheerfully around me like a bee up to that point. But all of a sudden, she wasn't there. So I thought, well, why even bring this up. If anyone asks, I don't lie. I say my son is ill. If they are interested and ask more questions, I will tell them, but I just don't bring it up for no reason.... I don't because we're fighting a stigma and it's there, and people are simply not educated.

Recalling that moment, Linda's face clouds over, "I don't fall apart. I just go on. But isn't that awful?"

Yoshiko Takeda is a typical Japanese mother who worries about how her daughter's mental illness will affect the future of her other children. It was around May 1991 when her 22-year-old daughter, Emiko, began being late for work. One day she followed a strange woman she met on a commuter train to the woman's house. She would also phone a friend or relatives and ask them to let her stay overnight. Then she would disappear from the house and not come back for a day. Anxiety-stricken, but relentlessly seeking an appropriate doctor for four months, Yoshiko finally found one whom she could trust. The doctor's diagnosis was schizophrenia, and it was a most shattering experience. Even though Emiko has been given a good prognosis in recent years, Yoshiko now worries about her 29-year-old son's future, as she is very well aware of the stigma attached to mental illness in Japan: mental illness in the family is abhorred by prospective in-laws and can become a reason for canceling the wedding plans.

It's about his marriage. It will definitely be affected by his sister's illness. If he has a good relationship with someone and gets engaged, he may be able to tell the woman that his sister has a not-so-serious psychological problem. But what if the future wife's parents investigate our family, if they find out that my daughter was hospitalized for a long time? It will be bad. I wish he would find a woman who can understand this sort of thing, but....

Sociological Perspectives

Thus, the implications of having a mentally ill person in the family are enormous. But what can families do about their situations? Will they continue to feel devastated by this diagnosis and the additional social implications?

First of all, the structural–functional perspective of sociology reminds us of the power of internalization through socialization that we experience from our childhood. One of the central assumptions of the structural and functional perspective is to look at social phenomena as systems. A system is an entity composed of different, but interrelated parts. Therefore, no part of society or no human being functions independently. Like an organism, each part constantly affects another and works toward an equilibrium of the entire system.

From a macro standpoint, we acquire shared values and beliefs of our society and learn to conform to its norms. A society's most important agenda is survival as a functioning and stable whole. So, it is crucial for society to demand that its members share basic values and adhere to various social rules, even if it sometimes means personal sacrifice and loss of individual autonomy. According to structural–functional perspectives, however, everything will eventually fit well to maintain order and continuity in a given society.[4] Severe mental illness ultimately implies deviance from social norms, and almost every society has taught its members to abhor and fear such deviance, whatever form it may take. Family responsibility and commitment are another firmly internalized value of many societies, which gives a sense of the enormous burden experienced by families of the mentally ill.

Though the basic attitude toward mental disorders is equally negative, and expectations regarding families are equally heavy, Americans and Japanese have been socialized in different cultural contexts. This is precisely why we can anticipate different thinking patterns among individuals from the two cultures. For many Japanese parents, jeopardizing marriage possibilities for their healthy children or even relatives because of a mentally ill family member is one of the most serious concerns. Japanese parents would go an extra mile to prevent it from happening. As mentioned earlier, the social and political environment with regard to the treatment of mentally ill patients is also different in these two countries, which poses different kinds of constraints and obstacles for families to struggle with. What families can do is try to overcome them, but in a way that is appropriate within their cultural framework.

From a micro standpoint, family is a closely knit system. For a family to survive, members must share a family culture that gives them direction, especially early in life, and which often becomes a basis for dealing with various problems that arise in adulthood. Some families may choose to be united to cope with mental illness together. Some families prefer to avoid openly talking about it or even touching on the issue and continue to pretend that there is no problem at home. Children who grow up in this kind of avoidant environment may learn to think this is the only way to deal with problems.

Furthermore, being a system, any change in a family never fails to send waves into the rest of the family space, including family subsystems such as husband and wife, parents and children, and siblings. However, the system is intrinsically resistant to change as a whole. Therefore, in order to survive and maintain overall structural status quo, adaptation on the part of its members is required.[5] When families begin to deal with the mental illness of a member, they must make various adjustments within the home, changing their roles and taking on more responsibilities whether they wish to or not. If these adjustments aren't made, the family system may cease to sustain itself. In reality, this adaptation process is far more difficult than the structural–functional perspective usually implies. The onset of mental illness profoundly transforms many dimensions of family relationships. It is often a time that is filled with disagreement, a clash of ideas, and conflict within the system. From a conflict perspective, however, a family is understood as not always being a happy and harmonious unit.[6] Siblings of a mentally ill patient often grow up feeling resentful toward their parents because they do not receive enough parental attention, or they may disagree with the way the parents handled the mental illness. The presence of mental illness in a home is perceived in a variable way unique to each member's position within the family system. And the differences in these perceptions are bound to produce tension, conflict, and even competition in the process of eventually working toward a point where the family system is stabilized.

Thus, structural and functional perspectives present a rather deterministic view that focuses on how external forces such as position in society or in the family affect people's decisions and behaviors. However, this is only half the picture of what happens to human beings when confronted with a life tragedy.

As devastating as the effects of mental illness seem to be, however, families do not remain frozen by the catastrophe. They keep struggling to adjust to the incredible demands of the situation. Though the daily reality presented by the mental illness seems uncontrollable, unpredictable, and unresolvable in the beginning, many family members endure, go through different stages for years or decades, and grow to acquire new interpretations, beliefs, and perspectives on their lives.

Ken Morris admits that once he finally reached the realization of his son's illness, it helped him tremendously, and he regained his usual self as a constructive problem solver.

> From then on, the world opened up because I had finally accepted what it was. I could get my son into different programs; I could read books about schizophrenia; I could get the proper medications; I could get him on SSI.[7] I could do all these things. But, to finally get to the realization of what exactly was going on was very hard. Because you don't want to accept it.

Events and the physical environment do not simply impinge upon an individual. Human beings have the capacity to eventually process these stimuli and construct the world according to their own perceptions. Despite incredible odds, hardship, and obstacles, the effects are not in absolute terms but are relative to the various mental filters each individual develops through life. Thus, being hit by a certain catastrophic event results in different responses, depending on the individual.

Crucial to this process is the individual appraisal of stressful events in life. Symbolic interactionism, another sociological perspective, provides a good framework for understanding this process. The essence of this perspective is best summarized in the work of W. I. Thomas (1863–1947), as expressed in the Thomas theorem: "If situations are defined as real, they are real in their consequences." This means that one is affected by the events only in the way one perceives the event. Even negative life events and various occurrences become stressful only when one perceives them as stressful. Our perception becomes the basis for our responses and actions toward the situation. According to symbolic interactionism, we are not an entity the external world imposes itself upon.

Rather than passively responding to external stimuli, human beings actively process through their minds various verbal and nonverbal symbols and respond to their interpretations and perceptions of the situation. Symbolic interactionism points out the power of our mental capacity to create a reality for ourselves. Despite the initial devastation experienced as a result of a diagnosis of mental illness, many family members eventually refuse to be passive victims of the situation.

Hearing the doctor's diagnosis for the first time, Yoshiko Takeda was completely shattered. She felt that even the anxiety that had tormented her for the preceding four months was better than this verdict.

The word *schizophrenia* made me feel hopeless. I felt I was hit on the head by a hammer. I was speechless. My head drooped down and I could not raise it for a while. Then the doctor said, "Look, it is only my guess, but your daughter's schizophrenia may reflect the situation of your family: the whole family is not in unity. Everyone in the family is scattered and their feelings are apart from one another. By everyone getting together again and working together on your daughter's illness, something good can come out of it." He was trying to console me, but I thought to myself, "This man does not sound like a doctor," and looked around his office. I found a cross on the wall at the corner of the room. I thought to myself, "Is this man a Christian? Is that why he says something so unlikely for a medical doctor?" What he said was true. We were a family of four, but each one had gone their separate way for a long time, especially after the children grew up. My daughter has this kind of serious illness, but if we come back to become one family again, we might be able to change the situation for the better. That's where I found a shaft of light.

As they go through the perception phase, people use various strategies, based on their past experiences, in order to eliminate, modify, or control emotional distress.[8] Depending on the situation and the person's disposition, there are various coping behaviors. One may turn to social support or one's own psychological resources (such as personality characteristics, positive self-image, sense of control, self-esteem, and pride) as expressed in the concept of "personality hardiness"[9] or "sense of coherence."[10] One may also turn to cognitive techniques that control or neutralize the meaning of the stressful event.

Looking back on several decades of dealing with her son's mental illness, and the death of her husband and her mother, both of which occurred within a six-month period, Linda sometimes wonders how she managed.

I have been looking back on it. I think I have great inner strength and I had a mother who had that too. I think her influence on me was very strong.... My strength is spiritual.... Well, we're Jewish, but we're not Orthodox. We're not observant. But I've always believed in a higher power. I think that we all have to do our very best. It's there, but it doesn't get everything into motion....

The following chapters will reveal how each family member came to grips with their lives by mobilizing their inner strength, and the malleable and autonomous nature of a human mind that is always capable of creating its own reality.

Notes

1. G. L. Weiss and L. E. Lonnguist, *The Sociology of Health, Healing, and Illness* (Englewood Cliffs, NJ: Prentice-Hall, 1994), 87–109.
2. M. I. Herz and S. R. Marder, *Schizophrenia: Comprehensive Treatment and Management* (Philadelphia: Lippincott Williams & Wilkins, 2002), 3.
3. G. K. Terkelson, "A Historical Perspective on Family-Provider Relationships," in *Families as Allies in Treatment of the Mentally Ill: New Directions for Mental Health Professionals*, ed. H. P. Lefley and D. L. Johnson (Washington, D.C.: American Psychiatric Association, 1990), 921.
4. C. A. Winton, *Frameworks for Studying Families* (Guilford, CT: Dushkin, 1995), 44–85.
5. Ibid.
6. Ibid., 86–108.

7. N. Dearth, B. J. Labenski, M. E. Mott, and L. Pellegrini, *Families Helping Families: Living with Schizophrenia* (New York: Norton, 1986), 122–124. Supplementary Security Income (SSI), provides a monthly cash allowance for the needy including senior citizens and physically or mentally impaired individuals with no ability to maintain employment.

8. L. Pearlin and C. Schooler, "The Structure of Coping," *Journal of Health and Social Behavior* 19 (1978): 2–12.

9. S. C. Kobasa, S. R. Maddi, and S. Courington, "Personality and Constitution as Mediators in the Stress-Illness Relationship," *Journal of Health and Social Behavior* 22 (1981): 368–78.

10. A. Antonovsky, *Health, Stress, and Coping* (San Francisco: Jossey-Bass, 1979).

PART II

The First Signs of Mental Illness: How the Symptoms Emerged and Became Permanent

CHAPTER 2

Early Impressions

Yes, it was very painful. It was very ... I was very overwhelmed.
I didn't know where to turn to, who to ask. I was so scared. I was
afraid of exposing myself and my daughter. I didn't want my
daughter to be classified as mentally ill. — An American mother.

Introduction

The symptoms of schizophrenia have been well documented and its classi-
fication criteria have been established for more than five decades. The
essential features of schizophrenia, as noted by *DSM-IV-TR*, are a mixture
of characteristic signs and symptoms, which include positive symptoms
such as distortions in thought content, perception, disorganized language
and thought processes, and grossly disorganized or catatonic behavior, as
well as negative symptoms such as restrictions in emotional expression, in
thought and in speech, and avolition.[1] People who have schizophrenia are
believed to experience alterations of the senses, such as increased acuteness
of audio and visual perception; inability to sort and interpret incoming
stimuli (which results in difficulties in watching television or movies);
delusions and hallucinations; an altered sense of self, which makes them
confuse their bodies with those of others; and changes in emotions and
movements.[2]

The onset of schizophrenia typically occurs between the late teens and
the mid-30s.[3] Three-quarters of patients have onset between the ages of 17
and 25.[4] Though having an initial onset before age 14 or after age 30 is

considered rare, of those interviewed for this study, there were two American mothers whose sons with schizophrenia had already shown various signs during childhood and one Japanese husband whose wife was diagnosed as having schizophrenia in her late 50s.

The delusions are caused by the misinterpretation of perceptions or experiences. The themes of delusions can vary, ranging from those of a persecutory nature in which a patient believes that he or she is tormented, followed, or spied upon by others, to delusions of a referential nature, which make the patient feel that the contents of the media, for example, are directed at him or her. Somatic concerns that reach delusional proportions may also occur. Various disorganized behaviors that can be childish or agitated sometimes leave the person disheveled, dressed in a bizarre manner, or lead him or her to behave inappropriately in public.[5] Furthermore, the display of inappropriate affects, such as depression, anger, phobias, and high anxiety is also a commonly observed symptom.

Although schizophrenia is perhaps the most striking mental disorder that has been studied and well documented by the psychiatric community, for the average person it does not stand out first as a disease, even when someone begins to show signs of affliction. It is simply a strange and scary change happening to their family member.

Parents' Perceptions

When the first signs of mental illness become apparent, its elusive nature tends to cause both the patient and the family to delay in confronting this grave reality. Every parent can pinpoint several critical episodes no matter how many years ago they took place that marked their lifelong trajectory as the family of a mentally ill patient. There are different paths through which the first signs of abnormality in a son or daughter were discovered. Roughly four patterns have been found among the parents interviewed.

Adjustment Problems

Typically, the pattern of recognition is that the child begins to show various adjustment problems during adolescence. The teenager begins to have academic and social problems in school, or there are difficulties at home and sometimes at work. The onset of puberty introduces an emotionally unstable period of life, requiring major adjustments in the course of growing up. Graduating from high school, leaving home, going on to college, or starting a first job are all particularly stressful turning points. Therefore, when symptoms coincide with these transitional stages, it is not uncommon for parents to at first ignore the changes in their child and to see them simply as growing pains. But there comes a time when these signs can no longer be ignored.

The details of each breakdown episode depend on family background, the living conditions at the time, and the type of mental illness, sometimes complicated by the patient's involvement with drugs.

When Wallace Green, 63, a successful doctor, looks back, there were some strong signals of aberrant behavior that he did not pick up at the time but that were clearly leading to his son Mike's first psychotic breakdown several years later. In retrospect, Wallace thinks that his son became symptomatic probably as early as high school. Mike was 30 at the time of the interview with Wallace. Although Mike successfully graduated from high school with an excellent academic record and eventually went on to Cornell to study music, he always had difficulty in completing projects. But interactions with his peers were even more difficult for him. Wallace felt that his son was often manipulative and a liar, which had been basically perceived as a personality problem. However, he and his wife were divorced when Mike was in his teens, and because Mike was living with his mother most of the time after the divorce, Wallace thinks that there might have been more obvious signs that he was not exposed to, and that, not wanting to admit there was a problem, his ex-wife covered up a lot for Mike. Four and a half years ago, when Mike dropped out of graduate school, he was already showing occasional signs of being delusional. One day at his mother's house, he broke the television set and then removed the CRT, which he believed was planted by the FBI. Twenty-five-year-old Mike was clearly and acutely psychotic. When Wallace finally went to see him, his son had been hospitalized on an emergency basis on a psychiatric unit and was "totally delusional and in a horrible shape."

Robert Kirk, 71, vividly remembers the 18th birthday of his son, Ben, which he and his second wife organized, together with her own three children. Ben was clearly acting strangely: he was giggling to himself and making motions up into the air as if he were talking to someone else, although no one was there. Not too long afterwards, Ben was found by a neighbor talking loudly and hollering up on the roof of the family home. Despite his wife's caution, "Something's wrong," Robert denied it. This also coincided with the time when Ben had a bitter argument with Robert, moved out of the house, and lived on his own. It was a move that Robert recalls with enormous regret today. Ben soon began drinking and taking drugs, switching jobs, and moving frequently, and eventually he was evicted from his apartment. It was after he moved into his grandmother's house that the breakdown occurred. He would creep up behind her with a pan and a spoon, bang them together, and give her a horrible fright. Robert finally contacted mental health authorities.

Drug habits developed during adolescence can also lead to or magnify the effects of mental pathology. Frank Brown, 66, thought that his 35-year-old son Dan's personality problems and inability to cope with life originated from his upbringing. But today he believes Dan's drug addiction and the bad crowd he hung out with triggered his mental illness. Dan's brother Mark was much bigger than Dan physically and excelled in sports and at many other activities. When Dan attended Mark's school, some of his teachers compared Dan unfavorably to his brother. Frank thinks that being compared to his older brother was a strain on Dan and thus he developed a chip on his shoulder. Dan started hanging out with pot smokers and other people who were "not in his best interest," as his father said, and began missing school. Naturally his grades suffered. At 13, he stole pot leaves from a neighbor and got in trouble with the police as a result. It was a tough time for his children, as Frank and his first wife were divorcing, which was traumatic and stressful for everyone. Frank gained custody of the children, all of whom were supportive, except for Dan. Despite his excellent skill in solving any kind of mechanical problems, Dan could not get along with others at work and quit his job, which made his father take the stern measure of telling him to move out. At this point, he was already in his late 20s. "I wish he would have gone in the military as a matter of fact, but he never did," Frank says. "I was in the army and it didn't hurt me a bit. It was very good for me." Frank thought that a tough, character-building experience would solve his son's problems. Dan changed jobs a number of times and moved to the area where his old drug-user pals lived. And when he met Georgia, nicknamed "the Speed Queen," it was the beginning of the end. He had only been smoking grass up to that point, but after meeting Georgia he began using methamphetamine, and his behavior deteriorated. He was paranoid as well, and that's when the possibility of mental illness finally came to Frank. When he visited Dan's apartment, he was shocked beyond words. His son became very explosive and started yelling. Frank thought he was "definitely a mental case."

For Japanese parents, drugs are not yet as rampant a threat to their children's lives as it is in the United States. But poor school attendance and poor performance are often the first indicators of their children's failing mental health.

Reiko Matsuoka's husband and his relatives are all highly educated people, graduates of prestigious universities. Naturally, Reiko, 56, and the whole family had high expectations of her oldest son, Shigeru, who was not only a wonderful student academically but also good in sports. But at 14, he began to skip school and stay home, doing nothing. He would leave for school in the morning, and then return home at once. Soon he stayed home all the time. He would stay up all night and sleep all day. His concerned mother would meet with the school counselor. The counselor patiently listened to her concerns, but could not provide any fundamental solution. Then, on Christmas day, Shigeru, who was by then quite big, suddenly became violent, kicking Rieko, and shouting "I'll show you how stupid you are!" She had bruises all over her body, and she thought her son was going to kill her. Another time, he set fire to a curtain. The family home became a shambles. He also expressed great hatred for his father. "I wondered how I could survive those days," Reiko recalls, with tears in her eyes. But both the parents and the counselor thought Shigeru was going through a phase of so-called school refusal and intrafamily violence, a very serious but not uncommon psychological problem of school children in Japan.

"Tôkô Kyohi," school refusal, is a well-known phenomenon, which is representative of problems the Japanese education system is facing today. Japan has almost the same school system as the United States: nine years of compulsory education and three years of high school, which a majority of teenagers complete. However, the Japanese educational system, especially at the precollege level, has been criticized for its competitiveness and over-emphasis on uniformity. The strong pressure to conform to many school rules and survive frequent academic testing has led to adjustment problems for many Japanese students, which has been an ongoing problem since the mid-1970s. Unlike most truancy problems in the United States, "Tookoo Kyohi" is often regarded as a psychological problem of stressed-out students who develop a type of school phobia. They typically come from highly educated families and have been good students. These students know very well that they must attend school and feel extremely ashamed of not being able to do so. They somehow cannot get themselves to go because of neurotic symptoms or somatic discomfort. It is reported that the total number of school refusal children reached over 139,000 in 2002.[6] Sooner or later, not a few of these frustrated, home-bound students resort to the behavior known as intrafamily violence. Not all school refusal children become violent, but quite a few of them exhibit violent behaviors at home after a period of time. The motives and the cause of the behavior are entangled with various problems of family relations. The duration of the violent period also depends on the individual child, but the target of hatred and violence is most often a mother or father. Again, this is most likely to appear in relatively wealthy and well-educated middle-class families. Parents are severely beaten by their own children and the whole family lives in fear of a violent outburst and abuse by the child. Usually out of shame, the family tries to hide this domestic situation and refuses intervention from the outside until the point when it becomes uncontrollable. There have been incidents where overstressed parents ended up killing a violent child. Although school refusal and violence are quite serious matters, Japanese parents or teachers usually do not connect these manifestations to a psychiatric problem. It never occurred to the Matsuokas that the problem of Shigeru, who was only 15, was a psychiatric illness, even though she consulted with three doctors, who recommended letting Shigeru live alone. Then one day, after he started to live by himself, Shigeru was found sitting on the sidewalk and apologizing profusely to passersby. This was the point when Rieko decided to take him to a psychiatric hospital for the first time.

Of Japanese parents interviewed, at least three reported cases of escalating violence at home, which began with failing school performance. School refusal often begins during the junior high school years. Failing a university entrance examination is also a trigger.

School refusal does not necessarily develop into intrafamily violence, however. Osamu Kinoshita's 15-year-old son, Noboru, reported constant somatic problems. His intense mental discomfort was always expressed as a bodily complaint such as "I cannot do anything because my glasses are bad," "I cannot see things well because I cannot integrate what I see with right eye and left eye," or "My right brain and left brain are confused." There were times when Osamu had to call an ambulance, but there was never evidence of physical illness. Noboru also began spending a lot of time washing his hands and he became slow in getting anything done. But all Osamu could think about was that his son was going through a phase, which would pass with time. He placed Noboru in a private school for children with adjustment problems, but his son could not continue. Because school refusal and intrahome violence are the major psychological problems among Japanese teenagers, parents, teachers, counselors, and even doctors often fail to detect signs of a more serious psychiatric illness. Particularly confusing is the fact that it occurs around critical transitional points: childhood to puberty and puberty to young adulthood; therefore, it is more likely to be interpreted as a social adjustment problem, which delays the needed medical intervention.

The Child Who Was Always Troubled

While adolescence is one of the turning points when parents notice their children behaving differently, some parents think their children always showed various behavioral and personality problems from early childhood, such as hyperactivity, compulsive behavior, and violence. In other words, as long as they could remember, their son or daughter was always a troubled child. These parents had sought help from child psychologists and psychiatrists for a number of years, but even so they never imagined that the child might be suffering from a psychiatric illness. In addition to the fact that developing schizophrenia during preadolescence is not typical, it is extremely difficult to make the diagnosis in very young children. Children are not yet capable of explaining their delusions and hallucinations. Other symptoms, such as communication or behavioral problems, can be mistaken as signs of other childhood developmental disorders.[7]

Maria Hafer, 61, thinks that her son, Jeff, already had difficulty with other children around four years of age, and signs of extreme irritability and maladjustment were sufficiently evident to put him in a special education program in public school. When he was 11 or so, Jeff began showing certain compulsive behaviors such as not stepping on the floor but moving from chair to chair, which began innocently when he was playing with his sister, but soon made Maria feel that it was no longer a game. By the time he was 13, it was very clear there was a serious problem. It was at the end of August, in the middle of the family vacation, that Jeff's compulsions went out of control. He became panic-stricken and ran off into a swamp, and his father followed to rescue him. Everyone in the family realized something had to be done.

Kelly Seeman, 72, can relive that day more than 30 years ago when she fell in love with a little boy of four at an adoption agency. As she recalls, "It was totally an emotional experience." Little Allan, just abandoned by his biological family, was playing with some toys on the table, intently manipulating them with considerable dexterity. He was a beautiful boy. But in retrospect, Kelly admits, there were a number of problems with this adoption. The licensed adoption agency, which saw Kelly and her husband as a desirable, stable couple, approached them at very short notice. A hasty and difficult adjustment was required from both the boy and the new parents. But more problematic was the fact that Kelly gave little thought to the practical side of raising this child. She now thinks that she was quite naïve.

> I also considered myself omnipotent. The one thing that the agency said to us was that this child is an angry little boy. And, instead of listening and heeding what they were saying, I took this as a challenge. This is an angry little boy who I was going to love and help not be angry.

The problem soon became evident. Allan started to act out his anger very aggressively. Right from the beginning he had difficulty playing with and relating to other children. He was a child of "Three A's, angry, anxious, and asthmatic," as Kelly described it. At 12, Allan became increasingly reluctant to go to school. He preferred staying home and, when feeling secure, he was able to focus and draw for hours. But most of the time he was labeled "hyperactive," "disruptive," or "unstable." Kelly would bring him to the emergency room in the middle of the night because of an asthma attack. The stress of just going to school and interacting with other children became a major task he could no longer handle. Kelly took him to a psychiatrist, but by the time he entered his teens, she had to admit that she no longer had the capacity to control him.

Pat Bryant, 57, another mother who adopted a boy, Nick, at two months old, remembers the child was hyperactive in preschool. He would break things and teachers would tell her that his attention wandered. Pat was already arranging regular sessions with a child psychologist for him when he was ten. Nick soon started drinking and smoking cigarettes and marijuana. By the time he was in high school, he was a regular user of all types of drugs, mixing them with alcohol. He would steal Valium from his grandmother. According to him, this was self-medication to keep himself balanced and calm. In spite of all these habits, he always managed his schoolwork well and went to college.

Miki Maeda, 65, in Tokyo, was frustrated with one of her twin daughters, Misa, who "just could not do ordinary things in an ordinary way." The signs of her mental problems were clearly perceived by her mother from early childhood. At ten, Miki noticed Misa was bothered by trifling things. For example, she would worry that the school lunch was poisoned. When a spot of soup was on the floor, she would insist that it was blood. Then she started to be afraid of going to school. Not being able to eat or sleep, she lost weight and weakened. Her obsessive–compulsive behaviors were incorrigible: once starting to brush her teeth or to wash her hands, she did not know how to stop. According to her schoolteachers, Misa seemed unable to concentrate. Miki had no hesitation in taking her daughter to a psychiatrist. The doctor diagnosed her as having "shinkeishou" (neurosis in Japanese), which Miki thought was a reasonable assessment. Besides, she was slightly relieved; if it was "neurosis," it could be cured.

During the high school years, Misa became a typical school refusal student, complaining about numerous somatic symptoms. Miki took her to many kinds of medical doctors, but no substantial physical problem was ever discovered. Even after Misa reached her late teens, Miki's daughter often acted like a little child, crying and making demands like a spoiled little girl. In fact, she still thinks that it was only the booming economy that at the time allowed "this incredibly childish daughter" to get a job. But after one year, Misa could not handle the pressure and the sense of competition from the other younger women workers in the office. When she broke down and was taken to the emergency room, she could not even move her body; it was as if she were paralyzed. She had not been able to eat, sleep, or keep herself clean for some time.

When the Signs of Illness Appear Out of the Blue

The third pattern of recognizing the first signs of abnormality was indicated by parents who thought they had a very normal, healthy child until one day life changed abruptly and they realized something was seriously wrong . In fact, these parents had considered their children excellent in many aspects; "a star" student or a promising young professional, as they tended to be highly intelligent and had been the pride of the families. One Japanese father described his daughter as "a golden egg" for him and his wife until she developed symptoms of schizophrenia. In these cases, the very first sign came unexpectedly, almost out of the blue, sometimes reported by a third party in school, a neighbor, or a law enforcement officer. Sometimes the sick child voluntarily asked for help and surprised parents by being fully aware that something was wrong. Usually, parents have no choice but to face the reality immediately, which results in quick, appropriate help seeking from a mental health professional.

Rosana Olmos, 64, had twin sons, Andy and Raymond, who were stars in every sense: handsome and attractive, good students, and excellent football players. One day when they were 17, Andy looked upset, sitting at the dining room table with his head in his hands. When Rosana asked, "Andy, what's the matter?" his response was "There's something wrong with my head, I can't think clearly. I feel kind of confused. If I walked out of my classroom and someone said where do you live, I wouldn't know what to tell them." Rosana immediately sensed something seriously wrong. They went to a psychologist who wasted no time in placing him in a psychiatric hospital for the next six months. Things happened very fast. After this incident, it was not even a month before Raymond, the other twin son said to her, "I had this great basketball game today. I was the star player, I have this microphone in my teeth that tells me how to play." He was also hospitalized at once.

Ann Berger's son, Stan, was also an exceptional child. His IQ was 150 and in sixth grade he was enrolled in a program for gifted children. But within six months after starting college, he became depressed and went for counseling. Then one day, he called home and said to Ann, "Mom, come and put me in the hospital and don't let me talk you out of it." He knew that something very serious was happening to him.

Linda Katz's son, Rick, also volunteered to see a psychiatrist. It was when he had just turned 20 and was starting his third year of college. Linda and her husband came back from a vacation in Europe, and Rick said, "Mom I want to speak with you. I'm not feeling well and I'd like to see a doctor." When Linda was about to make an appointment with their family doctor, he said, "No, not that kind of doctor. I want to see a psychiatrist." That was the first time she was aware that he had a serious problem, and she never forgot how surprised she was.

Kôichi Takagi, 61, was a typical workaholic Japanese company man who had little time left for his family. It had been three years since his wife had passed away. He had continued to concentrate on his work and never dreamed of facing his son Tamotsu's illness. "It was a complete shock!" he recalls of the evening he received a phone call from an officer of the

Tachikawa Railroad Station located in a suburb of metropolitan Tokyo. The station master said that his son was in custody. Tamotsu claimed that he was being followed by someone and was very scared, and he asked the station officer to protect him. He traveled all the way to Tachikawa, knowing that the Japanese Self-Defense Forces military base was there, and he thought that would protect him. Kôichi went to pick up his son at midnight. However, what came as an even bigger surprise was that Tamotsu suggested he should be taken to the Kunitachi Hospital, saying, "Dad, I know the doctor there. The doctor can be contacted immediately." "What is going on?" was the question racing through Kôichi's mind. Soon he learned that Tamotsu had been seeing the doctor at this hospital when his mother died. Kôichi had no idea. The following day the father and son were in a taxi on the way to the hospital. Tamotsu suddenly became agitated, shouted, and tried to get out of the car, which finally made Kôichi realize the seriousness of the situation. Upon arrival at the hospital, his son was immediately admitted into a closed unit. It all happened within 24 hours, and it changed Kôichi's life forever.

Shoko Inose, 63, was a widow for many years. She was just thinking to herself that her years of hard work raising her only child Mamoru by herself would finally pay off now that he had graduated from a top university in Japan and had gotten a job in a prestigious corporation. He was truly a son to be proud of and the precious treasure of her life. The future looked bright for both of them. It was three weeks after he started in the company's new employee training program when Shoko received a call from Mamoru, who said in a feeble voice, "Mom, people are saying bad things about me in a train. I can hear them." Almost instantly, she took the train, rushing to see her son who was in Kobe, hundreds of miles away from Tokyo. The sight of him made her speechless: he had been missing from the company dorm one evening and was found squatting down on the street. A senior colleague had already taken him to the hospital, where the doctor diagnosed him as simply having a "transient symptoms resembling schizophrenia" and advised him to have a good rest.

When There's No Real Pattern To Be Discerned

There are cases which do not clearly fit into the first three patterns: children who had already reached early adulthood, some in their 20s or even in their early 30s. A few of them had a normal life, with a relatively successful career, but most had a rather bumpy journey marked by much trial and error, in pursuit of the job or the lifestyle they felt most comfortable with. In some cases, the development of mental illness was compounded by their physical health problems, involvement with drugs, religious cults, or radical social movements. Although the parents had detected much evidence of maladjustment to society in their children for a number of years, it was difficult for them to link their children's situations to psychiatric illness, because in most cases they were functioning adults, at least at a minimal level. Like the first type of symptom recognition, it usually takes parents some time to turn to a psychiatrist.

Barbara Weiss, 65, was extremely worried about her daughter, Jessica, when she quit her job at a well-known airplane company and, despite her mother's efforts to talk her out of it, went off to Central America to start a new life with a group of other young people. Jessica was 24 and it was the age of "flower children." She came back after six months, feeling very ill, and hallucinating on some drugs. She was disoriented, hearing voices, and couldn't get her thoughts together. She also suffered from a serious case of hypoglycemia, so Barbara thought that was the main cause of her daughter's condition. Jessica went on an organic diet, without medication, and it seemed to be working for a while. But the voices came back as soon as she began eating regular food. It was not long before Jessica was diagnosed as having schizophrenia, and it was just the beginning of a number of hospitalizations for years to come.

Haru Morimoto, 64, and her husband were surprised to learn that their only son, Hitoshi, had been expelled from school. It had taken him three years to pass the competitive entrance examination, but he was eventually accepted into the philosophy department of Kyoto University, the most prestigious university in Japan. He ended up staying there for six years until the notification came that he had not earned enough credits to justify his student status and therefore would be expelled. He dropped out and came back to Tokyo. He ran a *juku*, a small private cram school, for about three years, but started drinking and quit the school business. Hitoshi was over 30 years old at that point and had not achieved substantial success in his career to match his pride and ambition. He began complaining that someone was watching him, that the TV was reporting his activities, and started making predictions about tomorrow. Haru and her husband did not take it seriously. But she still regrets today that neither she nor her husband had understood the gravity of the matter much earlier. Later, Hitoshi was diagnosed as "neurotic" at a hospital where he went for his constant somatic complaints, which is a euphemism often used in Japan for serious psychotic illness.

Dorothy, a daughter of Helen Hawkins, 71, had experienced no adjustment difficulty or personality problem. She had been healthy and active, and a model student in college. At 27, she was an attractive, popular woman, working as an executive secretary at a famous airplane company. Helen had no doubt that her daughter was enjoying life without any problems. So when Dorothy came home and said, "I think somebody's following me," Helen and her husband did not take it seriously. Then one morning when Dorothy was getting ready to go to work, she fainted, looking extremely fearful. During the next six months, she went for a therapy, but became increasingly paranoid and delusional.

Bruce, the only son of Timothy Rosen, 74, presents a mixture of many elements. Timothy always recognized discipline problems when Bruce was growing up. At age 11, the boy was seeing a counselor. Although he had a very high IQ and graduated from high school with honors, he started gambling and smoking marijuana, and his inability to make basic social adjustments became increasingly evident. He liked girls, but he wasn't able to relate. He became an unhappy, isolated young man. "And then this cult, the New Life Foundation, got a hold of his mind," Timothy says firmly, indicating that this was the turning point that triggered his son's mental deterioration. Timothy almost worried himself sick and tried everything to talk his son out of it, but with no success. Bruce went to their headquarters in Nevada and stayed there from time to time, and he began to have breakdowns. He would wander around the city, hearing voices and claiming a computer chip was in his brain and receiving messages. He would enter the mental health system, but would also go back to the New Life group again, until the group decided not to keep him any longer because of his symptoms.

The First Signs of Illness as Seen by Siblings

A mentally ill person's siblings report different perceptions of the first signs of the illness than their parents do. Many of the siblings were children in the middle of growing up themselves, so it was usually difficult to see their brothers' or sisters' condition as a sign of a distinctive illness. Rather, these siblings lived with a great deal of confusion and puzzlement because of their siblings' bizarre and antisocial behaviors, and at the same time were forced to accept them as a part of their families. If the siblings had already reached adulthood, they usually lived away from the parental home. In those cases, they did not have clear-cut memories of how the breakdowns had occurred; neither can they accurately pinpoint the onset of the illness. However, many of the siblings played a role in assisting and supporting their parents in the process of caring for their siblings.

Furthermore, some siblings interviewed had struggled with extremely dysfunctional family circumstances for a long time before mental illness surfaced, such as parents who themselves had serious emotional difficulties. For these people, mental illness was just another facet of the entire picture of family dysfunction. In any case, the siblings' experiences with their family members' mental illnesses usually began with less direct contact with the situation compared to the parents. How they perceive the issue depends on, and is complicated by, various factors unique to each family's structure, type of patient pathology, and the family's cultural and socioeconomic position.

Jane Wilson, 45, is the fifth of nine children. Her memories of her sister, Catherine, five years older, are entangled with her entire family situation. Their jobless father was a heavy drinker and once had been diagnosed as paranoid schizophrenic. She recollects that Catherine started acting out around the time their father had a major breakdown. Thanks to the right medication, which he took for the rest of his life, his condition was later stabilized. However, family life was constantly upset by the confusion Cathy caused. The earliest memory of there being something wrong with her sister went back to when Jane was around ten. Catherine and Jane were in the kitchen together alone, and Jane pointed out that Catherine was doing something their mother would not approve of. Catherine suddenly grabbed Jane, digging her nails into her arms, and said, "If you tell anything I'm going to kill you!" "The way she said it and the way she pressed on me, I knew she meant it, kind of," Jane recalls. "It was very frightening for me and it was one of those moments when I just thought, … 'Oh, I don't understand what's happening.'" Catherine was a Bo Derrick looka-like beauty, who attracted many different boys, but her extroverted manners were often embarrassing to Jane. She also frequently ran away from home. As a little girl, Jane looked at Cathy and her own home with fear, puzzlement, and detachment.

Marianne, 43, can more clearly distinguish the breaking point of her sister Emily, who is three years younger. Marianne, married at seventeen, was living one street over from her parents. The first recognition that something was wrong with Emily was a phone call from a neighbor, who said she was dead drunk and passed out on the neighbor's front lawn. Marianne was also shocked to find some written notes from her sister's girl friends at school, saying that she should not be sleeping around with boys. Emily would run away periodically. A few months after Emily and her parents moved to Washington state, Marianne learned from her mother that her sister was pregnant, which was just "mind-boggling" to her. Though Emily delivered the baby and even managed to graduate from high school eventually, she did not take care of her little daughter (her parents eventually gained custody of the child) and continued to have relationships with many different men. She would disappear for weeks and months, and at one point was working as a prostitute in Las Vegas. All this pained the family, especially her parents. No one knew what was wrong with Emily. She had not yet been diagnosed and was simply showing so many "strange and confusing behaviors."

Jodi Kramer, 59, remembers a shocking moment when her older brother Doug came over to her house, disoriented, saying TV characters were talking to him. After serving in the Air Force for four years, Doug went to mortician school and was working in the autopsy room of a general hospital. Jodi was already married then and had two children. His real major breakdown occurred when he was around 29. He became very hostile to his mother, who was living with him, and started to threaten to gas and kill her. Eventually, the police had to be called.

Mieko Maruyama, 65, the oldest of seven siblings, knows the true meaning of a dysfunctional family. A younger brother committed suicide at the age of 46. Another brother became alcoholic and was later found dead alone in his apartment. Their father, a violinist and a selfish tyrant, forced all his children to be perfect musicians to fulfill his dream of creating a family quartet. He was ambitious, but never a stable provider.

Mieko's mother was practically a slave to her husband and worked as a housemaid to support the family. Only Mieko escaped her father's oppression by marrying. Even after several decades, she talks bitterly and painfully about her family, which she says was "abnormal in all respects."

One of the remaining brothers, Yôsuke, a musician, started to skip out of restaurants without paying. He began stealing Mieko's money, too. He would wander from town to town, sleeping rough. Mieko was married and busy with her own family as well as her in-laws, so she does not know when the first hospitalization took place, but she imagines that he was hospitalized involuntarily a number of times. Sometimes he sneaked out of the hospital and she had to let him stay overnight. Other brothers all became ill almost at the same time and occasionally interfered with Mieko's life, but she never knew the details of how their illnesses developed. Her only sister, Yumiko, was also showing obvious signs of emotional instability.

Junko Nomura, 56, also feels that her sister, Chieko, could neither handle nor resist the control of their mother, a self-centered tyrant who Junko now believes always had a borderline personality disorder. After Junko married and had her own family, she did not see her sister for some time. When she came back to visit her mother and sister, she noticed Chieko's unusual level of apathy, but Junko did not take it seriously at that time. Although her aunt, a nurse, urged that Chieko should be hospitalized, no one took the needed action. Soon Chieko's condition further deteriorated: she became verbally abusive and even delusional. When Junko saw her sister harshly criticize others, she thought, "Oh, Chieko's changed! She's become like our mother!" One day when Chieko came back to her apartment, she was extremely high, and obsessed with talking about politics. She said, "Saga Sen (a famous political journalist) is stealing my ideas," and "Something is steaming out from the newspaper. Orders are issued from the transformer of the electric poles...." Junko at last realized that her sister was sick.

Instead of being a bystander of the family chaos, some siblings took a central role of intervening in the crisis at home because their parents were dead. In some cases, even if the parents were alive, they were incapable or totally unreliable. These siblings had to become the surrogate parents, or to act as the head of the household at a very young age.

Melanie Wood, 56, recalls the day almost forty years ago when she came back home from college, and noticed that her older brother's behavior had become bizarre and erratic. Joshua would lock himself in his room for days without taking showers. He began hearing voices and became paranoid. But her parents were "pretty uneducated about things and thought he was going through a difficult time as an adolescent." Her mother didn't want to listen or deal with it and her father didn't know what to do. One day when Joshua bashed his hand through the door and behaved in a very bizarre fashion, Melanie thought something had to be done. She called the psychiatric emergency team, and the rest was "a big scene."

At 21, several years after World War II ended, Shin Okabe, 70, was to all intents and purposes the head of the household. The family had lost everything, and in a few years, both parents passed away. As the eldest of five siblings, Shin worked hard to support his brothers and sisters. It was a tough time for everyone, and their main concern was how to survive each day. All his brothers and sisters worked hard, except for the youngest sister, Yasuko, whose arm had been badly injured in an accident during the war. She was severely handicapped and, feeling that she was of no use to the family or anyone, she became withdrawn at home. In the early 1960s, Shin noticed that she was staring at the ceiling with a strange glare. She also began to wander around the neighborhood, which worried Shin, who even followed her around the town. Yasuko became verbally abusive to their other siblings, too. These incidents bothered him but weren't taken seriously by anyone else. He and the other siblings simply thought that Yasuko was strange. But he could no longer think this way when she made a scene at another sister's wedding reception, becoming extremely upset and crying like a child, so Shin finally took her to the hospital.

The Spouse's Point of View

The spouse of a mentally ill person also noticed the first sign of illness in his spouse's personality changes or bizarre behaviors. The perceived symptoms are verified by their children, the spouse's colleagues, or others in their social circle. Some can trace a certain behavioral pattern that already existed when they first met and married, that suggested the later development of illness.

Gordon Collins, 50, met outgoing, beautiful, and assertive Andrea at a dance class and they started dating. But he was shocked to see her apartment for the first time because it was buried deep in trash, a mess like he had never seen before. He cleaned up for her, finding coins worth close to $200, which oddly made him feel she was an interesting challenge. In fact, she was not like anybody he had ever met, which stimulated him to continue seeing her and to find out what would happen next. Six months later, they got married. Andrea, a nurse, soon started to show problems at work. She could not keep proper patient records, and in private her mood swings were increasingly conspicuous. She would also sleep a lot.

Willam Baker, 58, was utterly bewildered seeing his wife Martha turning into someone he did not know. When she was a college student and came to work for his restaurant for the first time, he thought she was a charming, hard-working young woman. Years after they married, Martha had been promoted to manager of a duty-free shop in charge of a big budget. One night when William was out of town, she called him and sounded hysterical. When he got home a few days later, her colleagues contacted him and told him that lately she had been acting very strangely. He also realized she was involved with people from a cult group, studying witchcraft. He told her that if she didn't stop, he would leave her, which made her give up the cult. But she began behaving in increasingly erratic ways, being often disoriented and extremely aggressive. She would get into trouble with her supervisors and was eventually laid off. William was shocked to see her change and hear language she never used before. He thought to himself, "No, this isn't the lady I married!"

Kôji Yamada, now 73, was 28 when he married Hitomi, then 23, from his hometown Niigata, a rural prefecture in Japan. Although she was fussy about distinguishing her things and others, basically Hitomi was hardworking, honest, and a good partner for Kôji. A few years after their first baby was born, she began hearing voices and became withdrawn at home. She would also claim, "Our next door neighbor is saying bad things about me." Kôji was puzzled by Hitomi's shouting for no reason and talking to herself. The turning point was 1964, the year of the Tokyo Olympics, when she ran away from home to Atami, a hot springs resort about two hours from Tokyo, and was found by the railroad station officer, who contacted Kôji. At that point, Kôji hospitalized her.

Few of these parents, siblings, and spouses were aware that these incidences were, just the beginning of their years of struggle with their loved ones' mental illnesses.

Notes

1. American Psychiatric Association, *Diagnostic and Statistical Manual of Mental Disorders.* 4th ed. rev. (DSM-IV-TR) (Washington D.C.: American Psychiatric Association, 2000), 298–99.
2. E. F. Torrey, *Surviving Schizophrenia* (New York: Quill, 2001), 32–87.
3. DSM-IV-TR, 307.
4. Torrey, 121.
5. DSM-IV-TR, 300–304.
6. *Mainichi Shimbun* (Mainichi Newspaper), "Futookoo Saita 139,000" (School Nonattendance Record High, 139,000"), August 10, 2002.
7. DSM-IV-TR, 307.

CHAPTER **3**

Family Response and Family Feelings

Days of Uncertainty

As the first signs of abnormality are recognized, families experience turbulent feelings: intense stress, insecurity, and pain. The development from the moment of first recognition to the first major breakdown, which usually necessitates a decision to seek psychiatric help, varies greatly in its length. How individual family members live during this period also seems to depend on their location in the family and, most importantly, how they interpret the patient's abnormality. But parents, siblings, and spouses all live with enormous anxiety, puzzlement, and a sense of uncertainty, not knowing what is going on with their loved one. They watch powerlessly as he or she turns into "a bit of stranger," as one mother put it.

One typical reaction remembered by family members is that they simply did not have time to feel anything they could articulate or they cannot recall exactly how they felt because they were thrown into a state of confusion they had never experienced before. They were completely absorbed in trying to manage the chaos caused by the mentally ill family member. If the mentally ill person exhibited antisocial or embarrassing symptoms outside the home, they, especially parents, became frantic about picking up the pieces and trying to keep up appearances.

Tetsuro Isono's son, Teru, had recently started a job at a very prestigious corporation but had trouble in adjusting to the new environment. After several episodes of bizarre behaviors and violence at home, he went missing for five days, until the police called his parents.

Every time something strange happened with his son, Tetsuro thought that being an effective, strong father would help his son get back on his feet. But some months before Teru was finally hospitalized, all Tetsuro remembers was simply "desperately taking care of each incident, what was pressing at each moment," and how he "couldn't even afford to contemplate what caused my son's strange behaviors."

When her older son Kenji's intrafamily violence broke out and progressively intensified during his junior high school years, Miyoko Tajima, 65, was at her wits end. The Tajima family was a typical Japanese home: a workaholic husband and a full-time homemaker who had total responsibility for domestic matters, including raising the children. Kenji would constantly beat her up, verbally expressing his grudges from years past as well as enormous hatred toward her. Every day, she thought it her responsibility to maintain the daily routines of housekeeping, and take care of her husband. It was the occasional visit by her husband's colleagues that made her most nervous. "My son was on the rampage in the room next door, screaming," Miyoko painfully recalls. "It made me stone-cold with fear that the guests would wonder what was going on. Eventually I asked my husband not to bring his colleagues to our home."

The sense of confusion is so overwhelming that it seems as though some family members do not know what to feel, or maybe they subconsciously suppress their pain at an earlier stage in the chaos. Confronting reality is sometimes more difficult than living with unresolved fear and denial. It is also the case that the term *mental illness* is often not in their cognitive dictionary.

Martha's erratic behaviors confused and disoriented William Baker for a long time. He did think something was wrong with his wife, so he tried hard to figure out why she was doing things that did not make sense at all. He kept asking himself "Why? Why?" Unable to understand her problem as a disease, he could not help being very angry at her many lies and her verbal and physical attacks on him. Then there was the strangely clever way that she changed her behavior in front of others so as to appear quite unremarkable. Seeing her destroy everything they had worked for together appalled him.

Anger was also expressed by Osamu Kinoshita, 64, whose son stopped going to school and idled away the days at home.

> I was very upset and angry because he worried me so much, especially because he was destroying his precious life. He can do fine if he tries. I did feel sorry for him, so my anger was mixed with pity. The ages fifteen and sixteen are supposed to be the most youthful, beautiful time of life. But what is he doing? What is he thinking?

How can he be in such a miserable state? Nothing can be worse than this!

Underlining the emotions of extreme concern and anxiety is fear, as Maria Hafer says. She did not understand her son's compulsive behaviors, "I was afraid of losing him!" Her frustration with the system at the time was definitely an added stress, and it took months and months of wasted evaluation time before she found an appropriate doctor for her son.

Frank Brown, 66, was devastated to notice his son's continual disturbance. He felt he no longer knew what to expect from his son. I don't know if he's going to go this way or that way," he says. "Anyway, I was very emotionally traumatized when I saw what was happening to Don."

Kelly Seeman had just felt overwhelmed by her adopted son Allan who needed a psychiatrist's care from a very early age. She "grabbed and latched onto the doctor" who recommended that Allan should be hospitalized. Although he was not a specialist in child psychology, just hearing the word *hospital* was a great relief for her. When Allan's antisocial behaviors worsened, she even had to worry about her safety. "His anger frightened me because it was just frightening to see and not know whether he would turn on me." She knew that she had no control over him, which made her feel hopeless at one point.

> [There were times when] I wanted out. And it was too hard. It seemed impossible to help this child to take any responsibility, to take charge of his own life in any kind of a positive way. There were problems with the law, with the neighbors, with school.

Osamu Kinoshita too felt he had completely lost control of his son. He now admits that he should have hospitalized his son much earlier, though he wonders if he was ready to accept the diagnosis of mental illness in those days. In desperation, he joined a cultlike religious group that promised a miracle cure for any disease. He and his wife threw themselves into the group's meetings for a while, but soon realized that they were in the wrong place.

Some Japanese mothers had forced themselves into an isolated position in their families and struggled alone without the help or understanding of their husbands. Japanese husbands, especially of the older generation, tend to think they can leave all domestic matters to their wives. Division of labor based on gender is still a very powerful force in the Japanese home. After the early honeymoon years and the arrival of their children, husbands who are addicted to work and wives whose utmost priority is the children begin to organize their lives along separate lines. Unlike marriage in Western countries, marital companionship is less important than parental responsibility. But the parental responsibility is also divided along gender lines: father as financial provider and mother as someone who raises and disciplines the child. It is not unusual for a couple to have little in common after years of marriage. Kei Yamamoto, 81, is such a mother, who once felt "I wish I were dead" when her son's violence escalated at home. She was also exasperated and angered by his verbal abuse. With no help from her daughter, she thought no one would understand. The pain and loneliness was so intense that she felt like killing herself.

Kôji Yamada also contemplated suicide when the pressure at home became too much to bear. One hot summer day, he thought he could not take it any more and wanted to end it for the whole family. It was the innocent sleeping face of his little daughter, Mayumi, that brought him back to his senses. When his wife, Hitomi, started to act in a bizarre and withdrawn way, he tried everything to make her feel better. He would take her out to parks or department stores on weekends no matter how busy he was. He had a business to run and a little daughter to raise. It was unusual for a Japanese man to be responsible for all domestic matters, but there was no one else. Bewildered by the condition of his wife, he even turned to a fortuneteller and *Ogamiya* (religious prayer healer), which only disappointed him. All he could think about was how her condition could be improved. However, the thought that he might have to live like this for the rest of his life made him feel hopeless. He became worn out and neurotic: one day he realized he could not stop involuntary movements of his hands and whistling. He began taking a tranquilizer, and then asked his doctor to increase the dosage. The despair at home caused him to have a phobic reaction at the thought of returning home every night.

Siblings' reactions to early abnormalities are different from those of either spouses or parents, who usually feel this stage more keenly and take it very personally.

As a little girl in the midst of constant family turmoil, Jane Wilson was far more concerned with fending off harm from her sister's behaviors than with worrying about her sister Cathy's actual condition. The turning point for the entire family was when Cathy ran away after a big fight with her father and everything became explosive. It seemed to Jane that much of everyone's life was spent in huge battles or desperate efforts to find Cathy. When her mother would go looking for her sister, Jane reported thinking to herself, "Why don't you just let her go? It's so nice when she's gone. Don't bring her back here." As Cathy's abnormal behavior intensified, Jane would spend a lot of her time alone at the library, riding a bicycle, or just sitting on the porch and playing with her hair. The most important thing was staying away from home as much as possible. But she remembers she was also quite resentful.

> My security and my peace were being so upset. It just made me so angry at her, at everyone, at the needs of the people who were helping. I mean, I say helping now, but at the time, it was like well, I'm not the one causing trouble, how come I'm the one who gets ignored? I remember that very vividly as a young person. But what I did was I just went off and made my own life.

Marianne Schmitt was able to get away from home by marrying young and establishing her own family. But whenever she heard from her parents about her sister, Emily, she couldn't help but feel bad for them. The parents were handling the situation relatively well, but it was unbearable for Marianne to see them carrying the double burden of dealing with Emily's behaviors and taking care of the baby she had abandoned. In order to take some of the load off her parents, Marianne decided to let her sister live with her for a while. This was the first time she was directly exposed to her sister's breakdown and she realized then the seriousness of Emily's condition. In the beginning she tried to offer support and to accept Emily for herself. But when Emily came into the living room and cut her wrists in front of Marianne's children, Marianne thought, "Oh my gosh! I don't want my children to see this," and at once called for an ambulance.

On Diagnosis

When families can no longer keep domestic chaos at bay, they contact a medical professional, or an acute breakdown leaves them with no choice but to contact the psychiatric system, sometimes as a result of a patient's involvement with law enforcement. Even if they already have spent some time in seeking help from the system in search of an answer, with little substantial success or convincing results, one inescapable day arrives when families must face the psychiatrist who gives them the verdict on their loved one's condition.

Today there are a variety of measures used to confirm the diagnosis. In addition to the diagnostic criteria in the *Diagnostic and Statistical Manual of Mental Disorders* which lists the symptoms of schizophrenia that have continued for at least six months, neuroimaging and neurophysiological studies can show physical changes in the patient's brain, such as enlargement of the lateral ventricles, decreased brain tissue, and hypofrontality.[1] Family reactions to the psychiatric labeling of the patient by the doctor are not uniform. Typically, the diagnosis evokes intense pain and other types of acute distress, which family members reported ranged from "extremely frightening," "intense shock," "speechlessness," to "It felt like the end of the world."

Strong Reaction: Pain

When he heard the diagnosis of schizophrenia for his son, the emotion Robert Kirk felt was earth shattering.

> God Almighty, it's like he's dead. If it's schizophrenia, the life of my wonderful son is gone. I mean, it's just … his life is ruined. He's going to have no life, that's what I thought…. Just the word *schizophrenia* struck terror in my heart. I mean, my God, he's got schizophrenia. That's a terrible mental disease and it'll never be the same. And I'm sorry to say, but it's true: he's never been the same.

Wallace Green was devastated and anguished to hear his son had schizophrenia. Being a medical doctor made it impossible for him to deny the facts. He was well informed about the illness and particularly fearful of the implications.

> I was quite aware of the seriousness of the disease. I did a dance between being a physician and being a father. And that placed me in a very, very painful position because on the one hand, I knew the malignancy of the disease and the prognosis, and yet it wasn't really getting to me fully, but it was there subconsciously, and I guess I was in a controlled state of turmoil. I emphasize *controlled state*. Of turmoil.

Wallace would try to talk to his son every day, and see him several times a week. He recalls his feelings during those early days:

> I wanted to fix it, I wanted to control it. I was occasionally crying. I would always be hopeful. I always felt that there was a healthy portion of my son and if we could just embellish the healthy portion, we could get him somewhere. I was going through my own process of accepting the disease myself.

But there were practical concerns as well. Wallace did not know what to expect from his son any more. Unpredictability brought a sense of fear and anxiety, making him wonder if he could get his son to take medication or if his son could be dangerous.

Helen Hawkins had read a number of books in an effort to understand what her daughter Dorothy was going through, and the possibility of schizophrenia was in the back of her mind. Nevertheless, to actually hear the doctor utter that word was just "awful": it was her worst nightmare come true. A Japanese father, Ichizô Ohira, 82, tried to escape into drinking when his daughter Megumi was diagnosed as schizophrenic. No matter how much he drank, however, he could not get drunk. It made him even more aware and alert. "It only made my agony bigger," he says.

There is a powerful shock implied in a simple question with no answer, "Why?" Tetsuro Isono kept asking to himself, "Why? Why? Why my son? There's no one with mental illness in my own or my wife's family." When Naoyo Abe, 77, learned her second son Mikio had a mental illness, she found herself desperately reexamining what had happened to him since he was a baby, asking herself "Why? What caused it?" She kept thinking, "When he was a little boy and had a high fever, he had convulsions. During high school, he fell off a dive board and hit his head in the swimming pool. But his brain wave was found to be normal. Then why?" When Haru Morimoto, another Japanese mother, was told that her son had schizophrenia, it meant the "end of the world." For her generation, it meant that he was crazy, insane. She wondered if she had raised her son in the wrong way. Her husband quit drinking his favorite tea and she quit coffee, praying to God that they would give up anything if their son would get better. They would have done anything to see him recover.

When the experience of facing the diagnosis is too painful, family members simply do not accept the diagnosis at first. They keep going back and forth between utter refusal to accept the diagnosis and a brief moment of acceptance until they hit the reality that there is no other choice but to accept it. Often acceptance on a logical and intellectual level comes first, but the hardest part is acceptance on the emotional or gut level. However, some parents refuse to accept a diagnosis for much longer periods than others. Their denial is so complete that it may adversely affect the welfare of their children.

Simply because she could not accept the schizophrenia label for one of her twin sons, Yoshiki, Satoko Katagiri started on a long journey of doctor shopping. She turned to anything that promised a magic cure by "alternative" methods. The hypnotherapist's ad that boasted of curing any disease through *seishin-bunseki* (psychoanalysis), captured her attention on a train. She turned to this man in desperation and sent Yoshiki to see him for more than a year. An enormous amount of money was spent, but the worst part was that in the meantime Yoshiki's condition rapidly deteriorated, showing more and more typical symptoms of schizophrenia. "I was the one being hypnotized by this man in those days," she recalls. When she realized this man's "method" was nothing but quackery, she was completely devastated by anger and guilt. She says, "It is painful just to remember it!"

Relief at the Diagnosis: A Neutral Reaction

Unlike the family members so far described, some clearly remember a strange feeling of relief rather than pain when the diagnosis of serious mental illness was delivered for the first time. Particularly if the whole family had been tormented for years by the patient's endless "incomprehensible" and "bizarre behaviors" with no convincing explanations, and was just about to reach the limit of their patience, the diagnosis brought them to a point where the questions they'd been asking for many years were finally being answered. As one American father said, "In a way, I was relieved. It's something that you can put your finger on. You know, it suddenly made sense." Or as one American mother said about the diagnosis of manic depression for her son, "Well, I think I was surprised maybe, but then when you think back about it … it really wasn't a surprise. Especially when I started to learn more about the symptoms, it began to make sense. He had pretty much self-medicated himself because he had unstable chemistry. The whole thing sort of came together and that seemed right."

Her sister's diagnosis schizophrenia put a final end to the years of questioning by Marianne Schmitt and her family, "What's going on? Is it this, is it that? Was it her childhood, or was it some other factor?" and gave more perspective to the problem, making it easier for them to deal with it.

> That was kind of a relief, just being able to put a title on it, that there actually is something wrong with her, because then you have a little more sympathy for the situation and you have sympathy for her. It's something out of her control. She's not just being rebellious. So it's something that has control of her.

The sense of relief also came from the awareness that, based on their own observations and speculations, the diagnosis did not seem as bad as "other diagnoses." This even gave them a sense of hope. For years Glenda White, 56, had been distressed, scared, and overwhelmed by Shelly, her 16-year-old daughter. Knowing what it meant to be mentally ill herself, the last thing she wanted for Shelly was to be classified as mentally ill. When she heard the doctor say Shelly had a borderline personality disorder like her mother, it made Glenda sad, but at the same time she thought, "I knew it wouldn't be as devastating as some other diagnoses, like schizophrenia." In her mind, her daughter would be able to function if she wanted to, as she herself had done. Borderline personality disorder is characterized by patterns of unstable interpersonal relationships and affects, poor self-image, impulsivity, fear of imagined abandonment or rejection, and inappropriate anger. Symptoms are enduring and have a significantly negative impact on the person's life. However, it is not categorized as a psychotic disorder, which is often accompanied by hallucinations and delusions.[2] Glenda confesses, "They said this was a good diagnosis, because you are not 'crazy.'"

Though he did not know much about mental illness, Gordon Collins still felt his wife's diagnosis of bipolar-type II sounded slightly better than manic depressive, which meant, for his generation, that the only treatment was hospitalization. What Gordon's wife was suffering from was one of the mood disorders that were also classified in a separate category from the psychotic disorders. It is an illness that involves an extreme degree of mood disturbances. It is largely divided into two categories: major depressive disorder and bipolar disorder. While the main features of major depressive disorder are episodes of depressed mood that are likely to be repeated after partial interepisode recovery, bipolar disorder repeats the cycle of manic and depression episodes. Bipolar is further divided into two types: bipolar I and bipolar II. A person with bipolar I disorder has at least one manic episode in which he or she exhibits intensely high mood and extreme behaviors followed by depression. A person with bipolar II also has periods of highs and lows, but the highs are hypomanic, and thus not severe enough to create problems in the person's social or occupational life.[3] Gordon feels:

> Saying it's bipolar — everybody scratches their head and says, "What does that mean?" Nobody even really considers that a label because they don't have the foggiest idea what it means. It's pretty much the same thing. But it's a way of destigmatizing it, by putting a label on it that nobody really understands.

The sense of relief was most strongly expressed by parents and siblings who felt finally that their mentally ill family member would be properly taken care of. "It didn't matter whether it was schizophrenia or something else!" Reiko Matsuoka, a Japanese mother, weeps every time she remembers the struggles of those early days.

> Schizophrenia or whatever, I didn't feel anything but desperate for a way to help my son. Please do something! Do anything to help him so that he can live a normal life, without beating up his parents.

Kôji Yamada was also relieved to see his wife finally taken into the medical system. "She will be saved at last," he thought. Junko Nomura even felt hopeful that she could finally discover what was wrong with her sister after all those years, and thought, "Now, the treatment can begin."

A certain fatalism and a sense of resignation were expressed by some Japanese family members. These were people who had been aware that there had been mentally ill relatives in earlier generations. Some of them had grown up seeing or hearing about a "strange" grandparent, uncle, aunt, or cousin, who gradually lost the ability to function or disappeared for long periods because of repeated hospitalizations. Some family members might have suppressed these memories to this very day, or they might have been more or less living with the conscious fear that such an illness might strike their loved ones. Yoshimi Naitô, 78, was shocked to hear her younger brother's problem was schizophrenia, but she also thought her family genetics had something to do with it. There was no seriously mentally ill relative so far as she knew, but she thought her brother's problem was the inescapable result of certain personality tendencies common to many other family members, which were described as "weakness" and "instability," terms perhaps marking serious, but not formally diagnosed, mental illness.

When Miki Maeda heard the doctor mention the possibility of schizophrenia for her daughter, she thought to herself, "What was destined has come at last."

> It was hard, of course. But since I had these relatives, I thought it was hereditary after all. I guess I'm different from other mothers in this respect. I thought it was my turn. I grew up seeing my favorite cousin who was quite close to me in age losing her sanity. We had played together, gone to school together, taken trips together. We were close. I was young, so I did not quite understand the situation then, but I was aware something was going wrong with her. I remember I wanted to make her better.

No Special Reaction

There were also family members who were not at first greatly affected by the diagnosis of mental illness. This was because they had little or no knowledge about mental illness at that time and had no idea what the terms *schizophrenia* or *manic depression* might imply in terms of their relatives' lives. Many had heard or even read about these illnesses but never understood the serious social and personal implications. These people say, "It didn't mean much to me," "We were very ignorant," "I had no idea what it meant," or "I had no idea whatsoever, except it's supposed to be a serious disease." Even those who were slightly better educated about mental illness had difficulty in connecting the diagnosed disease to their mentally ill family member. As William Baker says,

> Oh, I had heard about schizophrenia. Yes. But, I thought that was someone sitting in the corner, withdrawn, you know, and kind of just crazy.... No, I didn't think she [my wife] was crazy. [Laughter.] I knew she was strange, but not crazy.

The schizophrenia label on her son didn't mean much to Ana Berger, either, because:

> You know, he didn't talk like a crazy person. His sentences weren't all mixed-up or whatever. He was just very depressed. And, in a way, he talked like a normal person, but he couldn't function really very well. So, the diagnosis was just a name and I guess we put that down to his depression, basically.

The First Psychiatric Hospitalization

The first psychiatric hospitalization can take place when the diagnosis is made or at another time. It can also take place long before the final diagnosis because an accurate diagnosis might not have been made at the time of an emergency hospitalization. Sometimes the patient will finally be hospitalized long after the diagnosis has been made. In this case, the family may have managed to take care of the patient or tolerate his existence at home with the help of medication and outpatient treatment, until the point where his condition deteriorated to such an extent that the family was forced to act. One of the features of schizophrenia is that the majority of patients have little insight into the fact that they have a psychotic illness.[4] Therefore, most of these cases involve involuntary hospitalizations.

The experience of seeing their loved ones locked in the psychiatric unit like prisoners, and having to leave them screaming and crying behind a closed door, causes families excruciating pain. They are tormented, going back and forth between an unbearable sense of guilt at "betraying" their loved ones and the rational view that the only way to help and keep their loved ones safe is by hospitalization. They have to resist an intense desire to immediately rescue their mentally ill family members and bring them back home. They force themselves to recognize that if they come home now it will be the same old situation, and they cannot handle it any more. For many family members, the first hospitalization stands out to this day as one of the most traumatic life events, and as many describe with tears, "The hardest thing I ever did in my life."

Strong Reaction

"Oh, yeah, that was traumatic," Frank Brown says, recalling that indescribably painful moment. When his son Don was threatening suicide, there was no other way but to get the police and PET team involved. But he had to watch his son being taken by force before his eyes. When his son resisted, it was "a terrible scene like out of a movie." They bent him over the table, face down, and during the struggle his arm was badly injured. He was eventually taken to the university hospital's psychiatric ward.

> Oh, for me, it was the worst thing I've ever done. But you know, I had mixed emotions. On the one side, I felt very guilty about betraying my son, but it was a necessary betrayal. My mind said, you know, that there is a doubt. I doubted that he was going to kill himself. But I didn't know 100 percent. I interceded and I felt that this was necessary because something had to happen to help Don. And even today that's exactly my thinking right now. Something has to happen to help Don and I don't know what it's going to be.

Helen Hawkins's daughter, Dorothy, has been hospitalized several times, but the first time was something the whole family can never forget.

> [I felt] awful. Oh dear, you know my whole family, I'm sure they were just as devastated, but it was awful. The first time she was hospitalized she was screaming. "Please don't put me here," and my niece had never seen anything like that, because quite a few members of my family were with me. At one time when she was hospitalized she didn't want any family members to come and see her. It was too embarrassing for her.

Some Japanese mothers, too, couldn't describe the episode without bursting into tears. It was truly the most painful thing they had done in their lives.

For days, Leland Miller, 54, felt completely and utterly helpless after his family had to put Rosalyn, five years younger than Leland, into a psychiatric unit for the first time. Being the responsible oldest son and caring so much about his parents, he assisted them through this traumatic process.

> Well, I'll never forget, after we got her in the hospital and everything was done, so to speak, I cried. You know, I just broke down and cried. I really didn't know what to think, but I knew that there was something seriously, seriously wrong with my sister. And it was very, very, very upsetting to me.

His son's voice still haunts Robert Kirk.

> It was a mental health hospital in Orange County. And he said, "Get me outta here." And I just felt so bad, but I couldn't get him out. I said, "I'll see you every day and do what I can to help you."

Anger was the emotion Barbara Weiss remembers most when her daughter Jessica was in the hospital for the first time. She just couldn't believe that the bright student who had aspirations for herself was in this state. Barbara needed to look for someone to blame. First she got very angry at her ex-husband, who had left her and then died, because she wanted him so much to be there to help her. Then the anger was eventually directed at God.

> I looked around for people to get mad at. But I was really mad at God because this happened. I didn't see why this should happen to her. Not thinking "Well, why should it happen to anybody?" But in those days, I was thinking about her. My life was just going to visit her. My whole life was her and trying to help her. When she was down, I was down. When she was up, I was up. And that's the way my life was.

Neutral Reaction: Relief

Just as some were relieved to hear the final diagnosis after a long period of confusion, other family members also felt more relief than anguish when they saw their sick family finally hospitalized. Although the emotion was always mixed with sadness, guilt, doubt, and anger, they felt that their mentally ill family member was now in a safe place. Glenda White remembers experiencing many kinds of emotions at the same time. She was glad to see her daughter hospitalized, but also felt scared of the stigma, what people would say. She kept asking herself several questions: "Was I really doing the right thing? Was I truthfully doing it for her? Was I doing it for egotistical reasons? Is it just an ego trip on my part?" William Baker mostly felt relieved. He felt like he had accomplished something and that now his wife Martha would get the help she needed. Osamu Kinoshita was also relieved to see his son hospitalized because his lifestyle had degenerated into "sleeping during the day and staying awake all night and doing nothing." That his son would be able to get some treatment gave him hope, especially because he thought in those days, before he learned more about schizophrenia, that the disease would be completely cured by the treatment.

For others, the mere absence of the sick person in the home gave them space to breathe and time to think about themselves. Kelly Seeman is honest about her feelings after placing her son, Allan, in the children's unit of a psychiatric hospital.

> The help was mostly the absence of the stress. I mean, somebody else had responsibility for this child. I had my own life. That was where the help was. The help in understanding the child was not forthcoming. The help was only that I could cope with the dailiness of my life. I could get some satisfaction from the dailiness of my life and I didn't have this angry, acting-out, anxious child to cope with. The relief was there. That's what it was: relief. Did I understand this child better? Not necessarily. Did I get some insights into myself? Some. I began to perceive how I am not — was not — that omnipotent. That I could not be all things to this child. I could not make a life for this child. I did not know how to help him make a life for himself.

His younger sister Yasuko's hospitalization gave Shin Okabe a great respite. The previous two years had been just too difficult. The daily trouble and chaos she caused at home ended at once. By the end of that year both his older sister and Shin got married and started new lives. In the following year, his younger brother also got married. No one in his family ever intended to stay single as long as they did, Shin says, or intended to get married around the same time. It just "happened this way," he says. But he also feels it was not an entirely by chance. What he implies is that perhaps it was an indication of how much of everyone's energy had been consciously and unconsciously spent on taking care of the mentally ill sister, and therefore they had no energy left for planning their own lives. With Yasuko's first hospitalization as a turning point, the close family of five brothers and sisters, which had stayed together and protected one another since the end of World War II, began to scatter, "as if it had lost centripetal force." "Until then, we were so close," he says. "We lived with this sense of crisis, that unless we had strong solidarity, we could not survive. Of course, we had quarrels sometimes, but we were always good to one another." He feels since that point, however, the family lost its center of gravity and everyone started to drift away. Maybe everyone was exhausted by that time. He says:

> It was like after this center of gravity was gone, a suddenly centrifugal force blew everyone away. And not only were we physically

away, our feelings toward one another weakened, too. It must have been most difficult for my sick sister.

The first hospitalization truly marked a new stage for the Okabes when they could each begin to think about his or her own life.

Feeling Unsupported

In the middle of the shock and struggle with the new reality of mental illness, family members try to seek support and sympathy from outside. This is a natural reaction to any stressful event in life. However, not a few people reported being faced with misunderstandings or sometimes even cold rejection from others whom they turned to for support. About half of the family members interviewed both in the United States and Japan expressed their sense of isolation, loneliness, and even humiliation at one point in dealing with the illness. Their sense of being "unsupported" was most acute early on when they were feeling most vulnerable. This unsupported feeling could worsen because it was compounded by multiple factors, which placed the families in a vicious downward spiral. First of all, it was because of the strong social stigma against mental illness: from the moment of diagnosis, the family members themselves were well aware of how society in general would react to mental illness. This awareness forced many of them to choose not to talk about it and to decide to hide the illness no matter what, which then made them hesitant in reaching out for further help. It was also their own ignorance about and prejudice against mental illness that tormented them.

The first people that the families expected to receive some sense of support from were doctors and the other medical professionals they were forced to come in contact with. Medical professionals are often the only possible sources of both hard information and compassion in the beginning. However, it was not uncommon to hear families recall several episodes of encounters with medical professionals that were more painful than helpful and only added further stress to their already anguished state of mind.

Yoko Tomita was never the type to shun help from various resources to cope with worrisome changes her husband had begun to show. But when she contacted the mental health section of the local public health center, the counselor asked her on the phone, "Don't you think he became strange because of you? Doesn't it occur to you?" "In retrospect, what a terrible thing to say!" she recalls.

When Wallace Green, a doctor, went to see his son, who had just been taken into the emergency unit at "the best teaching institution in the world," what he heard from a fellow physician at the height of his agony was chilling. He was shocked by how a doctor could be so unsupportive.

> And the psychiatrist, the M.D., was inept. Inept. When I was bleeding and needed somebody just to look at me, and say Dr. Green, I understand how you feel. Those are magical words, *I understand how you feel*. He said to me, I'll never forget it, "Dr. Green, I think you ought to see a psychiatrist."

Furthermore, because of the patient's right to confidentiality, Wallace was unable to discover which hospital his son had been taken to, except that it was in another city far away from Los Angeles. When he was eager to fly to his son, it was the psychiatrist who would not divulge to him which hospital Mike was in. "I could have strangled that psychiatrist under those circumstances," he recalls. Although Wallace understands these rules probably better than most people, this fellow doctor's attitude of going strictly by the book was terribly difficult. "I'm a doctor, I'm a human being. Why couldn't he tell me where my son was? I mean there's a sense of what's right and practical."

Through this experience Wallace has come to believe that when family members are breaking apart, the real issue should be the family. He also has a cousin in psychiatry, whom he contacted. However, he couldn't get the information he was searching for.

> He was helpful during that period of time. And even remained helpful, but even with Roger [the cousin], I see he was acting the typical psychiatrist. A little removed and a little distant physically and kind of, tell me how you're doing, how are you? You know, they don't interact as much as the behavioral, clinical psychologist.

Frank Brown, a father, feels that some doctors had no emotional patience. He believes that there must be many wonderful doctors, but in reality, he confesses, he has not come across any. Another father, Ken Morris also feels that some doctors are condescending.

In the Japanese medical setting, doctor–patient relationships are likely to be more traditional and authoritarian, and patients usually feel uneasy about exercising their right to information about the diagnosis and treatment. It is only in recent years that the patient's right to information and decision-making about the treatment began to be introduced in Japan. Therefore, for Yoko Tomita and some other Japanese family members, the most frustrating thing was the lack of explanations about the illness from doctors. She had long wished that her husband's psychiatrist would spend more time with her alone to explain about his illness.

> I was most intimidated to see the doctor annoyed when I asked questions. First of all, it took courage for me to talk straight to him. So when he didn't take my concern seriously, it was quite a blow. I think a doctor's attitude like this brings nothing but more chaos to the family.

She understands how busy doctors can be. However, she is convinced that if doctors are not available, there should be a system within the medical institution that provides support and care for the patient's family members. "Lack of time and explanation, and lack of caring for the family members' pain" were most often heard from Japanese parents and siblings who had stressful experiences with medical professionals.

The second group of people the families of the mentally ill may turn to for support are relatives. This endeavor also brought disappointment and loneliness to some. William Baker had to realize his wife's mental illness was something that his family and relatives would never understand.

> And, most people don't understand. And, that's why you can't talk to anyone because they don't understand what you're talking about. And, a lot of them give me some ill advice, like "Why don't you divorce her?" "Well, nothing's wrong with her"; you know, all that kind of stuff.

Takashi Ishizawa, too, once talked to his wife's family after she became ill. All her parents and siblings were surprised. When he mentioned the possibility of heredity, her parents were defensive and denied it.

Seeking help in the wrong places and feeling discouraged about reaching further support vonly aggravated families' sense of helplessness. From a very early stage, Maria Hafer was always willing to seek outside help for her son Jeff's neurotic behavior. When he stopped talking and going to school, the principal of his public school called her and her husband into his office and said that he could solve the problem for them if they would give him permission to paddle Jeff. He believed this would make her son start talking. The lack of understanding of the nature of Jeff's problem was just astounding to Maria. When she contacted the local health center when Jeff's problem became too serious for them to handle, she was referred to the children's clinic. Months and months passed by, and they just continued to evaluate him, only to reach a conclusion that they did not have a specialist to treat him. They ended up recommending a private clinic.

> I was angry at the system. Hurt and angry.... [It was] an improper amount of time, doing evaluations on my son.... Yes. [All this time was wasted.] And I am still sure that if he had been seen and treated quickly, that original break would not have been so bad.

Maria and her husband also went into couples group therapy with a psychologist and thought of trying a church group run by a pastoral therapist. However, neither one addressed the specific situation of the parents of a mentally ill child. In fact, Maria herself was not sure in those days what Jeff's problem was. She thought she was struggling to cope with a difficulty in the home like many other families.

After his sister's psychotic breakdown and hospitalization, Leland Miller was living each day with wrenching pain. He did go to a counselor at college, just to find out it was not very helpful, because "they didn't understand anything about mental illness." The lack of knowledge and perspective on this particular situation only reduced him to just another client who was having some kind of personal crisis. When he talked with his friends, it was again impossible to get the kind of support he needed so much.

Others simply didn't even try to seek help. Ruth Singer, 68, didn't want to talk to anybody about her son Paul, as she says, "because of the stigma."

Japanese parents were even more consciously determined not to talk about the illness to anyone. Tôru Yamaguchi, 72, and several other parents flatly say they felt they had to hide it at first. Tôru explains, "I had relatives living nearby. If it was an ordinary disease, I might have told them about it. But it was a mental disease. I thought I had to hide it." However, when he once hinted about the problem to his younger brother who lived just around the corner, his brother became very upset and told Tôru never to bring it up in front of his wife. "He is such a wimp that he cannot sleep when he hears something about mental illness," Tôru says. His brother's family refused to associate with Tôru or his family. Neither Tôru nor his mentally ill daughter Yuri were welcome in their home. Tôru and his wife decided to keep Yuri's manic depression strictly to themselves. Running a small drugstore, he felt it was even more important to hide it from the neighbors and customers. The Yamaguchis became socially withdrawn, which ironically affected his business, later forcing it to close down. It had never occurred to him that there were places where they could find publicly financed resources. They were having a lonely battle all by themselves. Haru Morimoto and her husband were running a small clothing store, and the decision to hide their son's illness was almost "instinctive," they say. "We had a service business." So they kept it to themselves and never talked to anyone about it.

The problem for other Japanese parents was that they had no idea of where to go to get help. They themselves were too upset about their sons' and daughters' diagnoses to be able to deal with practicalities, and as Yoshiko Takada says, "I didn't know what to say."

Ichizô Ohira, 82, also chose not to tell anyone about his daughter's schizophrenia. Being a Christian and a regular churchgoer, he once told his Canadian pastor who was working at his church in Japan. But he was quite disappointed later to find out that the pastor had told others about his daughter's illness. In addition, he knew about public sentiment toward mental illness. Ichizô says, "Basically it is 'craziness,' right? People can't stand it. Schizophrenia is a disease. But for them, it is nothing more than insanity." So he and his family decided to do everything possible to keep it a complete secret. The only people these Japanese parents were able to express their feelings to and discuss their concerns with were the doctors in charge of their mentally ill children. Even though not all doctors were helpful in giving comfort to families, at least they were the professionals who knew about the disease, and other people usually had little or no knowledge about it.

Melanie Wood doesn't remember talking to her friends at college about her brother, Joshua. "I just didn't confide a lot. I was pretty closed about sharing a lot of stuff, you know," she says. It was particularly important for her to say nothing to the man she was dating at that time because she was embarrassed. She now thinks that it was one of the reasons for their breaking up after a short while. The man was from her hometown and made her uncomfortable.

One very natural reaction to the illness of siblings is the fear of becoming sick oneself. Some studies have indicated various concerns unique to siblings about their future.[5–8] When one child in a family has schizophrenia, the chance of a sibling becoming ill is nine times higher than a person who has no one with the disease in the family.[9] Siblings of the mentally ill are particularly haunted by this fear and it may interfere with the development of a healthy self-concept. But rarely are their needs for resolving this fear addressed, or the accompanying pain eased. They not only have to grow up with a sense of secrecy about the illness of their brothers and sisters, but also with the recurrent nightmare that they may end up the same way. Worst of all, they have a sense of hopelessness that no one else could possibly understand their feelings.

Jodi Kramer describes her thoughts in those days.

> Way back, it worried me to see this happening to my family. I worried for my own.... It was like I was worried for myself too because I was just young. Uninformed and still going through

emotional things and insecurities and then it magnified those things. Magnified my insecurities because ... if I had an emotional feeling, I always had to wonder "now, am I going crazy, too?" I couldn't take it as easily as most people can take emotional ups and downs because I have this right in my face that I have mental illness in my family.... There was really no need to talk. I had my husband. I talked to my husband about this and that was about all. Certainly I didn't have a support group. I mean, that wasn't popular at the time. I didn't have a church that I went to, so I didn't talk to people at church about it. And so it was a very sort of an unsupported thing that I really didn't talk about.

As the Illness Develops

Shock, guilt, hopelessness, despair, grief, anger — a variety of emotional responses have been recalled and expressed by all family members with regard to their earlier years of encounter with the illness. Sooner or later, each family member realizes that having to deal with the mental illness of the loved one is no longer an isolated incident that goes away after a while, but is something that has to be faced on a daily basis. The number of years the families survived following the onset of illness varied at the time of the interviews, ranging from 5 years to more than 30 years. The new shocking reality that a family member suffers from a mental disorder becomes an inescapable part of daily awareness deep down, whether they accept it or not. Distress tends to lessen the longer family members live with mental disease. It may transform itself into different kinds of chronic pain. However, the duration of the period does not necessarily correlate with the change in their perceptions of and feelings about the reality of mental illness in the family. Rather, it is the prognosis of the illness that has the most substantial influence on the families' distress.

Different mental disorders take different courses of development. Schizophrenia, for example, takes several types of course over the lifetime of a patient: some never have more than one episode of psychotic breakdown, while the condition continues to deteriorate in others.

It is reported that the possible course of the disease over a ten-year period following the onset of schizophrenia divides into four outcomes: 25% recovered completely; 25% are much improved; 25% are modestly improved; and 25% remain unimproved.[10] The prognosis for 30 years following diagnosis is better. As a patient ages, positive symptoms such as hallucinations and delusions often decrease. "It is almost as if the disease process has burned itself out over time and left behind only scars.... "[11] Manic episodes of mood disorders can slow down with aging.[12]

However, the clear mechanisms responsible for the better outcome seem to remain mysterious to many families and even to doctors, except that effective medications and psychosocial factors can have a positive impact on prognosis. The common pattern is that many episodes occur intensely during early adulthood, and the condition gradually progresses to a more mildly chronic state as the patient ages. McFarlane writes: "The range in between is occupied by myriad variations."[13] Furthermore, multiple factors including time, degree of disability, hospitalizations, contact with professionals, and other life situations within the family all combine to determine family members' perceptions.[14]

Reliable medication use has been stressed as being of primary importance. Research on antipsychotics has made impressive progress since the 1970s. Though medication does not cure the illness, it enables most patients with schizophrenia to control the symptoms. In addition to first-generation antipsychotics that affect the functioning of neurotransmitter receptors, second-generation antipsychotics such as clozapine, olanzapine, and risperidone have been widely available since 1990s and are believed to have greater efficacy and relatively less adverse effects.[15] Medications such as lithium and SSRI are also crucial for mood disorders as well as psychotherapy in helping patients understand their illneses.[16] However, mentally ill relatives of the family members I interviewed were in quite varying conditions with different degrees of severity and the ability to function. In this sense, the reaction to the illness is unique to each family, depending very much on the later development of the patient's life, as well as the various resources utilized by the family.

After it took Maria Hafer so long trying to find an appropriate facility for Jeff, her son with schizophrenia, he went missing for nine years, during which there were only occasional phone calls, mostly silent. Maria and her husband lived through years of anxiety not knowing where their son was, or whether he was alive or not. "We would worry, we would be frightened when we heard news on the radio about something happening to somebody. In some ways we were relieved that we didn't have to deal with anything. Guilty. Because we couldn't do anything."

The fear, which seemed everlasting, was ended one day by a phone call informing them that Jeff was in a state hospital in Arizona. When Maria was finally reunited with him, Jeff was a changed person with long, wild hair, heavily medicated, but still with the same voice, which his mother had no problem recognizing instantly.

Kelly Seeman often wanted out. It was too much for her after her divorce, carrying sole responsibility for a violent son who was in and out of jail and board and care. She wanted to get away from Allan, and in fact she moved to another state alone at one point for a few years.

> At the most difficult time I wished he were dead, and then that passed.... With me, everything, especially as it relates to my son, is not an absolute. I wanted to get away from him, but I was always very concerned. I love him very much, but I would like to see him dead.

But she always came back to him. She couldn't ignore the fact that no matter how much of a struggle it was, he was still very much a part of her life.

Wallace Green to this day still agonizes about his son's diagnosis, which was made about five years ago. He is still working on accepting the fact both intellectually and emotionally that his son has schizophrenia, but he cannot help but feel frustrated when he sees his son unable to lead a normal life as a young man, despite his intelligence, aspirations, and insight, which touch him tremendously.

> And to this day, I am anguished. My process has been different. I mean, just today I'm anguishing again because my reserve and my capacity to handle his loss of function is devastating for me. And on the one hand I want to strangle him and on the other hand, I love him.... I'm going through many insightful moments personally, as a result of my son's illness, and I have grown immeasurably. The pain has produced a great challenge for me, and as we talk, I'm going through it. And this is day by day.

No matter how many years pass by, her daughter Jessica's verbal abuse pains Barbara Weiss. Even though Barbara knows it is the illness, not her true self, that makes Jessica act abusively and violently toward her mother, it becomes unbearable to hear her say quite often, "I had a dream that you died," as if she were trying to kill her mother with these words.

> I actually sometimes have thought, "Why don't you die, Jessica." But you see that isn't where it's at. Or I've thought to myself, "Well, I'll die." Because many times I've thought, "God, take me. I don't want this anymore! I can't stand it anymore! And I can't seem to do anything about it! And so, take me! I've had it! If this is what you wanted me to learn, I don't ... I've learned whatever I'm gonna learn. It's my time to go." But you see, it doesn't work that way.

The sense of guilt never stops tormenting Reiko Matsuoka about her son, Shigeru, who was diagnosed as schizophrenic five years ago. Now she feels that she will have to take care of him for the rest of her life. She still regrets every day that she put too much pressure on him to achieve academically and keep up with the level of other highly educated and successful relatives. "I feel if I had not pushed him to go to cram school so much, he might not have become sick!" She cannot speak without tears. "I did a terrible thing to this poor boy. I really did. I just feel sorry for him."

Torrey, a psychiatrist, writes that guilt is a common reaction among parents of schizophrenic patients but that it is detrimental to their coping.[17] Some families, especially the ones with other children who are still young, are reluctant to give up blame and guilt, because guilt provides them with an illusion of control that they can prevent it happening to their other children. Another type of family Torrey writes about is the one that will not give up guilt because it has become an essential part of the family's way of life: Oddly, some families "thrive on guilt, wallowing in it and blaming each other as their principal pastime." I did not encounter such families in this study, but parents, especially Japanese mothers, report an overpowering sense of guilt, even after years had passed since the start of the illness.

After decades, however, parents tend to stop struggling to resist or fix the situation, but begin to accept it, and reach a sense of resignation and peace. Since the onset of his daughter's manic depression, Tôru Yamaguchi has gone through a lot. For the first few years after the diagnosis, it felt as though his life were on a roller coaster: Yuri would repeat the cycle of first a manic state, which usually lasted three months, and then a depressive state, which usually lasted for the remaining nine months. Particularly difficult for him was her manic state. He and his wife had to keep their eyes on her all the time because she could act out her violent energy at any moment: She would fall down the stairs, burn her hair, or become aggressive to her mother, which eventually made it impossible for him to keep his business open. "It just became unbearable." Within six years, his distraught and guilt-ridden wife died of stomach cancer. Tôru thinks she died of stress. "It may have something to do with the fact we fought in the first year, blaming each other for our daughter's illness." He did everything to keep the family going, encouraging his wife and working hard to keep the business, hoping his efforts could make a difference. But everything failed. "I just resigned (*akirameta*). I thought it was my fate. That's the way it goes, I thought." After he closed his business, however, he was able to spend more time with his daughter, which improved her condition as well as their relationship.

Looking back over the 30 years since his daughter became ill, Ichizô Ohira somehow feels "time heals a lot." It was truly devastating to him and his wife at first when Megumi was diagnosed. But in ten years, he and his family had adjusted to the new reality, he thinks. His daughter, Megumi, now 53, is occasionally able to work, but basically repeats the cycle of being in and out of the hospital. The total length of her hospitalization totals almost ten years.

Siblings

Siblings of the mentally ill are not only profoundly influenced by the illness of a brother or sister, but many were also forced to grow up fast to be self-sufficient and independent in the chaotic home situation created by the mental disorder. From initial efforts to make sense out of the family chaos, they have also developed numerous emotions that they do not even comprehend themselves. Shame, a fear of being seen as different, grief, and depression are all common reactions.[18, 19] Some siblings become over-achievers out of a desire to make up to their parents for the loss of their mentally ill child.[20]

Their parents' and indeed the whole family's attention was focused on the mentally ill member with little time and energy left for them. Parents may expect the healthy children to play an unreasonable role for their age, to shoulder an enormous burden that they had no choice but to accept. This also causes siblings to have feelings of frustration, resentment, and even the guilt over their own anger and their own well-being.[21]

However, their "survival-oriented responses" are "to shut down parts of their emotional lives, to become overresponsible or to disengage from the ill member or the family as a whole."[22] The long-term consequence of this coping action can be deep emotional scars on people who have experienced this kind of life as children. They might well be left with a lingering sense of abandonment and a feeling of having had a deprived childhood, partly because their feelings were ignored at home. When they look back on their emotional responses to years of struggling with the sick relative, many siblings recall sadness, fear, and pain, all of which had been suppressed because confronting it at that time would have been too much to handle. Eventually, they realize they have suffered tremendously from the effects of the illness. American siblings have been most articulate about their feelings.

Jane Wilson describes her response to the family chaos when she was a child:

> When I found out that she was trying to commit suicide, my first question was, did she succeed? I was like, okay, good. [Laughter.] I mean, that sounds terrible, but that was the only answer that I could seek to this whole chaos was if she would die. That would be the only way to end this. And, so I must have felt terribly tormented.

Melanie Wood can now recall the feeling after her brother Joshua was diagnosed as having schizoaffective disorder. But she could not talk about it for many decades, because her family required her to "numb it out."

> I think, I probably stuffed a lot of my feelings, you know. I think I did. I think I sort of tried to attack it from a pretty cerebral perspective and you know, did a pretty good job of stopping all my feelings about it.

Particularly noticeable is the resentment toward their parents. If their parents gave the patient more attention than the other children, the well children often grew up feeling angry and jealous. If they had to be the rescuer, intervening in the family crisis for some reason, instead of their parents continuing to take the major role in caring for their sick child, the feeling of unfairness haunts them, even though they may continue to be forced to play those unwanted roles. Furthermore, the anger can be against the way their parents handled the situation. Or the anger may be directed toward parents who they believe were the very cause of the dysfunctional home and therefore the illness of their mentally ill siblings.

Melanie was only 17, when she called the PET team because of her brother's psychotic breakdown.

> Yeah, I didn't want to do it even in a good sense. You know, I just felt it was their responsibility but like I said, I think my mother has incredible limitations being an adult and being a parent. And I think my father had many limitations too. So yeah, I got the ball rolling and my dad finished it and my mother I remember, she hid in the closet when they took my brother away.... I wrote in a diary or journal that night because my feelings were just pretty bad. I mean, pretty overwhelming. First of all, I felt pretty guilty that I did something that maybe I shouldn't have started. And it wasn't appropriate for me to be doing that. So I felt I was scared. I felt guilty. I was frustrated. I was angry I guess at my parents. I was scared for my mom. I was angry maybe at my dad because he hadn't taken more initiative. I was worried about my brother. I felt way over my head as far as having to deal with something that I didn't feel all that equipped to deal with. You know.

Despite her confusion, Melanie continued to play the parent's role for her brother. She moved out of state for many years, but even from far away the home situation and her brother's illness continued to be a secret, frustrating, and dark part of her life, which can still make her feel resentful toward her parents.

> Well, just off the top of my head I remember that it wasn't good and I felt my parents weren't really addressing Joshua's illness appropriately or effectively enough, so that's one of the reasons that I would talk to these doctors, you know. And sometimes he would be in the hospital, sometimes he'd be at home. But you know I had my own difficulties with my parents. I hate to use that word, it's so terribly clichéd, but — dysfunction. My family was terribly dysfunctional.

In addition to fearing the biological implications of her brother's schizophrenia for herself, Jodi Kramer had been very distressed by seeing what her family as a whole had to go through.

> Oh yes. Saddening thing. Always has been for me, and I lost trust in my parents and my parents' guidance, or I wouldn't really pay much attention to what they said because I didn't see them handling this very well and I did lose faith in God because my thinking was, how could this horrible thing happen to my brother if there was a loving God. Because I saw that this was a living hell that my brother was in and my brother couldn't get out of that living hell and it was affecting the whole family. It was very difficult. A lot of energy was drained and it was embarrassing. Caused confusion, unclear thinking. A lot of ignorance, denial in the family. It seemed like we didn't live in reality. I know, I remember now that I'm talking to you. For a long time, something about that reality. I remember being very angry at my parents for accepting this abnormal behavior as normal.

In most cases, parents are the major caretaker of the patient if the patient is not married. However, as years go by and parents age, it is inevitable that some healthy children start to feel the pressure to take the load off their parents, particularly if they have a relatively good relationship with them. Marianne Schmitt could no longer see her parents burned out from taking care of her sister Emily and stepped in to take the role of caretaker.

> I think it was a mix of emotions. I was angry again, because I was always going back to "Look at what you're doing to our parents." And I saw it as maybe she's doing this on purpose and how cruel

that was of her to hurt our parents that way. I was angry. I was probably frightened, and this was all new and I didn't know how to handle it, yet I have always felt a responsibility for her. For whatever reasons, the responsibility has fallen on me. I felt being her sister, I had this responsibility. Somehow I had to fix her, somehow I had to work out this situation. You know. I had to fix this. And you know, that's kind of been quite a burden. It was a burden for quite a while, so I had to find the answers to relieve my parents and somehow find a place where my sister fits — and what do we do with her? So you know, anger, confusion, and responsibility, I felt.... At the same time, I never felt I could turn my back on her. I wanted to. I was dealing with emotional issues in my own life and that was kind of compounding it. But I never could turn my back on her. There were periods of time that I had to withdraw from her and just say I can't deal with this right now. I have my children, my husband, and it always came back because she would always call me from the hospital and contact me, so again I had to come up with answers.

Responses by U.S. and Japanese Families

There is no question that both American and Japanese families of the mentally ill have been tormented by the onset of illness in their sons, daughters, siblings, and spouses. Worries, sadness, despair, guilt, shame, and many other painful emotions they suffer are equally intense and devastating. Particularly when the parents recalled the agony of the first hospitalization, they sounded exactly the same in describing that moment. For more Japanese families, however, it seemed to have taken a longer period of time before they reached proper medical help. In addition, Japanese parents were more likely to feel isolated in the beginning without the help or understanding of others in dealing with the abnormality of their sons and daughters. The delay in getting appropriate help only intensified their distress. This is probably due to the general lack of information about severe mental illness in Japan and the lack of visibility of psychiatric professionals. Not a few parents initially resorted to religious or spiritual help or fortune-tellers for their family problem before it was officially defined as mental illness.

There are many types of new religious organizations in Japan and fortune-telling services are found everywhere. Religious organizations are readily available and advertise widely or people find them by word of mouth. Many of these religious groups are Buddhist-based, some are derived from Shinto, the indigenous Japanese religion, or they can be a completely new creation. It is true that some provide true spiritual consolation. Unfortunately, it is also true that, despite appearing authentic and trustworthy, a few organizations exist for the sole purpose of making a profit by manipulating their followers' sense of hopelessness and by giving false hope for a miracle. Some Japanese parents admitted having become the victims of these fraudulent schemes at least once.

Furthermore, from a clinical standpoint, any delay in seeking help is highly problematic. The earliest possible detection and pharmacological intervention, and other psychosocial treatment, can produce better clinical results as well as relieving the burden on families.[23]

Not a few Japanese parents also mentioned contemplating suicide, saying "I wanted to die" or "I wanted to kill myself," while no such reaction was heard from any of the American family members. With a Buddhist and more fatalistic orientation in Japanese culture in general, suicide is a more acceptable choice for resolving a serious life problem. In fact, Japan has a very high suicide rate.

American siblings were particularly analytical and expressive about their feelings of being hurt by the childhood experience of growing up with a mentally ill family member. This is probably because many of them had received psychotherapy at one point and learned to articulate their feelings and discuss any problems. It is likely that there are many families of the mentally ill who have no interest in any therapeutic approaches. However, the American interviewees were recruited (like the Japanese participants) from support groups, so they were already preselected for their willingness and motivation to seek outside help and to make a change in their lives. The fact that they willingly participated in the interviews confirms that none of them was any longer shy about facing mental illness in the family, even if they might once have been. Although psychotherapy is mostly accepted among middle-class, relatively well-educated Euro-Americans, there is a willingness in American society in general to try psychotherapy.[24] Whether people understand the concepts accurately or not, a psychological vocabulary and perspective is part of everyday life through the mass media and ubiquitous mental health services. On the other hand, such a culture does not exist in Japan, at least not in the mainstream. When I repeated the question several times during the interview, "What did you feel at that time?" many Japanese family members had difficulty describing and even finding the right vocabulary for their response. It seemed some, particularly Japanese men, were slightly surprised, even a little irritated, by such a question. Certainly, Americans and Japanese have different styles of communication and also differ in their methods of resolving problems. However, family members seem to go through basically the same process in both cultures on the way toward gradually adjusting to the reality of the illness.

Notes

1. American Psychiatric Association, *Diagnostic and Statistical Manual of Mental Disorders*, 4th rev. ed. (DSM-IV-TR) (Washington, DC.: American Psychiatric Association), 305.
2. Ibid., 706–10.
3. Ibid., 369–87.
4. Ibid., 304.
5. D. L. Johnson, "The Family's Experience of Living With Mental Illness," in *Families as Allies in Treatment of the Mentally Ill: New Directions for Mental Health Professionals*, ed. H. P. Johnson and D. L. Johnson (Washington, D.C.: American Psychiatric Association, 1990), 31–63.
6. N. Dearth et al., *Families Helping Families: Living with Schizophrenia* (New York: Norton, 1986), 32–55.
7. A. B. Hatfield and H. P. Lefley, *Surviving Mental Illness: Stress, Coping, and Adaptation* (New York: Guilford, 1993), 82–84.
8. J. T. Johnson, *Hidden Victims, Hidden Healers* (Edina, MN: PEMA, 1994).
9. E. F. Torrey, *Surviving Schizophrenia* (New York: Quill, 2001), 143.
10. Ibid., 129–30.
11. Ibid., 134.
12. http://allpsych.com/disorders/mood/index.html
13. W. R. McFarlane, *Multifamily Groups in the Treatment of Severe Psychiatric Disorders* (New York: Guilford, 2002), 3–17; at 6.
14. K. G. Terkelsen, "The Evolution of Family Responses to Mental Illness Through Time," in *Families of the Mentally Ill: Coping and Adaptation,* ed. A. B. Hatfield and H. P. Lefley (New York: Guilford, 1987), 151–66.
15. Torrey, *Surviving Schizophrenia*, 155–210.
16. http://allpsych.com/disorders/mood/index.html
17. Torrey, *Surviving Schizophrenia*, 320–21.
18. Hatfield and Lefley, *Surviving Mental Illness*, 82–84.
19. Dearth et al., *Families Helping Families*, 32–55.
20. Hatfield and Lefley, *Surviving Mental Illness*, 82–84.
21. Dearth et al., *Families Helping Families*, 42.
22. Ibid., 32.
23. K. T. Mueser and S. R. McGurk, "Schizophrenia," *Lancet* 363 (2004): 263–72.
24. R. N. Bella et al., *Habits of the Heart: Individualisms and Commitment in American Life* (Berkeley: University of California Press, 1985).

PART **III**
What Happens to the Family System?

CHAPTER 4

Intrafamily Interactions: The Marital and Parent–Child Relationships

When my mother, my sister, and my younger daughter met, they wailed, "She [my elder daughter with illness] cannot have such an illness! How can she end up like this?" They kept crying. This is what I still remember so well that I can never erase the moment from my mind. It was so painful. Especially, my younger daughter insisted, "My big sister is not mentally ill!" — A Japanese father.

Introduction

What happens to the family as a whole? How is each major relationship within the family affected? Is it possible to survive the distress brought on by the trauma of mental illness and remain unchanged? The answer to all of these questions is "probably not." The central concepts of structural–functional theory as well as the enduring foundation in family therapy theories are that the family is a system and that, as a result, the parts within the system are interrelated.[1] The smallest social system is composed of two people, and the family is clearly one kind of social system. These systems do not function independently, but interact with one another. Thus, a family is not simply an aggregation of more than two separate individuals, it is a dynamic organism composed of subsystems of individuals with different roles and expectations, as well as the multiple combinations of units that these individuals join to create: husband and wife, parents and children, father and one child, one sibling and another, and so forth. They are also situated within an environment of extended kin such as grandparents, aunts, uncles, and in-laws. All these individuals with different degrees of closeness create a world that directly and indirectly affects each of his or her experiences and decisions. Each member of each unit, and each unit in itself, are so interconnected to one another that a change in any part of the family is bound to have repercussions throughout the entire family system. Although the system also tends to be persistent and stubborn in maintaining the status quo, existing roles, and already established patterns of behaviors and interactions, those patterns in each subunit are also influenced by forces from outside and become responsive and adaptive to the changes.

Naturally, a highly stressful event such as the onset of mental illness not only affects each individual family member who has a close relationship with the patient but also affects the characteristics of the family as a whole. It furthermore affects the subsystems within the family: the marital relationship, the parents' relationships with their healthy children, and even with extended family such as in-laws. In an ideal world, everyone concerned should be mutually supportive and cooperate to overcome the crisis. However, in reality, each human being will necessarily have his or her perception of the illness, feelings about it, and ideas as to how the situation should be dealt with. This can bring discord and conflict between the respective family members. The discord creates rifts within each unit and within the system as a whole, which in turn develops more stress in the system as a whole as well as the individual units.

When a child becomes mentally ill, both parents mourn, but they rarely accept the illness in the same way. Although it is too hard for them to articulate why they mourn at the time, the sources of mourning come from their acute awareness that their child's future has been changed permanently, with the likelihood of severe limitations in terms of both work and finding a partner. Many parents in their initial despair may only see that their child's life is over, and this was how many parents who participated in the present study felt when the diagnosis was made. Parents may feel that they have failed in raising their child, that the illness is somehow their fault. The diagnosis may also mean the loss of the parents' dreams for the future of what they had wanted to accomplish through their child, such as grandchildren and being able to pass on the family business to the next generation. Furthermore, social stigma attached to mental illnesses and the implications for other family members grieves parents deeply. In this process, while one parent is more willing to face reality, the other may stay in denial and may refuse to have anything to do with the illness or the patient. The defense mechanism of denial can be positive in a sense that it prevents the person from being completely crushed by the stressful event, especially when there is nothing much to be done. But the positive effects of denial are regarded only as a temporary solution.[2]

However, from the family system's standpoint, the spousal (or sometimes ex-spousal) relationship suffers a great deal. When one person does something, the other does the opposite, like two people going up and down on a seesaw. If this becomes a pattern in which one family member reacts to another's problem, it only makes the problems more insoluble.[3]

In the interviews, these discrepancies were often expressed. Since the interviews took place individually, I was not able to observe how two or more people would interact with each other at home. The individual interviewees' accounts only present what one person thinks about his or her relationship with other members of the family. However, their perceptions about how their partners in the subsets have responded to the tragedy only tell us the magnitude of the complications the development of mental illness can bring to family life.

The Marital Relationship: How Partners View Each Other

One common reaction of the parents of a mentally ill child is that one of them understands the reality as inescapable while the other does not. Some researchers report mothers as being the stronger partner and willing to face the fact of mental illness, while fathers are in general less able to do so. Fathers also tend to seek other explanations for their children's abnormalities in character problems or drug abuse, and sometimes even choose to completely withdraw from the problem.[4] Though this may indicate an interesting gender difference in coping, the limited number of parents interviewed for this book did not necessarily show this pattern.

When One Partner Is in Denial

Glenda White's husband never wanted to accept the fact that their daughter was mentally ill. Having had a borderline personality disorder herself, Glenda was very familiar with mental pathology and how to get appropriate help. She took all the necessary actions to get her daughter into treatment. Her husband had also had episodes of depression in the past, and in Glenda's view he was still a very depressed man. While Glenda is a go-getter and outgoing person, he was the opposite. The difference between their personalities, which might have been the source of their mutual attraction before marriage, now seemed to be a serious obstacle in the long struggle with their daughter's mental illness. Even when the diagnosis was made, Glenda could never discuss it openly with her husband. Her resentment was clear when she mentioned that he was "never there when things got really messy." This has made their relationship as a couple very difficult.

> I'll bring it up to him. Well, you know, sometimes he'll be kind of condescending and she should be doing this, whatever. Doesn't he realize that she is ill? I mean, she can't be on track like other kids. He doesn't want to give her any slack.... He doesn't say no, but he's not supportive in that sense. He doesn't participate.... I buy books on the subject and he doesn't even bother to read them.

Divorced couples often feel isolated by their ex-spouse's flat refusal to take any part in the grieving over their child's mental illness. Wallace Green's ex-wife, who lived with their son Mike while he was growing up, "did not accept what was going on, but functioned with a lot of denial," particularly when Mike's psychotic breakdown became so acute that no one could deny the reality. When her son became ill, Ruth Singer had been divorced for many years but had some communication with her ex-husband on the phone; he had remarried. According to Ruth, he neither gave her any word of encouragement nor support, nor did he even want to talk about it with her. Ruth had to struggle alone to cope with her son's illness. She talked bitterly about her ex-husband's nonsupportive attitude while she was the one to pick up the pieces and provide a place for their son to live when he had nowhere else to go.

> My husband is a person that I believe is in complete denial. He knows that my son has a mental illness, but he would never go with me, he would never get involved in educating himself about it or understanding it. In looking back, I have remembered that my husband himself had moods or depression, and in looking back, I try to get the history of his family and everybody is closed mouthed. So, if there is something that has been passed on to my son, it has to be from my husband's side of the family.

When their adopted son, Allan, became utterly out of control, Kelly Seeman's husband at that time erupted, saying "I didn't want him anyhow. It was the fault of the agency. They shouldn't have given him to us." It's true that Kelly was more willing to take Allan and persuaded her husband to adopt the little boy. In Kelly's view, however, he never showed opposition, so she went along with the adoption. What she wanted to hear from him was, "We took this responsibility on ourselves." But her husband always had "great difficulty in taking responsibility for his own decisions."

After they were divorced, he was completely out of the picture with respect to her life and Allan's. Kelly believes this has left a grave void in Allan's life and caused him to suffer to this day.

> [I feel] Sad. Guilty. What else? Angry at my husband — ex-husband. He just turned his back on the whole thing. And to this day, he lives in Los Angeles and he doesn't visit Allan (who lives in the same city) and Allan still hungers after him.

Mutual Blame

It's not uncommon for a husband and a wife to blame each other following the onset of mental illness in their child.[5] Neither discord nor conflict are strangers in any family's life. According to conflict theory, conflict between the more powerful and the less powerful is a natural and endemic reality within all social systems as well as between social groups.[6] Therefore, as some conflict theories of family state, the conflicts and clashes within families are both inevitable and constant, a built-in part of the system.[7] Being so shocked and traumatized by the diagnosis of mental illness initially, some partners take their pain out on each other. They blame each other's genetic background, the way the mentally ill child has been raised, or some other factor they do not agree upon, for the development of the illness. This is, of course, a useless activity, and it makes a very bad situation even worse.[8] This is a tragedy that is probably unique to parents of the mentally ill. No physical disease would cause exactly this type of conflict in the marital relationship. However, it can be seen as an indication of how upset the partners are over the illness and how vulnerable they are and how overwhelmed by despair.

When their first daughter was diagnosed as manic depressive, Tôru Yamaguchi and his wife were shocked beyond words. His wife kept crying for days and then an ugly argument broke out.

> It was about the genetic background of our families. We began accusing each other, I was blaming her family and she was blaming mine. We both brought up things like which family had a mentally ill person. This was only in the beginning, you know. We didn't do it after a while. But I said terrible things to her, that she had a mentally ill relative with the same illness. She'd say, no, it was on my side. So I'd say, "You bitch, how dare you!" We said horrible things to each other. It was so bad.

As he said, this argument didn't last for long. But his wife continued to be tormented and devastated by the illness and even contemplated suicide.

When she begged him to die with her, it was Tôru who convinced her that they could not do this because they couldn't leave their daughters. Tôru's wife died of stomach cancer a few years after their older daughter became ill. Tôru thinks that it was the stress that made his wife sick and killed her. But he still blames himself for having those ugly quarrels with her. "If we had been kinder to each other, she might not have become sick and died. Of course, I will never know...."

Naoyo Abe also regrets that she once accused her late husband of causing their son's illness. While she was active, outgoing, and hard working, he was a very quiet man. She knows he died deeply regretting the fact that he could not see his son grow to be an independent adult.

Although she can now say that it was completely "ridiculous," Helen Hawkins also remembers she and her husband blamed each other for a short while right after the diagnosis of their daughter's schizophrenia. She thinks "it was just awful." Her husband was totally devastated by the diagnosis, while she, despite the enormous shock, tried and managed to keep her sanity by getting intensely involved with her job during the day.

Rosanna Olmos greatly disagreed with her husband, not only about the cause of the illness of their twin sons, but also how to manage this illness. Her husband came from a very quiet, calm Hispanic family where they never argued. She came from a family of three close sisters, who are all very vocal and outgoing.

> [We would argue] probably with regard to what caused it. My husband has always wanted to blame it on drugs rather than on some reason, you know.... We knew it was an illness. We didn't know anything about it. We just didn't. You couldn't find out about it either. In the seventies.... At first we just tried to cope and keep them at home and everything. But eventually it got to the point where they were abusive and threatening and.... And I don't know how many years after it was that I said it's either them or me. They say in every one of these families, there's a marshmallow and a hardened one. In my family I was the hardened one. I was the straight up. My husband was the "keep them home and take care of them" one.

Rosanna knew that Hispanic families very much preferred to keep their children home, but could not help but be frustrated with her husband's simplistic view of their sons' condition. When one of the twin sons joined the Navy (to her surprise by managing to pass himself off as someone suitable and trustworthy at the recruiting office), she could foresee what would happen. "And I said to my husband, he should not go," Rosanna says, "he will fall apart." But my husband's attitude was always "It'll straighten him out. He'll be fine." I said "no he'll fall apart." It didn't take long for Rosanna's prediction to come true: the son cracked under pressure and revealed his mental condition to the Navy. He was placed in a psychiatric ward and then discharged from the service, which only confirmed her husband's inability to accept that his son had a mental illness.

Conflict theory also maintains that conflict, although it is natural, normal, and inevitable in social systems, can be functional. If the family never fights, and sweeps its problems under the rug, then the unresolved problems linger and will take their psychological toll on all the family members.[9] The positive function would be that it can work as a safety valve for occasionally letting off steam. It can also foster communication and interaction. However, parents of a mentally ill child who blame each other seem to be more deeply scarred by the experience than by, for example, the physical illness of a child, and sometimes marital conflict caused by mutual blame can leave serious, irreversible damage.

They Are Not in Denial: Each Has a Substantially Different Perception

Whether the outburst of distressed emotions between husband and wife functions as a safety valve or not is unclear. For some couples, it might work as the outlet for intense conflict within the relationship, because when couples go through this phase, they quickly realize the futility of name-calling and fault-finding. Then the spouse who has been in denial usually joins with his partner in at least accepting that their child has a serious mental disorder. However, many couples still keep their separate views of the illness. Even though neither is in denial any more, substantially different perceptions of the illness can still bring strain to the relationship. As Maria Hafer says, the presence of her husband was helpful in her ability to cope with her son's illness, but at the same time made it more difficult. He took their son's illness extremely hard. This was partly because he was completely unfamiliar with mental illness, while Maria had done some volunteer work in this field. Furthermore, the husband was an A-type personality, a workaholic who spent a lot of time away from home, which also made Maria angry.

> He did not understand the nature of the illness at the beginning. I mean, he did and he didn't. From the time that we were on that vacation (when our son's compulsions went out of control), he really didn't understand that it was an illness and not misbehavior. We've just had so much to deal with.

Anna Berger admits that her ex-husband has been there a lot for their son, Stan, but "in a different way." Her husband has accepted the illness and seems to know about schizophrenia. But he is not as empathic as she wants him to be.

> He's not anywhere near as active or assertive, you know, or does as much chauffeuring, and doctoring, and phoning, and researching — you know, all the stuff that I've done. He has come to visit Stan wherever he is. And his main point of view — one of the reasons we're divorced — is that he thinks that all you have to do is tell somebody what to do and they're supposed to do it. And to this day he does that. My son has had a characteristic of his particular illness. You know, they're all different. Even though they're alike, they're different. My son does not use his voice at times; he doesn't speak. There's nothing wrong with his articulation. It isn't the words that he has any problem with. He claims it hurts his voice. It strains him to talk. So he doesn't talk. He'll write notes.

It has been speculated that this voice problem is psychological. Whatever it may be, Stan cannot tolerate emotional intensity with the voice around.

> So, my ex-husband says this to him…. When my son whispers, "Sorry, Dad, I can't use my voice." So his father says, "Listen. Talk to me or I'm not going to talk to you." So then my son will try; he'll raise his voice a little. My ex-husband says, "See? All I have to do is tell him what to do and he does it." But it … so, he still has that sort of idea. In spite of the fact that my ex-husband is a social worker.

Yoshiko Takeda never discusses their daughter's illness with her husband. He is supportive, as are other family members, but still he doesn't quite understand the seriousness of the illness. Yoshiko has attended family support groups and many study groups to understand the importance of continuing medication. But her husband doesn't take it so seriously and even says, "Maybe she [his daughter] doesn't have to take the medication any more," which surprises Yoshiko and makes her wonder, "Doesn't he remember what the doctor said to us so many times?"

Kay Yamamoto feels the same way toward her husband: He doesn't seem to take it so seriously. Or as she says, "He may not simply understand what to do," about their son's illness. He may be just pretending to be relaxed about it and instead leaving all the work to her. It was, in fact, always she who went to the doctor and participated in the family support group. She wants to think that he is very concerned at heart with his son, but he has never shared the responsibilities needed to better understand their son's illness. Kay has been the only caregiver, which has sometimes made her feel so lonely that early on in the illness she wished she were dead.

An Active and an Inactive Caretaker

Maintenance of structural equilibrium and balance is in the nature of a system according to functional–structural theory, which sees social phenomena as systems made up of many interrelated parts. When the family system is shaken up by a tragic life event, a member will often change his or her role to the one with new expectations and demands; otherwise, the family as a system would eventually break down. Although this adaptive process is one of the automatic mechanisms of the system, it proceeds at a different pace and level of flexibility, depending on the individual. Like the differential acceptance of a mental illness diagnosis, some are quicker to adjust to a new role, while others may not be so flexible and instead withdraw and become completely inactive with regard to dealing with the illness. Winton writes, "The adapting partner provides the adaptation to the system and thus the family may survive, as long as the adaptive person continues to give in or accommodate."[10] These newly adapted roles tend to become rigid if the family is to survive. However, the system seems to be built on rather thin foundations. If the adaptive person feels unfairly burdened, he or she may choose to withdraw his or her function, in which case the family system will be in danger of collapse.

Some couples share the same understanding of the illness and they mourn together and try to support one another in the beginning. However, one of them soon ends up taking all the active roles, while the other has little or no involvement with the care of their mentally ill child. There are different reasons for this clear division of labor. Some may find it an efficient arrangement, or one of them may be totally incapable of handling the patient's practical needs. Some may find the responsibility too overwhelming to face, and express this honestly, which leaves the remaining partner with no choice but to take all the responsibility.

Timothy Rosen has been the sole care provider for his son, Bruce, who has schizoaffective disorder. It was quite surprising to him when his ex-wife revealed sometime after their son's breakdown that she had several cousins with schizophrenia and that her grandmother had committed suicide. She was very matter-of-fact about it, although she herself only learned about it over time, and was not aware of this family history when they got married. Timothy and his ex-wife would go to the family support meetings together in the early stages, but soon she decided not to get involved with the care of her son. She was extremely open and candid, saying that she had spent 18 years with their son and felt it impossible to get involved any further. Timothy, on the other hand, was willing to accept and respect her decision. He even strongly defends her position and admires her as a successful career woman. For a divorced couple, they have what Timothy himself calls "an anomaly of anomalies" relationship that even makes his present girlfriend jealous: Timothy and his ex-wife stay in touch regularly and he is happy to give her encouragement and support for her career. He believes that it is much better that he takes care of their son, because he is able to feel so rewarded by doing so. His ex-wife also has complete trust in Timothy with regard to their son.

> No, I can't [tell her to be more involved] and I'll tell you why. Because I know it's impossible. Why beat a dead horse, as they say? Why ruin my communication with her and my acceptance of her? She has a right to do what she feels she has to do or is only able to do. And I have to accept that. Oh, I would like to see, maybe, a little more acceptance, a little more willingness to accept him. Yes, I would like to see that, but I know it's not possible, so I don't dwell on it. I don't dwell on it.

Ken Morris has a close relationship with his wife and can discuss anything about their son's illness. However, she has remained withdrawn from support groups and has been reluctant to get involved in the same way as Ken has done. However, Ken accepts her, as he understands that this is particularly hard on her.

> And primarily, I think the reason why is because there is a history of mental illness in my wife's family — not my family.... Her sister — two years younger than she, has schizophrenia, paranoid schizophrenia. And her brother, tragically — is now fifty-five years old — I am positive that he's got the disease, but he has never been diagnosed. So therefore, he lives in squalor. It is just a family tragedy.

Pat Bryant says that everyone in her family accepts and offers support for her son's illness. But she cannot help but admit that she has been the one who was most proactive in dealing with her son. She wants her husband to read about manic depression, but he won't. She rented the movie *Mr. Jones*, but he wouldn't watch it, saying "I don't want to know: it's too scary."

Well, he knows some things. And he [my husband] likes the new doctor because the doctor is very direct. He tells him everything directly depending on what he asks, so, you know, he likes that. But, like he went once to an AMI meeting and he said, "I can't go back again. It's too hard for me to sit there for two hours and hear these horrible stories of families with children who are forty-five and are still living at home. And the ones that are locked up in institutions and are never going to get out. It's too scary. I can't bear it. It's too emotional. I'm just drained afterwards." Somehow, the educational part of that makes me feel okay; it helps me. But it doesn't seem to help him, so I don't force him to go.

Kazuo Takenaka is a survivor of one of the fiercest battles in Burma during World War II. He has lived his life believing that the man should be the head of the family, literally. So he regards it as his responsibility to take the initiative in the care of his daughter Shizuka, who developed schizophrenia. Besides, his wife was too upset to deal with the situation in a constructive way. She did try to be involved in the beginning, but eventually the stress burnt her out. One day she said to Kazuo, "I can't do it anymore, dear. It's hopeless. Please take care of the rest." Since then, he has accepted being in charge, which he thinks is a good thing.

I don't want to sound like a dictator. But I see those mothers in the family support group who say they wish they were dead because it is so hard. They say such things because they just feel completely helpless. But I tell them, "Why don't you bring your husband?" Men are different. Men can look at the problem from a broader perspective. They go to work and have to make many decisions for themselves. So they have learned how to think not only about the patient, but also about the surrounding environment. Once they make a decision, men are better able to follow through. So these mothers should bring their husbands. But most husbands don't want to join. Of course, men get disturbed and bewildered by the situation, too. But they don't think about the worst possibility all the time. They can take a more detached attitude, like you never know what will happen to anyone. It is also true that there are many patients who have become well enough to work as healthy people do. So it's important to be farsighted, not see things in the short run. It's important to keep going and doing what one has to do. My generation has been educated to think this way.

Solidified Relationships

The mental illness of their child did pose a serious strain on otherwise amicable husband–wife relationships, but there were others who stayed close during a crisis, which further strengthened their bond as a couple. Some wives say their husbands are very helpful and the two of them are just like "a three-legged race" team, meaning they work closely hand in hand with each other, and some husbands say they and their wives agreed on how to deal with their child's illness. One Japanese couple admitted they had some differences in their approach, but it was clear they were able to develop a more solid relationship in coping with their child's mental illness together.

Linda Katz remembers her late husband as a partner who was "terrific in helping." They would discuss and share worries about what would happen to their son when both were gone. Her husband, who was a businessman, started to set aside some money to secure his son's financial future. Miki Maeda remarried a man 30 years older when she was a struggling divorced mother with twin daughters. He passed away many years ago, but she has no doubt that he was a great father and support when one of her twin daughters, Misa, had a breakdown. She thinks it was because he was not their biological father and was capable of seeing Misa's condition more objectively.

> He was so good to all of us. That's why we didn't all go under. It was his decision to bring her to the psychiatrist. He took the initiative. He used to say "I am not their real father, so I can look at them from a slightly detached standpoint. You get too involved with them to see them objectively." I was so grateful to him. Maybe I looked like I was going crazy about my daughter's condition. But he was able to make a sound judgment.

What Illness Does To the New Relationship

Some American parents who are divorced from the mentally ill child's other parent are under great pressure in trying to balance the relationship with the current spouse or partner along with the commitment to the mentally ill child from the former marriage. Usually a lack of understanding from the current partner and the energy absorbed in caring for the mentally ill child make the new relationship extremely difficult. Nancy Hoffman just feels helpless when she is torn between her current husband, who can't accept her son's mental illness, and the needs of her son, which she cannot ignore. "Of course [it hurts]. I am in the middle," she says, anguished.

Frank Brown also describes how he is torn between two different kinds of commitment.

It was affecting my relationship with Christy [current girlfriend] terribly. Even now, now that my son is there. She is very ticked off. And that concerns me. I don't blame her for being.... It's not her problem. And she has no children. And we met a few years ago in a tennis club and.... She had a house and I had a house and so she's living with me. But now that my son is there, she's doing fairly well, but I know this can't go on. Because it's going to affect my life tremendously.

Robert Kirk says his current wife supports him by being loving and taking good care of their house, but not his mentally ill son.

[Having a mentally ill son] changed my relationship with my [present] wife. And it's changed my relationship with my son. And so, I have been struggling for some kind of unification theory. In other words, I want my wife and I want my son. And, I don't think it should be an "either/or." And so my wife has been at almost all the meetings with me. And we've been talking about all those things, but I don't think it's sunk in with her the way that it's sunk in with me. So I'm spending a lot of time on this. I'm not spending as much time as I would like to on this with Ben. Now with the unification theory, we have an apartment and we have somebody working there. As far as I'm concerned, I have two households. I feel partially a member of the other household and partially a member of my household.

But even as he perceives the conflict of interest between his son and wife, Robert has decided not to confide in his wife any more about his feelings, anguish, and concern about his son, because he knows what her reaction will be.

Because she would let me know that she thinks that I'm doing some things wrong. And frankly, after my brother's death and after I came into the money, I felt that I really had to take her out of the loop, so far as confiding in her and getting her input because I knew what the input would be. And the input would not be in my son's favor. So I felt....

The Parent/Other Children Relationship

When one of the children becomes mentally ill and the parent's attention is focused primarily on that child, the dynamics of the relationships between the parent and the healthy children go through changes as well. The well children are also disturbed by the development of the illness in their sibling and have to cope with the family crisis. As in the husband–wife relationship, there can be discrepancies in perceptions of the patient's illness. Parental expectations of the other children may change and at the same time they may try to protect them from any added strain.

Wallace Green understands well that the breakdown of his son Mike was extremely traumatic for all the other children, including his 12-year-old son. It was no secret to any of them. He remembers that all the family members got on a plane together to go to see Mike, and family solidarity was an important force at that time. However, believing that "each one probably reacted in proportion to their own strength emotionally," Wallace didn't go into great detail about the illness with his other children.

Ken Morris took a courageous step as a father and talked very openly about his son's illness to his daughters. He believed in the power of knowledge and education, and wanted to make sure that there would be no confusion among them. He decided to discuss the issue with his children in an open and direct way, including the issue that many would not have the courage to face easily: the genetic consequences for the other children.

> We are a very close family. I brought them along step-by-step. I would say at least once a week, we would have an hour or two meeting to explain what was going on and what the problem was. So, I think that they've accepted it. They feel bad about it. I feel bad for the genetic consequences to their young families. But, there's nothing I can do about it. And I've advised them about those genetic consequences.... In other words, my daughter has a daughter. The chances of her getting it are 10 percent. That's huge. And my daughter knows that. Her husband knows it. And so they are very in tune with that.

Ken's strength and leadership has become the central rock of the family even more than before. His daughters accepted her brother's illness and reached the agreement with their father. Ken's specific guidance, determination, and the action were invaluable.

> I think they perceive the problem in a very logical way. That is, they're at a crossroads in their lives. They're starting jobs. They're starting relationships. They're starting their adult lives. And although they feel very sad for their brother, it is their brother's problem. And I feel that they feel very sad for their parents, but they feel it is their brother's and their parents' problem. And I'm

thinking that's exactly the way they should take it because there is nothing they can do to help me — help the problem. They call their brother when they call him. They help their brother as much as they can, but they need to get on with life. And that's what we have instructed them to do, and that's exactly what they've done.

Furthermore, Rosanna Olmos's daughters and her other sons were all helpful in her efforts to take care of her sick twin sons. They were the precious support for Rosanna during many difficult times.

However, it is not common for a parent and other healthy children to have such open communications and create a very supportive relationship network. In many cases, parents, or one of the parents, are left alone with the entire caretaking responsibility for the sick child. The other children tend to be indifferent, if not hostile, or stay uninvolved with the mentally ill sibling's difficulties. This makes the parent sad and frustrated, but at the same time, he or she understands how the other children feel. Some parents showed a mixture of emotions, trying to defend the position of unsupportive children on one hand, but on the other hand, hinting at their frustration.

In his family, Frank Brown has been the only one to take any responsibility in the care of his son, Don. Everyone, including his ex-wife, has implicitly expressed reluctance to get involved. He says:

But you've got to remember that all my other children are married and they've got their families. You know, your first obligation is to your own family. And I can't blame them. And they all love Don. And they're all very concerned about Don. But they're very disappointed about Don.

Nancy Hoffman has a daughter who is a school psychologist and she doesn't want to be involved in the case of her brother Barry, who has schizophrenia. Not only is she unwilling to help Nancy in any way, she is also extremely critical of Nancy's way of dealing with Barry. She keeps saying, "Mother, he doesn't want to get better. I can't treat him." She thinks her mother is indulging him too much, which makes Nancy very sad. Although she says, "I can't allow this to stand between us," the mother–daughter relationship has been severely damaged by Barry's mental illness. Nancy confesses that she gets very angry at her daughter but tries to remind herself that her daughter has a right to her feelings.

Glenda White knows that her son, who is four years older than her mentally ill daughter, is ashamed and afraid of his sister's illness. He doesn't want to participate in the group therapy that Glenda has been involved with. They did go to a session once where about 50 people, parents, siblings, and children of mentally ill patients, gathered, but Glenda realized that it was too ugly and raw with pain for her son to face.

Ruth Singer also understands the fear felt by her healthy son. He took his brother Paul's illness very badly, and Ruth perceived him to be worried in the beginning. He seemed to have thought that there was something wrong with him, too. However, Ruth and this son never openly talked about it. She is also frustrated with the influence of his wife, who would not accept Paul in their home or around her children. The attitude of her daughter-in-law makes Paul feel completely cut off from membership in the family, Ruth imagines.

Timothy Rosen never pushed his daughter, Sylvia, to deal with his mentally ill son, Bruce. Timothy understands that she has gone away to school and has been busy traveling all over the world. But he cannot hide his relief in seeing Sylvia lately showing more genuine concern and understanding for Bruce's illness. She has taken more interest in his condition and in mental illness seminars. Timothy wishes that the three of them, he, Bruce, and Sylvia, could someday get together, but it has to wait until the time is right for everybody.

Many Japanese parents expressed their wish that their healthy children would not be badly affected by the mental illness of their sibling. They seem to feel that, as parents, they have an additional responsibility, which is to protect their healthy children from the added burden that may devolve to them in the future. At the same time, these parents were seldom open about the illness with their children. If possible, they would prefer to hide it from their healthy children. "My other daughter [or son] is married and has her [his] own life" was repeatedly heard from many parents. They are also worried about how the family's mental illness is perceived by the spouse of their healthy children and the children's in-laws.

Tôru Yamaguchi is both sad and happy to see his younger daughter married and living in a city far away from Tokyo.

> This way, her husband will not know that she has a mentally ill sister. He still doesn't know it. If he had known it before the marriage, he might not have married her. We decided never to reveal it to him. He is a doctor. If he had known about the mental illness in our family, the engagement might have been broken. I didn't want to see her move to a place so remote from Tokyo — it takes more than seven hours by bullet train. I really didn't. But, considering the other possibility, I can put up with her living far away from us.

Ichizô Ohira has also determined to protect his second daughter from the stigma of mental illness in the family, and instead, he takes all the responsibility for his oldest, mentally ill daughter.

> I wanted my second daughter to have a normal life. That's why I sent her to get married. But if she marries into a family with no knowledge about our problem, it may become very difficult later. So I saw to it that my former colleague, a high school teacher's son would marry her. His father and I had known each other for a long time. So even if he found it out later, I expect he would be more understanding. I have seen in some cases, siblings of the mentally ill give up any thought of marriage. I didn't want that to happen to her. I decided to carry as much of the burden as possible all by myself.

Though these children may not actively help out their parents with regard to their mentally ill siblings, they share an understanding with their parents of the seriousness of the problem. However, there are also many Japanese parent–child relationships with no direct communication on the central issue in the family. At best, they guess what each others' thoughts are on the situation.

Yoshiko Takeda worries about how her daughter's history of mental illness will affect the possibility of making a good match for her son, but she has never discussed it with him.

> I know I should talk to him. But we have been avoiding that subject. Probably we don't want to face that yet. I don't think he is taking it so seriously. But if I were on the side of the family of his future wife, I would worry about the implications. They say it is not strictly hereditary, but a certain disposition can be handed down — so.

Tetsuro Isono has never talked about his son's illness with his married daughter. He is not sure how much she knows. She has not been informed about her brother's psychotic crisis at home and at work, which even involved law enforcement. Unless the daughter asks directly, Tetsuro thinks it is better to keep it this way.

Haru Morimoto thinks someday she and her husband will have to explain to their daughter about her brother's illness. But their daughter is currently separated from her husband and struggling to raise a child by herself. Haru doesn't want to burden her further with this problem. "But someday, we will have to talk. It is important to choose the right moment."

These parents have a strong desire to keep their well children from the "contagion" of mental illness, as if exposure to the reality of disease will harm their well children. However, from the standpoint of these well children, these parents' protective gesture also makes it extremely difficult for them to have any honest discussion and communicate their painful feelings. They may feel unaccepted, stuck, or frozen, and even unable to get on with their own lives.[11]

While Satoko Katagiri was so busy with the illness of one of her twin sons, she had no time or energy left for the other son. He became a juvenile delinquent and notorious at his school. One day his schoolteacher surprised Satoko saying, "He must be going through a really hard time at home." It turned out that her son wrote an essay that explained why he had black and blue marks on his body. It was because his mentally ill brother, tormented by hallucinations, would beat him up. Only then did Satoko realize how traumatized the other son had been by the illness of his twin brother. She still can't talk openly about it with him. She doesn't want him to feel burdened by bringing it up to him, as she knows he has his own life to take care of.

On the other hand, Reiko Matsuoka remembers what an angel her youngest son (Akira) was when the oldest son Shigeru became disturbed. Akira was only a first-grader. He did "all the things that parents couldn't do for him." He would tell his big brother, "Let's play with the computer games," or "Let's go out and play catch." Another younger son, Tadashi, also made it easier for her at home, hugging, riding on Shigeru's shoulders, and asking his big brother to play with him. Shigeru didn't feel so bad being depended on by his younger brothers. It is unknown if these small children were really aware of their brother's problem. However, it is also reasonable to assume that they, too, had been exposed to Shigeru's volatile condition and the parents' distress. They may have become sensitized to the tension at home and felt they needed to do something within their capacity. These kinds of interactions among children certainly diverted some tension from otherwise unbearable home situations. Reiko feels extremely grateful to her younger sons.

When the mentally ill patient is the spouse, the healthy spouse's relationship with the children becomes extremely complicated. The bond established between parent and child is strong, mixed with various emotions. They are not only a parent and a child, but also become comrades and fellow soldiers on the battlefield, or sometimes enemies, rivals over family resources, and at the same time, close friends who know each others' pain better than anyone else.

William Baker's only daughter Lynn is angry with her sick mother and simply ignores her. But William knows very well what Lynn has had to go through since her mother became schizophrenic. It is this daughter's presence that kept him going and encouraged him to stay married despite his wife's terrible symptoms. He had to become two parents for Lynn. He has taken her to support meetings and given her materials to read about her mother's illness. He cannot forget one essay she wrote in high school about her mother, describing how she saw her mother and how much she still loved her. "It was pretty touching," he recalls. Lynn used to be too embarrassed to bring her friends home when her mother was around, but now she is able to explain the illness to them when they come. William absolutely adores his daughter.

Kôji Yamada also has an extremely special feeling for his only daughter, Mayumi. He had watched her grow and overcome enormous odds in her life. Since his wife Hitomi's breakdown, Mayumi had to grow up without a mother. Even during her relatively functioning periods between repeated breakdowns, Hitomi was very stubborn, difficult, and egocentric toward her daughter. He had always tried to keep his wife living with them and to perform the impossible task of taking care of his wife, his business, and his little daughter. But Kôji was aware that this situation forced Mayumi to put up with so much. He felt that she had reached the limit of her patience and "if she had to take any more of it, she would be the one going crazy." That's why he could no longer ignore her request when she demanded that he divorce her mother. She was 17 years old.

> She said to me, "That woman is not my mother. Put her in the hospital or divorce her." This was the last thing I thought I would do. It's not because my daughter asked me to get a divorce, but she made me realize that we could not go on like this as a family. It was a decision of me and my wife's, two grown-ups, that we got married years ago and built a life together. [It was not my daughter's decision. She does not have responsibility for this.] But the unfortunate illness made it impossible. What my daughter said made me feel very sad. It also made me realize how much of my energy had been spent on my wife with little left for Mayumi all these years. I felt terribly guilty. I felt so sorry for her. Me and my daughter hugged each other and cried together. I just told her "I am so sorry, dear. I am sorry."

Even after he divorced Hitomi and placed her in a long-term care hospital, he continued to visit and take care of her. For some time, Mayumi was not happy to see him keeping ties with her mother. She would sulk, saying to him, "Why do you have to go and see someone who is not your wife?" He understood that it was teenage rebellion, a sensitive period when she felt her mother was her rival. He would simply say to her, "I will go to see her. I may not be related to her anymore, but she is still your mother. So it is okay that I go and see her. You can stay home if you want." Mayumi refused to see her mother for the next eight years. Kôji understood her feelings and never pushed her. One day he and Mayumi were out together. He said to her, "I'm going to the hospital now, so you go ahead and return home as usual." All of a sudden she said that she would go to the hospital with him.

> I thought it would be an incredibly dramatic and touching scene. The mother and daughter who had been separated, meeting for the first time in eight years, right? I expected they would hug and cry together. But they were nonchalant. Nothing dramatic happened. My wife said to her, "You've grown." Mayumi simply said, "It's been a long time." That's all.

"I was a bit disappointed," Kôji says half jokingly. No matter how the scene turned out, there was no question but that it was one of the most touching moments for the Yamada family. Since then, Mayumi has been joining Koji regularly to visit her mother in the hospital.

Notes

1. M. P. Nichols and R. C. Schwartz, *Family Therapy; Concepts and Methods*, 5th ed. (Boston: Allyn & Bacon, 2001), 122.
2. A. B. Hatfield, "Coping and Adaptation: A Conceptual Framework for Understanding" in *Families of the Mentally ill: Coping and Adaptation*. ed. A. B. Hatfield and H. P. Lefley (New York: Guilford, 1987), 60–84.
3. Nichols and Schwartz, 123.
4. N. Dearth et al. *Families Helping Families: Living with Schizophrenia* (New York: Norton, 1986), 66–77.
5. Ibid.
6. J. M. White and D. Klein, *Family Theories* (Thousand Oaks, CA: Sage, 2002), 148.
7. C. A. Winton, *Frameworks for Studying Families* (Guilford, CT: Dushkin, 1995), 92.
8. E. F. Torrey, *Surviving Schizophrenia* (New York: Quill, 2001), 319.
9. Winton, *Frameworks for Studying Families*, 91–92.
10. Ibid., 71.
11. Dearth et al. *Families Helping Families*, 34.

CHAPTER 5

Other Dimensions of Family Interactions

Relationships Between Siblings

In addition to the husband–wife and parent–child dyad, the patterns of interactions and feelings within the subunit of siblings will definitely be disrupted and changed by the mental illness. Not only are parents worried about their own relationship with their healthy children, they are also concerned about any change that takes place among their children. However, they can only guess, being outside the siblings' loop, as to how their children see one another and especially how the healthy children feel about the mentally ill sibling. Closeness and friendly relations seldom exist between the mentally ill child and the other children. The parents are well aware that their healthy children have been disturbed by their siblings' mental illness and have struggled with it on their own. However, their attitude toward, or oftentimes their utter rejection of, the mentally ill sibling distresses most parents. At the same time, the parents also know that there is a limit to what the healthy siblings can do. The only thing the parents can do is to observe the situation and try to understand how it is affecting their healthy children.

It has been painful for Barbara Weiss to see how her children interact with one another. Her healthy sons want nothing to do with Jessica, their mentally ill sister. Barbara is sad but understands all too well how each son feels, which only puts her in the middle, feeling powerless. Glenda White has also been torn between her mentally ill daughter, Shelly, and her healthy son. The brother and sister cannot get along with each other. Shelly's mood swings and verbal abuse definitely make the sibling relationship very difficult. There seems to be nothing Glenda can do, except for struggling to teach her daughter to refrain from this behavior.

Pat Bryant's healthy children appear divided when it comes to her son, Nick. Pat understands that her daughter, for example, is carrying a lot of unfinished business with Nick and now wants to avoid him as much as she can.

> Our daughter, she is married and has a five-year-old. She really would probably not want anything to do with Nick. She understands about the mental illness; she understands about it. But, I think she spent so long when he was using drugs at home and we were doing nothing, that there is a lot of unfinished business with that…. She resented the fact that he took all of our attention. But I also think that she has problems of her own: marriage, her health…. So, she's got her own problems. She doesn't want to deal with it.

However, Nick's younger brother is the opposite, remaining optimistic and supportive regarding his brother. He is a college senior with a major in music. He may still have a problem accepting his brother's illness, and Pat thinks she should get him some books so he can get an accurate understanding of the illness, but she's happy to see his positive attitude, which also helps make Nick feel more at ease.

> He says, "Oh, you guys make too much of this. You know, what he needs is somebody to do stuff with, you know, a friend or something to do." So, when he comes home from college, he's his buddy. "Let's go do this." And, that has worked up to now fairly well.

Anna Berger also sees her children divided in their feelings toward her son, Stan. Both her daughter and another son understand the nature of Stan's illness very well. In the early years another son, Harry, would go to visit Stan with Anna. Because the way Stan became psychotic was humorous, in others' eyes, despite the illness, they were able to take it lightly to some extent. But as the years have gone by and Stan has not been getting any better, they have begun to feel more and more helpless.

> My son's brother Harry is more willing, I think, to take it on. He talks about it, you know. He says, "Oh, I'll take care of Stan." But I don't know if it really comes down to doing it, if he really will

want to. He's just gotten engaged himself. He hasn't been married yet. He's forty-one years old, but he will be married soon. And he might have his own family and he might not really want that responsibility. My daughter, Stan's sister, is still angry with him for things he did to her, quote-unquote, when they were little kids. And she's never been able to really let go of that yet. So, she probably would not be very happy to be responsible for him. But, we'll see. We have to deal with that, I think, in a little more depth.

Reiko Matsuoka never fully explained it to her two other sons when her oldest son Shigeru became mentally ill. One was still in elementary school and the other in junior high school. The only thing she said to them was, "Your big brother has a very serious disease. So will you be good?" But she knows very well that Shigeru himself tries to avoid his brothers when he comes home from the hospital.

> Shigeru must feel inferior to his brothers. He has been in the hospital, while his brothers have gone on to college and high school. He feels his brothers don't like him. He knows we as his parents care about him, but he feels that his two brothers have different feelings toward him.

Parents are aware of the repercussions of one child's mental illness for the other child or children. However, they mostly feel helpless. They usually have little energy left to help the healthy children resolve those conflicts, which is another dimension of the tragedy of mental illness in the family.

Relationships with Extended Family

In our modern, postindustrial age, the role of extended families in taking care of one another has substantially weakened. Still, the idealistic view about the extended family remains, with expectations that they will help when a catastrophic event such as mental illness suddenly hits a family member. However, the discrepancies in the perception of the illness as well as ways of dealing with the situation are not uncommon. And the reactions from relatives outside the immediate family often cause disappointment or add strain to the primary family's struggle with mental illness. After all, these relatives can stay away from the central chaos, remaining safely in the outfield if they so wish. Loss of contact with extended families was another unfortunate result of the mental illness in some cases.

Rosanna Olmos knows that her husband's relatives became critical of her approach toward her twin sons. "My attitude toward my sons is, the best thing I can do for them is to teach them to live without me. That's my goal. Now my husband's family, they want you to be very dependent on them."

William Baker is sad about the denial of his mentally ill wife's mother. She knows something is seriously wrong with her daughter, but just cannot accept the fact that she is mentally ill. She won't even come to see her daughter. William thinks since his wife and her mother never had a good relationship, he cannot push this frail old woman. But what is particularly annoying is his own relatives' responses when he divorced his wife.

> My family simply adore her and they know she's ill — they tried to make me promise that I won't leave her, but I won't promise that. Because when she was normal, she was a very loving, beautiful person.... My family is very religious and God is going to take care of everything. Whereas, I share a little different view. Not that I don't believe, but I don't believe God can take care of everything, and I have to watch this day in and day out and I've been doing this for a long time. Well, they will probably be a little irritated with me [when I leave her]. But it's my life. I'm the one that has to deal with this you know. They don't have to spend one day putting up with this craziness. [Laughter.]

Ironically it was her husband's illness that made Yoko Tomita finally accepted by his family. She remembers vividly that when her husband, Eiji, was diagnosed as having schizophrenia, her mother came to see her and flatly asked whether Yoko was going to stay married or get a divorce. The question itself was surprising to Yoko, as she had never even dreamed of leaving her husband. Yoko was doubly surprised that not even the slightest idea of divorce had ever occurred to her. Various family conflicts, including strong opposition to his marriage, made Eiji sever all contact with his parents and siblings. For a long time Yoko had been feeling guilty that Eiji had to lose his family because of her. Sometime after he became sick, she got the courage to visit his parents' home and ask for help. Although Eiji still refused to meet with them, Yoko's devotion and sincerity touched his family. Now his family members, who used to dislike Yoko, express deep gratitude to her. Since Eiji is still angry and cannot have a reasonable relationship with his family, Yoko keeps her contacts with them secret.

What They Wish Other Family Members Would Do

Even if the newly adapted roles have become more or less fixed within the home, many parents and primary caregivers of the mentally ill, when prompted, confess that they in fact wish other family members would be more willing to offer help. They have accepted their role of taking major responsibility for the sick one, but they also wish they were not the only one with this burden. For example, Wallace Green wishes his ex-wife had "more strength and honesty." He has been concerned that she has a tendency to swing emotionally from smothering their sick son with maternal feelings, to letting her anger get out of control. Interviewees in both countries often brought up the wish that healthy children or other family members would show a little more sense of connection, by making visits or phoning, keeping in contact, and expressing acceptance and understanding, at least to the caregivers. What William Baker wants is "just a little bit more understanding" from his wife's mother, brother, and sisters, none of whom are in contact with her. Maria Hafer says she wishes that her daughter would be a little more willing to have contact with Jeff. These caretakers are reserved about expressing their wishes and are extremely cautious in admitting their demands. They know too well the hardships involved in taking care of a mentally ill person and cannot tell other loved ones to go through the same ordeal.

Ken Morris's two daughters had accepted his son Charles' illness. They had been very well guided by Ken who showed strong leadership in the family as a father and made sure there would be no confusion among the family. But he admits that he wishes they were a little more generous to Charles.

> The only thing that I wish they would do is be a little more helpful to him. I wish that they would simply pick up the telephone and call him a little more often, invite him over to dinner a little more often, go over to his apartment and help him a little more often, call his friends and tell his friends to go over and see him a little more often. That's the only thing that I wish they would do a little better. But, again I understand the reason that they don't. I mean, when they're trying to buy a new house, when they're thinking about having another baby, when they're thinking about inviting people from Europe to their wedding — there's just not enough time. That's the way it is.

Family Interaction from the Siblings Point of View

Being the brother or sister of a mentally ill patient is particularly tricky. A view of the sibling's point of view presents a very different picture of family dynamics. Whether the mental illness hit their sibling in childhood or adulthood affects their response. Generally, siblings of the mentally ill patient have been able to observe the situation more objectively than their parents, having a wider view of the situation. Therefore, they can often be the best narrator/reporter/witness of the chaos in the home. However, none escapes the serious scars and mental anguish that the illness brings to family members. If they were still children or adolescents at the onset of the illness, their home life was constantly disrupted by the patient's symptoms and breakdowns, and they had fewer resources than adults in coping with this distress. Being adaptable creatures, children in such an environment learn various survival skills to adapt to the extremely demanding situation. However, they are often deprived of the chance to develop a healthy sense of self and well-being. Without adequate protection from parents, who are usually too busy or overwhelmed by their child's illness, or without a feeling of security, their early life can be filled with "chronic loss and abandonment," as psychologist Claudia Black calls it.[1] Black describes the cumulative effect of chronic loss and abandonment during childhood and maintains that the various protective strategies we develop when young are carried over into adulthood and manifest themselves in many other areas of our lives. They can even become the driving force, telling us how to live. As a result of this condition during childhood, we may develop cognitive defenses, denying, minimizing, or rationalizing our negative emotions. Excessive behaviors such as overeating and drinking may be used to distract us from our pain.[2] We may also develop a distorted sense of self-worth such as "I can't make a mistake or I will be worthless" or "I have to produce to be of value." When a strong sense of victimization is unwittingly acquired, we may never develop the ability to judge what is not normal. Furthermore, some may develop serious depression, substance addiction, and other compulsions later on in life. In times of distress, family can be a risk factor as well as a protective factor for children.[3]

I was able to interview only six siblings in the United States. All of them were extremely well educated about the issues surrounding mental illness, and while their views of the mental illness and the family situation were tragic in many ways, they were also very vivid and inspiring. Four of them referred clearly to a sense of instability and unhealthy factors at home, but these were issues that they felt existed before the surfacing of a brother's or sister's illness. And they directly and indirectly touched on the psychological and behavioral effects of their family member's mental illness on their childhood as well as their lives as adults. In particular, two of them (Jane Wilson and Melanie Wood) had to overcome extraordinary odds because their childhood and adolescent years were marred by obviously dysfunctional family situations. Despite the hardships, they have both gone a long way toward acquiring the ability not only to see things in perspective but also to be highly articulate about them.

Interestingly, most of these siblings mentioned a certain family culture that they were socialized in, which both impeded or helped the resolution of the problem at home. Families should not in any way be blamed as a causal agent for psychotic illness itself. However, the way they handle the suspicion of mental illness at home is a crucial factor for whether the family will survive as a system and whether siblings will be protected from irreversible scarring. For these siblings, the center of their family culture was their parents. When their parents failed to deal appropriately with the issue of mental illness, well siblings often became critical of them and their home culture.

Diane Nelson can clearly describe the Nelson family culture with its roots in Canada and Iceland. She believes that it had a lot to do with the way family members dealt with the early signs of her brother Warren's mental disorder. It took several decades before Warren was recognized by everyone as mentally ill. Diane says that her family was a very tight and close one, but not an "interfering family." When Warren started his typical rebellious phase during the 60s, going into the hippie mode, his father was disgusted, while his mother still adored her son, believing he could do no wrong. But the family never directly discussed and confronted the situation. The Nelsons had a strong belief in respecting individualism, protecting each others' privacy, and not being involved in other people's problems.

> I realize now that my family didn't discuss things in detail. Even though I was doing things that my mother didn't approve of, she would have never sat me down and told me that I was wrong and that she wanted me to do something else. And it's not that we weren't interested in each other. It's just that we as a family gave each other a lot of latitude. We were not an interfering family at all.... My mother never discussed with me any problems that Warren had, because it would have been too personal. She would not have discussed it with me because those would have been Warren's problems and personal for Warren and she would not have broken the confidence. Even among the family. So that's what I'm saying.... And I look back and I think, I didn't realize we were weird. [Laughter.]

Diane had her own trials and tribulations, developing her career, marriage, having a daughter, and getting a divorce. In the meantime, her brother's unconventional behavior had become more conspicuous and problematic, and the house he lived in with his mother was rapidly decaying. Diane was always willing to come back to offer both monetary and emotional help to her ailing mother and brother. "That's just what families do," Diane says. But she was caught between the love for her mother and the love for Warren, sometimes making up stories so that the reality would not hurt any of them too much, and so that the family could still be a family. But there were the lies, which she jokingly says "kept her nose growing and growing like Pinocchio." The biggest crisis she had to handle was when Warren informed Diane that he had gotten into trouble with police in a bar and was getting out of town. He asked her to take care of their mother for him. Mother was in the hospital at that time but was scheduled to be released the next day. Diane wanted to protect her mother and told her, "Warren says he's got a job out of state." The mother said, "Diane, don't lie to me. I know about your lying." And that's all they said about Warren leaving home. By early the next morning, her condition suddenly deteriorated and she passed away.

> She just died. Her heart just stopped. She was seventy-two. And I know why. My mother chose to die. My mother literally chose to die. Warren was off on another one of his toots. She couldn't take care of him anymore. I had been up a month before and discussed what my mother would do when she couldn't live by herself anymore. I had given her the option of coming and living with me. She laughed at that. She said, "Diane, we could stand each other for thirty minutes" [laughter] and she was so independent she would not go into a rest home.

When Warren called and learned that his mother had died, his first response was, "Oh my God, Diane, I murdered our mother," which Diane recalled as a nondelusional thing for him to say.

> I said, "No Warren, she didn't know you were gone." So I lied again. So my nose grew again. That's that family protection. You know. But I told him that no, she never knew you were gone. And that was the right thing for me to do because you know, because his going did have mother choosing to die.

This was the family where everyone cared deeply for each other but never confronted the issue together. The bonding of each member was Diane's role. She played the role willingly but sometimes very painfully. However, by the early 80s, she came to the full realization that her brother was mentally ill. "You could only go so long and blind yourself," she says.

In Diane's case, it seems that her inner personal strength kept her from being badly damaged by the family experience. Probably the biggest factor was that she was a mature adult when she faced her brother's mental illness. The strong presence of her parents also brought order and peace to family life when she was growing up. It is not a typical story of a sibling scarred by family turmoil. She never sounds bitter about the family background she had to deal with, which in fact might have caused serious delays in dealing with the reality. On the contrary, she loves and cherishes her family and their experience, including the struggle with her brother's mental illness. But it is true she has become the major caretaker of the family problem and had to take the role of guardian and protector of her own parent and her sibling. This experience is common to siblings of the mentally ill, and the development of family dynamics was similar to those in many of the families in this study.

Jane Wilson can vividly describe the family culture she grew up with, and which in her mind clearly had no positive effects on dealing with her sister Cathy's mental illness. Her story is that of a typical child who was abandoned chronically at home. Before the onset of Cathy's illness, the family had already suffered from the father's mental illness and alcoholism. Thanks to medication, he later stabilized enough to keep his job and somehow managed to be "functional in a very odd way." But the family continued to be terrorized by his abusiveness, irrational behavior, and extremely dogmatic way of thinking. When he died, it was a relief for everyone in the family. "He was just an oddball," Jane recalls. "He had enough children so that we could do things, to take care of the house. You know, shopping. We functioned as a unit more than as individuals." As for Cathy, Jane did not understand the details of how her illness developed, but remembers how she felt as a little girl who keenly observed everybody else in the family from a corner. It was her older brother in those days who had to be called upon to be a rescuer in a family crisis.

> When something happened, it was mostly, Jane, you watch the children, we have to go get your sister. I was home taking care of the little ones while they went off to go deal with whatever. Cathy was picked up by the police quite a few times. She would. I mean there were just too many… when the police started picking her up for doing things you shouldn't do in public.

One of the hallmarks of the Wilsons is that the whole family denied the problem and always pretended to function by helping and covering for each other. In her house there was this big family secret and everyone was united in a strange way to keep the secret deep within their home. This kind of response is not uncommon in many dysfunctional families. It requires everyone to exert enormous effort to pretend that everything is fine so that the entire system can escape total collapse. But it is at a cost of the most vulnerable members of the system, namely the children.

As pointed out by Black and others, denial is a natural defense mechanism to protect against pain and shame, which are perceived as impossible to deal with.[4,5] However, what this family culture may do to children is to implicitly teach the rule of silence: they cannot speak the truth, but instead, pretend things are different from the way they really are, and they cannot betray other family members by speaking up and expressing their honest feelings. Jane looks back on one of many incidents caused by Cathy.

> I mean, my family is a very supportive family. Everybody, everybody is. But you know, there's healthy support, as I've learned in the past few years, and there's unhealthy support. And so, that's one of the things that I realize now. Oh boy, we should have done something different! Whatever. Cathy tried to commit suicide after the baby [out of wedlock] was born, and Cathy ended up back in the hospital. And the baby came [to live with Cathy's family]. She must have been about three months old. Of course, my youngest sister was about seven at the time. So this baby came to our house and it was like nothing had ever changed. [Laughter.] We just had another baby in the house.

Her mother continued to take care of the baby even when Cathy was released from the hospital and moved back home. One evening Cathy became extremely hostile and violent and got into a fierce physical fight with her mother. She lashed out and literally bit her mother all over. "Nobody thought anything was wrong with that," says Jane. Most of the time, even during the time she was married or divorced, Cathy was always living close to home, often in the same neighborhood. That's why Jane, or one of the three younger sisters, was always called to come home to help. Even after her mother died, "It was almost like one of them became her." While three of her four brothers moved away, all the girls stayed near home in the Los Angeles area. Jane can now realize how much she squashed her anger way down deep because the family was supposed to be very forgiving, "a very Christian family, one of whose tenets was to turn the other cheek and to forgive."

The early socialization creates a lasting influence that continues into adult life. Discounting and rationalizing their painful feelings sometimes becomes an established pattern. In a sense, this has been an important emotional survival skill. Although many of these children grow up to be responsible, functioning adults, their inner sense of despair, anger, and disappointment makes them "closeted depressed" or someday acutely and overtly depressed. It often happens that some contemporary stressful event or the experience of loss can be a trigger to realize the existence of this deeply suppressed sadness, and suddenly the depression sets in.[6] This was exactly what happened to Jane when she was around 40. It eventually made her seek therapy and learn to think more objectively about her family culture, which had traumatized her for so long.

At the same time, when Jane encountered a family support group and discovered the place where she could talk about her family problem for the first time, it was a true lifesaver. Her life was transformed from constant denial to allowing her to be herself and confront the core problem. However, Jane's reawakening and recovery ironically meant the disruption of the unity of the Wilsons. She explains,

> The rest of my family, however, labeled it [the support group] a cult and felt very threatened by it. I brought home brochures. Look, here's all the answers, we're not alone. She'd say [one of Jane's sisters] no, no, that sounds like a cult to me, those people sound mean.

Her membership in the support group marked a point when Jane began to alienate herself from her original family culture. It is common, according to Black, that after one finds a "family of choice," learns healthy patterns of communication, and starts one's process of recovery, it is difficult to stay connected with the original family.[7] While Jane's siblings adamantly keep to their ways, she feels a wider and wider gap between herself and her brothers and sisters.

> The one the closest in age to me is trying to step away from it. But she still has that you know, "you gotta take care of your family" feeling. I think a lot of it is based on her own needs. She needs a lot of help herself because she has something that is kind of like chronic fatigue syndrome but with a lot more pain in the connective tissues of the joints. You know, you just get into this whole dynamic of taking care of each other. [Laughter.] Unfortunately, I'm very healthy, so guess what....

Now other family members are still very much involved in taking care of Cathy, crisis after crisis. She overdraws her account, but the family is always there to help pay it off, although realistically she shouldn't have a bank account. Even though Jane told them to stop reaping the harvest of her mistakes, they continued to pick up the mess. Jane just decided to detach.

> Well, we had other complications in the family that made me decide that I needed to detach. It's been very hard. My younger sister and I disagree very much on the way to handle some situations, like this. Taking care of Cathy. If she needs taking care of, that's what her board and care is for. That's not my job. That's not what I was brought into this world to do. And so, that's a real departure from the family, so to speak.

Again, this departure means the widening rift between herself and other siblings, which is now so big that they do not understand each other anymore. It still makes Jane sad and worried, particularly with regard to the perception of Cathy's illness, that they are so far apart. Some brothers and sisters still are not able to accept that Cathy has schizophrenia. They believe it was caused by the drugs. But Jane learned that one of their nephews has developed schizophrenia. Although the family had believed the father was only alcoholic, Jane has been speculating that there is some genetic cause for the mental illness in her family. However, no one is willing to accept Jane's theory.

> I think that they feel that it's something that they can get better from. I've talked with my rescuer sister about my niece, how I just did not see a future for her as a mother with a child. She kind of indicated that this is something that she's just acting out and that if she has somebody watching over her and everything, she'll get better. And I just was dumbfounded to hear that kind of — dumbfounded. I was just struck with the thought that it just doesn't work that way. You can have levels of functioning. So part of what I've had to do was, well if that's what you guys think, enjoy your life, you know. And I get accused of not being supportive.

Asked if there is anything she wishes for her siblings, Jane said, "I wish we could all just talk about these things. Openly." [Laughter.]

Jodi Kramer remembers how her whole family has been devastated and made to feel hopeless because of her brother Doug's schizophrenia. Doug was the oldest child and the parents' most promising son. He was a loving and outgoing young man, involved in a choir and with other talents in music. The illness totally took any motivation away from him, making him completely withdraw from society. Jodi also refers to the general orientation of her family, which was set by her parents. They reacted in different ways to their son's illness, but neither of them was constructive and helpful for facilitating the family to cope with this situation. Jodi was a smart young woman and could not help but feel critical of her parents. She saw her mother as uneducated, unreasonable, and unsupportive of Doug's problem. Her mother, an active member of the Presbyterian church, blamed many things; the religion of "self-realization" that Doug was involved with, the college education he was getting, and the therapist he was seeing. Jodi thinks that despite her devotion to church, her mother never talked about this to her minister, which she thought was very hypo-critical.

> I feel she was very private and embarrassed about it because in the fifties people were always worried about what the neighbors would think and I had a feeling that she hadn't even told the people at church and it made me ... I didn't respect my mother so much because I thought it was like being two faced. Like hell going on at home but you're putting on a front to the people at church. And spending effort on church activities, when we needed more help at home. So I became very critical. I had no right. In some ways I had no right to be so critical, but I became a very critical person, observing these things.

She remembers her father always drank a lot, usually behind his wife's back because she wouldn't allow it, but Jodi didn't know that he was an alcoholic until he told her so later.

> And so for years I was also critical of my dad because if I went to visit him, over there, he'd be sort of sitting in his chair and all he could say to me was have a nice day. He wasn't busy, active in the world, being in clubs. And he was just sort of passive.... [He was always a drinker and] he escaped from that problem too by drink-ing. He pretty much escaped everything. All situations. I don't think it was just Doug.

However, an educated younger brother (second brother Steven), who was seeing a psychologist one day took action to obtain information for the whole family. He organized a meeting for the family with a UCLA psychiatrist to learn about Doug's problem. The doctor clearly told her family that Doug had schizophrenia and would always be this way, and that the family had to accept this illness as lasting forever. Although it helped clarify things for the family, it was a cruel sentence, which made everybody give up hope and let Doug do whatever he wanted to do. He no longer had any advocates for himself in the family. Doug's problem was no longer a focus at home but was brushed aside.

Well it was sort of like hopelessness then. Being told something like that, sort of grew hopeless. So everyone just sort of forgot. Sort of like, okay then. We don't need to be putting him in any programs or finding day care for him or sending him to expensive psychologists or therapy. I think it had that effect. And that was not the intention of this doctor. And so my brother was allowed to go back home and live there for all these years. First of all he lived in the garage at my mother's house. That was like fifteen years. Just lived out back in the garage. Didn't work and just got some money. Veteran's money. But didn't go out, didn't socialize, didn't have friends.

This meeting for the Kramers occurred in the 70s when there was little support or education for families of the mentally ill. Doug continued to live in the garage, basically "doing little strange things off and on." His daily activities were walking down to buy cigarettes, watching TV, and eating meals his mother cooked for him. Basically he ended up vegetating all this time. When her father died about ten years ago, Doug moved in with his mother in the property she owned across the street. She is still a main caretaker for her son today. Jodi feels her mother is still very much in charge to the degree that Jodi cannot step in to improve Doug's lifestyle, so that he can be helped to make use of programs he is eligible for, as her mother refuses to try new things. Jodi gave up trying to help.

Jodi also realized her other siblings became estranged after the meeting with the doctor. They also responded to the family tragedy with a lot of pain, but differently. Steven, who organized the meeting, basically ran away from the family, married four times. She thinks Doug's illness was more difficult for Steven because he identified with his brother. Though he was the one who organized the meeting between his family and the psychiatrist, he is still in denial about the nature of Doug's illness. Other siblings had somehow accepted his illness, but Jodi thinks:

> I feel like all the brothers and sisters felt that it made the family an unpleasant place. I'm not close to my younger sister. And a lot of this has to do with Doug. We're all in sort of .... Also, we didn't get too much attention from mother and so we've been all sort of competing for mother's attention. And I think we're all.... We're not happy with the family. Like sort of unhappy with the family.

The basic hierarchy between parents and children should be the foundation of the family structure. However, in a highly dysfunctional family, this order is often broken. Instead, the pattern of "incongruent hierarchy" often emerges in which the child cares for his parents' emotional needs rather than vice versa.[8] If one has to grow up with unreasonable burdens and expectations from parents, an individual may not be able to develop a healthy sense of boundary with others. The child will only know less healthy ways of interacting with other human beings. Some siblings whose parents were incompetent in dealing with mental illness in the family seem to suffer from this consequence for a long time. However, as vulnerable individuals within the family with no other choice but to accommodate the task inappropriate for their age, they try to live up to the demands of the home situation at every moment. This can be the only adaptive response to the family environment they were exposed to.[9]

In the case of Melanie Wood, who was introduced in the earlier chapter, she was only 17 when she had to take the parental role to solve a family crisis. At the time of her brother Joshua's first psychotic breakdown, neither of her parents had any clue as to what to do. Melanie intervened and called the PET team, which took her brother away in a straitjacket. She was the only capable one in the family, but the incident left a deep scar in her. She recalls feeling scared, confused, and resentful of her parents because they did not take any initiative in dealing with the situation or protecting her from this overwhelming family burden.

For the next 20 years, Melanie always took responsibility every time Joshua caused a crisis at home. Her parents never changed or adapted themselves to face the reality. No matter how many times he had breakdowns, her mother always looked the other way and didn't want to see what was going on. Her father wasn't willing to look at anything either. Their denial made it totally impossible for them to appropriately address Joshua's illness. Melanie now realizes how she suffered from chronic emotional abandonment from her mother. Her mother was not able to look at Melanie as a separate being and expected her to see things in the same way as she did. She would say that Melanie was a spoiled brat and there was something wrong with her. Emotional abandonment can also occur when parents violate children's boundaries or impose a distorted sense of boundaries between themselves and their children.[10] It causes the children to develop a sense of inadequacy and shame, making them believe that they are not worthy individuals with their own feelings, desires, and needs. It affected Melanie's self-worth, too. But she had to wait until she reached middle age to realize her own pain. She is still struggling to heal from the damaged self-image.

Marianne Schmidt did not have to play the parental role from the beginning like Melanie. But now that her parents are old, she has become the major caretaker for her sister, Emily, because no other siblings are willing to help. Despite her mental illness, which had not yet been diagnosed in those days, Emily was able to graduate from high school. Being a single mother, she was able to collect welfare and rent an apartment just a few streets away from her parents. However, the parents became increasingly concerned with Emily's continuous erratic behaviors, such as taking off with a series of undesirable men and leaving her baby alone. The parents gained custody of their granddaughter, without Emily's objection. She would disappear for weeks and months on end. At one point she was a sex worker in Las Vegas, which pained her parents enormously. Without any medical diagnosis, the whole family was simply confused. When the diagnosis finally became apparent following her major breakdown, the parents had already burned out. Marianne thought they had reached their emotional and physical limit, and therefore, she could not help but step in. This was the beginning of her caretaking role for many years to come.

Marianne was the middle sister of three, with one older brother as the second child. They would share their frustrations with each other. Although they never had any answers, at least they could talk to each other about it. Since Marianne's husband was quite supportive and helpful, she ended up having them lean on her and she accepted the role. The oldest sister was much older and was close to Emily. That was another reason Marianne told herself, "So I just took the role." Their parents moved to another town for retirement, some distance from Los Angeles. They continued to raise Emily's child, but gradually left the picture in terms of Emily's care. Emily also went into the state hospital system for longer periods of time. It also became Marianne's role to inform her parents of what was happening. Though her father passed away a couple of years ago, her mother is doing quite well. She cares for her granddaughter, who is now in her teens and a joy to her life. Marianne became the focal person, and most of the responsibility for Emily's welfare landed on her shoulders. She has accepted the role, but she also feels that there is quite a deep rift between her and her other siblings.

> My brother basically has nothing to do with it. He doesn't want to talk about it. And he has no, you know, real concern about it. He lives with my mother. My mother, out of my concern for her, I convey to her positive things to assure her that my sister's taken care of, that she's doing fine. You know, when I visit her, I let my mom know of the visits and try to put a positive slant on it so I don't bother her or worry her. So I just, whether it's the case or not, I just say she's doing okay. You know, we get along and I keep it at that. I don't want to bother my mother. But she's open. She asks. She's interested.

But her brother has refused to offer any help. Marianne wishes that he could be more helpful, but has not been able to discuss it with him.

> When I bring it up, he seems disinterested and almost agitated. He seems angry about it. Probably because he was there much of the time during the early years, and he saw what she did to my parents. What they went through. And he's emotionally confused.

Her older sister has not been involved either.

> I think she feels it's something that she either can't or doesn't want to cope with. She feels comfortable that I'm taking care of it but she really doesn't want to be involved. And I don't know what the reasons are for that.

Although she says she will not push her sister, Marianne honestly wishes that her sister were a little more willing to share responsibility and that they could support each other. On the other hand, she has the generosity to understand better than any member of the family that all her sisters and brothers have been deeply scarred by Emily's mental illness.

> I think our family, just because of our background, our dysfunctional home, we're each dealing with our own issues. I think my brother's quite emotionally... how can I say? Immature? And he's dealing with his own issues and then, much like my older sister, she has her own issues that she's dealing with, and maybe I think it's just too overwhelming and it's just too much to take on anything else.

Marianne sees them not equipped with the ability to take on any more. She also had periods when she withdrew for a while and needed to seek help for herself. Now she feels she has been placed on earth to help her sister. "If I don't, who will?" she asks.

The same conflict within the family about the understanding of mental illness was raised by Japanese sisters and brothers. Their sense of resentment toward their parents, as well as pity for aging parents who were losing the capacity to take care of the patient, were also expressed. Like siblings in the United States, some fully accepted the role that the mental illness forced them to play, and others still feel frustrated with it.

Yoshimi Naitô became the focal person in the care for her mentally ill younger brother. She felt sorry for her mother, who just could not cope. After all, she was the oldest child and was expected to take charge. She also believed she should be the major caretaker. But she could not reveal the diagnosis of schizophrenia to her mother.

> My mother couldn't cope. She was in total despair. My brother had been living with her, exhibiting so many strange behaviors, but she whined that she wouldn't be able to take care of him anymore. When I came back home from work one day, mother cried, "Yoshimi, will you do something, please!"

This made Yoshimi feel she had to help her mother. Yoshimi immediately called the hospital and arranged hospitalization. As for help from her other siblings, she doesn't expect much. But she thinks their relationships are not bad at all. She has never been married or created her own family; however, she believes other brothers are willing to take care of her in the future when she becomes too old.

Since her mother died, Masashi Ichikawa has played the role of mediator between his father and his brother Hideo. When Hideo was diagnosed with schizophrenia, Masashi was living away from home, but always felt frustrated with the way his parents treated his younger brother. They were not at all educated about mental illness, nor were they equipped to handle Hideo's various sensitive needs. His mother was loving and devoted to Hideo, the youngest child after she lost the second in an accident, while his father was very strict and critical of everything. It was rare that his mother and father cooperated with each other on anything. The diagnosis was shocking to the parents. But Masashi was angry that his father left all the responsibility to his wife. He thinks neither his father nor mother had any understanding as to how to treat their mentally ill son.

> My father has never changed all these years, even after his son got sick. He was not at all cooperative with his wife. It's like he gave up on Hideo. He left everything to our mother, and just concentrated on his work. Our mother simply loved him and was often willing to take him back home even when he needed to be in the hospital for treatment. They had no idea that Hideo needed medical care. But I didn't fully understand it either in those days. Now I have learned that the family's interaction with the patient is an important factor. But in retrospect, we knew nothing in those days. We were not doing anything constructive....

But the mother's death five years ago forced Masashi to intervene more directly. The critical role that mother had played in this small house was now Masashi's. He has a career and a family of his own and lives at a distance, constantly worrying about his father and brother, who live together despite their hatred for each other. One lives on the first floor and the other on the second floor, and they avoid each other as much as possible. When Masashi visits them, he has to listen to each complain and criticize the other. They are still fighting over the same things they fought over more than ten years ago. Masashi is fed up with being a communication pipeline between the two. But he knows the inability of his father to understand the illness and also his brother's limitations. Hideo once tried to live by himself, but it did not last. Masashi is extremely concerned about how Hideo could manage to live alone after the father dies.

Junko Nomura has been frustrated with a widening gap between herself, her mother, and her brother in understanding her sister Chieko's schizophrenia. When the doctor delivered the diagnosis, it was her brother Yoshihiko who was most devastated. This family of three children had lost their father at an early age and were raised by a "tyrant, and extremely self-centered," mother. The inheritance dispute after her husband's death had also caused their mother to develop a strong persecution complex. Junko is now convinced that their mother always had a borderline personality disorder and that all her children grew up deeply scarred by her pathological control. Unfortunately, Chieko was the most vulnerable of the three children, Junko believes. Chieko could not handle or resist their mother's control and basically became her victim. Junko was able to resist, leave home, get married, and have her own life and family. As for Yoshihiko, he must have had a very difficult childhood, too, but never showed his scar. With a strong sense of responsibility as the oldest child and only son of the family, he worked hard and has become an executive in a prestigious corporation. Now the aged mother lives with him, his wife, and their children.

> My brother's shock was enormous. He was so shocked to realize that our family had produced a mentally ill patient. I was shocked, too. But I was prepared for it somewhere in my mind. Chieko had not been able to have decent human relationships with anyone for many years. I knew something was terribly wrong with her. But my main concern until that moment was how we could successfully bring her to the hospital. When it was done, I was more relieved, now that I knew they were going to start treating her. But for my brother, it was like the earth collapsed under his feet or something. As for my mother, her pride was so badly hurt. She said nothing to the doctor, but she hasn't accepted Chieko's mental illness. She has refused. She still says today, "How come that intelligent man with a medical school education can say such a

stupid thing?" On the other hand, once Chieko was hospitalized, it seemed that our mother couldn't care less about her. She even said, "I don't want Chieko back any more."

For years, Junko has been the only one in the family who was willing to face the illness and educate herself about it. Since she felt accepted and empowered by the support group, she has been an active participant. Now she is also involved in aiding the mentally ill and is in charge of an occupational training project for patients. But the rift between her brother and herself remains seriously deep. Chieko sometimes made harassing phone calls to his office, which infuriated Yoshihiko. He offers financial help for her, but says, "It is nauseating just to think of her." He doesn't want to do anything for her himself.

He is so angry at Chieko. Because he wouldn't understand her illness. He cannot distinguish the illness from the person. It must be very hard for him. So I told him about the family support group. I told him it will make you feel relieved, like it did me. But he said, "No kidding!" He doesn't even want his wife to go, although his wife has to deal with our mother on a daily basis and sometimes with Chieko, too. My brother is afraid of how others would see us. On the other hand, I am not living in my hometown now, but my brother has never moved away. So it may be easier for me and harder for him. But what's important for him is to get out of this old mode of thinking that he doesn't have to do anything.

In the beginning, Junko was upset thinking how stubborn her brother was. But now she has come to understand that her brother is afraid of being the victim of the pervasive social stigma regarding mental illness. Many members of family support groups are closed mouthed about their mentally ill family outside. This is the reality. She thinks, "I wouldn't easily say to anyone, 'Why don't you go to the support group. It is good!' It is also important to protect people who cannot be open about mental illness in the family." She feels she should not torture her brother any more.

Family Interactons in the United States and Japan

The United States and Japan are highly industrialized, urban societies with predominantly nuclear families. Despite this surface similarity, the basic values of the family can differ greatly between the two societies. While the American family ideal upholds the husband–wife unit, based on conjugal affection and companionship, as the center of the household, Japanese families are less concerned with conjugal intimacy than with the closeness of mother–child relationships and generational interdependency. The division of labor based on gender is still strong within the home, which explains the intense isolation experienced by some of the Japanese mothers who were discussed earlier.

Divorce is the most common form of resolution for marital problems in the United States, which has one of the highest divorce rates in the world, while it is still harder for Japanese families with children to take such a step. Of the eleven American mothers who participated in this study, four have been divorced and one has remarried. Of the five American fathers, four have been divorced and two have remarried. One of the two husbands was preparing for a divorce in the near future. On the other hand, only one of the eleven Japanese mothers has been divorced and remarried and none of the six Japanese fathers has been divorced. One of the three subjects interviewed as spouses of patients got a divorce but he remained as guardian of his mentally ill wife who was permanently hospitalized.

The breakup of the original family where the patient grew up complicates the family interactions after the development of illness. It is more difficult for the patient's parents, or former spouses, to communicate. Physical separation simply makes it more difficult to achieve any cooperation. If one of the patient's parents does not want to, or has found it impossible to be involved with the child's illness, he or she can vanish from the picture completely, leaving the other spouse with full responsibility for the patient's care. The American mothers and fathers I interviewed who were in this situation had to accept the caretaker role whether they wanted to or not. The distress of balancing the current relationships after divorce, including a new family, and the illness of the child from the former marriage was also seen only among American interviewees. The sense of added strain and frustration was painfully perceived by these individuals. However, Japan has been witnessing a rising divorce rate in recent years. It is not yet known how the increased incidence of family breakup will affect families of the mentally ill. At least, it is unlikely that it will make the Japanese families' adjustment and coping any easier.

Nevertheless, how mental illnesses affect various family relationships seems extremely similar in the United States and Japan. Here again, the same emotions, concerns for, and resentment of other family members and the sense of unfairness about the caregiving role were expressed. Few Japanese siblings articulated psychological effects as clearly as did the American siblings. As mentioned earlier, this is probably because they had not been in therapy and were not accustomed to explaining themselves by means of a psychological vocabulary and perspective. In fact, one Japanese brother of a patient broke down in tears for a moment during the interview, but quickly collected himself to continue talking about episodes in the family's life. Japanese interviewees were more willing to describe their roles and various conflicts in family relationships than their inner feelings.

The family is never a unitary whole. Each member of the family looks at, interprets, and deals with the event in his or her own way. The arrival of severe mental illness brings enormous distress to intrafamily relationships as well as the chance to solidify and improve them. It is difficult to predict how family life will be affected by mental illness, but it seems that not only is an individual level of coping important, but also that a "collective" coping process is crucial. How a family can best survive this catastrophe seems to depend on both its material resources and the social support the family possesses. However, it seems to me that the outcome ultimately hinges upon the "culture" of each family, not necessarily the culture of the society as a whole.

Notes

1. C. Black, *Changing Course: Healing from Loss, Abandonment, and Fear* (Center City, MN: Hazelden, 1999).
2. Ibid., 3, 25–26.
3. D. R. Hawley and L. DeHaan, "Toward a Definition of Family Resilience, Integrating Life-Span and Family Perspectives," *Family Process* 35 (1996): 283–98.
4. Black, *Changing Course*, 9–10.
5. A. B. Hatfield, "Coping and Adaptation: A Conceptual Framework for Understanding," in *Families of the Mentally Ill: Coping and Adaptation,* ed. A. B. Hatfield and H. P. Lefley (New York: Guilford, 1987), 72.
6. Black, *Changing Course*, 30–32.
7. Ibid., 113–35.
8. M. P. Nichols and R. C. Schwartz, *Family Therapy; Concepts and Methods*, 5th ed. (Boston: Allyn & Bacon, 2001), 125.
9. Ibid., 127.
10. Black, *Changing Course*, 20–21.

PART **IV**

Learning to Understand the New Reality of Illness

CHAPTER 6

Why Did the Illness Strike?
Families Look for Meaning

I'm just amazed that people who have Ph.D.s are so ignorant about mental illness. Unless it's touched somebody a lot, it's not something that people can understand. — An American sibling.

Most families know little if anything about mental illness until it hits a loved one. The terminology, system, and body of knowledge of psychiatry are puzzling and confusing. While they go through many kinds of emotional turmoil over the symptoms, diagnosis, and prognosis, family members also struggle in their own way to objectively understand the disease. Eventually, families make what at first seemed like a monstrosity into a manageable entity that it is possible for them to understand in their own way. Their grasp of the sick family member's condition may not be necessarily accurate in scientific terms. But even in the midst of psychological confusion, they observe, think, interpret, and construct their own explanations in order to better understand the new reality.

One of the key questions family members ask is why the particular family member was struck by the illness. Coming to some plausible explanation greatly helps them adjust to this otherwise too stressful and disturbing reality. It is essential for human beings to make sense out of a chaotic world. The causal attribution process plays a major role in the process of cognitive adjustment, which eventually helps family members adjust to the emotional aspect as well. It is a process that involves family members regaining a sense of control. In struggling to understand the mental illness of sons, daughters, sisters, brothers, and spouses, they eventually come to terms with the fact that the problem is real and to understand the true nature of the illness.

Learning about the Illness

The primary caregivers in my study, or the ones who interacted most closely with the mentally ill family member, came to learn about and be alert to a flareup of the symptoms of the illness better than anyone — even the doctor. Their eagerness to understand this unfamiliar field sometimes led them to make very careful observations regarding the patient's condition, and some family members became expert on their family member's illness. Again, their "theories" about the illness may not be scientifically accurate, based as they are on daily impressions and mostly nonscientific interpretation. Nevertheless, these views have become a part of their belief system about the illness, which helps them keep going and sometimes sustains hope of recovery even in the midst of despair.

Patterns of Relapse

Kôichi Takagi now understands his son Tamotsu's problem is auditory hallucinations:

> He hears in his brain something that is not there. I think instead of calling it schizophrenia, another name like "Auditory hallucination syndrome" would explain it better and people would understand the patient's problem. He would be someone simply with "auditory hallucinations," and that would sound Ok. For example, the sounds of a refrigerator, which we don't normally notice, sound like words or something to him, it seems. You know, it's a symptom which can even happen to ordinary people when they haven't slept for three or four days and are completely exhausted. It's not something we would never experience, you know. That's how I understand it.

With the support of his psychiatrist and hospital staff, Tamotsu, who majored in social work, managed to graduate from college. Though he started working at a new rehabilitation facility in Tokyo, which his father helped to establish with a sizable donation, the hard work that required meetings with many clients gave Tamotsu too much stress to handle, and his symptoms came back. In order to work through the night to meet a deadline, he often skipped his medications. When he was hospitalized again, it was the beginning of a cycle of repeated hospitalizations. "In retrospect, these hospitalizations have occurred about the same time of the year, January. I wonder if he has relapses under the same climatic conditions." Kôichi says. A number of recurrences are making Kôichi lose hope for recovery. But he keeps his cool-headedness and sense of humor.

> When I review the length of his hospitalizations, the first one was for twenty-four days and the second one was for twenty days, about the same length, right? Then the following ones were for seventy-seven days and seventy-nine days, again about the same length, but about four times longer than the first two. Then the next one was for 338 days, roughly four times again. The next one was for 567 days. This was almost double the previous one. I thought it was a "doubling game." You know it's like trying to quit smoking. Every time you quit smoking, you end up smoking twice as many cigarettes. I thought these figures had profound meanings. [Laughter.]

Through the struggle with his daughter Yuri's manic depression, Tôru Yamaguchi has figured out by now that her relapse follows a very predictable pattern. She needs to be in the hospital for three months of every year when she is in a manic stage, and when the manic stage is over, she can come back home with depression for the remaining nine months of the year. "The toughest time is during the manic stage," Tôru says, "when she talks a lot, calls anyone regardless of time." Tôru's chiding would just make it worse. So later he would contact those people Yuri had called and apologize for her lack of manners. She also goes on shopping sprees and ends up buying many expensive and unnecessary items. Tôru feels he cannot do or say anything to her about this, either, but leave her alone. He says that the transition from the depressive stage to the manic stage is so sudden and critical that even one day's delay in bringing her to the hospital would lead to an irretrievable mess at home. Some years ago, when she was still in the depressed stage, Tôru expected Yuri to soon return to the manic stage. He thought a few days of anti-manic medication would enable her to stay at home a little longer. However, she lost her sense of balance, falling down the stairs, unable to go upstairs by herself, or walk straight. He says he never wants to see her like that again. It is crucial to get the timing of hospitalization right, he believes.

Leland Miller also found out that his sister Rosalyn's psychotic breakdowns occurred in a certain pattern during the first decade after the onset of the illness. Although she was hospitalized a number of times, she married and had a baby. When she would disappear, leaving the baby, Leland was always there to offer help to his sister, but her condition never substantially improved.

> And so then, she lived in the apartment and raised the baby. And it seemed like every two years, you know, there would be a crisis stage and we would have to go in and pick up the pieces and so on and so forth. It's almost like clockwork. It was amazing.

Ruth Singer, who is convinced that his son's manic-depressive relapse is triggered by stress, says, "Always caused by stress. Some stress of some kind. Financial stress, girlfriend stress. He had to sell his car. That brought a big stress on him because he had no means of transportation."

Yoshiko Takeda sometimes suspects that her daughter Emiko had in fact suffered from some mental ailment for many years before she was officially diagnosed. Her prognosis is unusually good right now and Emiko looks as if she has almost recovered.

> Up until the first year in junior high school, she was an extremely active girl, but from the second year, she became very quiet. It's like, you wonder, "How come she became so quiet?" Although she became ill at twenty-two, when I listen to stories from other families about how their children's illness can start, and also look back on how my daughter changed, I wonder maybe whether there were signs of illness already. Many years earlier, she had stopped talking, you know. She didn't have many friends. She was in a marching band during high school and the team used to win a national championship. But she was told, "You are so quiet" by her teammates. So in retrospect, she might have been suffering from schizophrenia already. I have read that some people have a long incubation period for the illness. I wonder if my daughter had something like that. If that is the case, many things make sense to me now. She was so active and enjoying her life during the first year of junior high. Then slowly schizophrenia was creeping up on her. But the long period of medication eliminated much of, maybe 99 percent of her illness, and brought back her original liveliness. Her own, original energy. But she was a quiet girl for so long that she thought that her passivity was a part of her own personality and because of the illness and treatment, her personality changed. But I think she has simply gone back to how she was in the beginning....

Other Unique Perceptions

Kôji Yamada remembers that when his wife Hitomi had a hysterectomy caused by complications from an ectopic pregnancy, and then further surgery, she did not have any hallucinations. "But when she recovered, the hallucinations came back, and she complained that nurses or hospital attendants were saying bad things about her. It is strange, isn't it?" Koji wonders. "When she was physically ill, she was busy with that. She didn't have problems with strangers, either. It seems that when she got used to new people, she began to have hallucinations."

It took Barbara Weiss quite some time to realize her daughter Jessica's problem was a mental disorder, as she had long believed that Jessica's erratic behavior was caused by hypoglycemia, a physical condition. After more than two decades, Barbara still struggles to establish a relationship with her daughter, who is now in a board-and-care facility. Jessica's persistent hostility toward her mother is unbearably distressing to Barbara, although she would do anything to mend the relationship. But she began to have second thoughts about shedding too many tears on that: her whole life had been only centered on taking care of her daughter. At the same time, she developed an interesting view about mentally ill, which helps her cope with the illness of her daughter.

> I'm beginning to think about me more because I may live longer than my daughter. I don't know. I never hear anything about how long people live who have mental illness. We've never discussed that — even in any of our support groups. But, a lot of them are getting up there in their late forties, so you don't know how long. Of course, they're not stressed; they don't have stress…. It's the medication they're taking. What has been said to me is that they don't suffer like we suffer looking at it. They're out of it. And, you've got to take care of yourself…. I would think they would suffer. I should think they would, but you never hear of any of them having heart attacks or anything…. Parents have heart attacks, but you don't hear about them having heart attacks. It's kind of like a cop-out. You're in another world. But anyway, I wasn't that great. I probably look better right now than I did then. I was just a zombie, walking around, trying to find a miracle for my daughter. Like a magic wand, you know?

Helen Hawkins becomes enthusiastic when talking about what has happened to her cousin, who was once mentally ill. This cousin had been in and out of institutions all her life, although she married and had a child. When she got throat cancer in her 50s and had radiation therapy and other treatment, her mental illness was gone. Helen calls it a miracle story. And it gives her hope for her own daughter's illness.

They don't know that it's radiation, but she got cancer and I tell this story because that's an encouraging story to me. She's a doll, and her whole family, they said it's a miracle. We couldn't believe that it happened but we've seen her, and she took care of her mother, who she used to beat up. She took care of her mother when she was ill and now she's taking care of her sister-in-law and she's fantastic. So there is hope. We have seen a lot of them that have improved a great deal. Now this one is just like, well you'd never know. She couldn't raise her daughter. Her sister had to raise her niece because she was just incapable. But I tell that story at support meetings because it's a true story and I witnessed it with my own eyes and it's hard to believe. They don't know because she had several other treatments, the cancer gone, and they have no idea. Well, you know, they don't have any idea what even causes this [mental illness] other than it's genetic; however, they don't know which gene is causing it, so who knows?

Nevertheless, hope is also sustained with cautious realism, on a continuing basis, by Anna Berger about her son, Stan.

I've accepted that he probably will not do better. Although I am always hoping for that to happen. There have been several studies that show people with these illnesses in their fifties and sixties do much better.... The illness seems to sort of "burn out" as they get older. The people who did these studies were quite surprised to find people in these ages — fifties and sixties — who were doing as well as they were doing. Some of them were no longer taking medication. Some of them were working or were much more functional than they were when they were young. So that may happen, I don't know.

As a physician, Wallace Green tries to be objective in observing his son Mike's current condition. At the same time, he is tormented by the paradox that with the improvement of Mike's illness, his son may become more depressed and unhappy.

Seemingly his interactive skills are a little better. But the hallmark of schizophrenia is loss of will. And that still is present. He almost doesn't have energy to brush his teeth. You know, the simple things everyday…. No motivation. It's called avolition…. He's isolated, withdrawn, depressed. And the catch-22 is, as these people gain more insight, and become more aware and functional, the degree of depression can increase. Because when they're sicker or psychotic, they don't have the insight.

Another father, Timothy Rosen, also shares a similar view. Since the medication is working well, his son has shown substantial improvement over the years. However, Timothy worries that, if it works too well for his son so that he becomes insightful and knowledgeable about his own illness at the same level as his father, he doesn't know how his son would be able to go on. His son may find himself in complete despair. Timothy wants to see him get better, but that may mean something different to his son.

Another thing bothers me: If he gets to the point where his medication has made him understand his illness. If it were me, it would put me in despair: just knowing that I have this illness. I think there's a certain element of keeping up the denial. There's been no question in my mind for a while that he's been in severe denial: "I'm not sick." But, on the other hand, I think he knows he's sick. I think he knows he has schizophrenia. He knows the word. But if it were the point where he had to confront it so definitely to the point where he understood clearly that there's no cure…. If he went into what *I* know about schizophrenia, if that doesn't put him in depression, I don't know what would. So, I think it's a dichotomy that is very difficult to deal with. So, on the one hand, I want him to be well enough to be able to take care of his resources, take care of his personal hygiene, to…

Questions about Diagnosis

However, the big question persistently remains among some family members as to whether the diagnosis was an accurate one or not. Particularly if the sick family member was addicted to drugs, parents and others remain unsettled about the presence of the mental illness itself. In fact, comorbidity of various mental illnesses with chemical abuse such as alcohol and other substances is common. For example, it is reported that the likelihood of a substance abuse diagnosis is 4.6 times higher for persons with schizophrenia compared with the average population.[1] Powerful street drugs produce hallucinations, delusions, or disorders in thinking, which can lead to the diagnosis of schizophrenia if the history of drug abuse is not communicated. It has also been proven that chronic use of mind-altering drugs can damage brain function.[2]

The dual diagnosis is a complex one, but it means hope for some, because relatives can tell themselves that any problems were due to the effect of the drugs. A perception seems to exist in the minds of the general public that *drug addiction* sounds better than *mental illness*. The effect of drug addiction can in fact be as devastating as severe mental illness, but it seems less mysterious than schizophrenia. Drug addiction projects an image that makes it appear more controllable, perhaps even "curable." It does not sound like something that one has as an intrinsic attribute — it sounds like something that can be resolved with various types of treatment. There is also less stigma attached to drug addiction. Interestingly, I heard many American parents talking about the dual diagnosis with a strong wish that it would be a drug problem.

With a medical doctor's caution, Wallace Green thinks his son Mike's breakdown had something to do with his drug use. "We don't know [if it was caused by drugs]," he says. "I should like to think it was. It might be more hopeful. My intuitive sense tells me that people have this vulnerability. Given certain environmental condition, stressors like drugs, it might flare it."

From the beginning, Frank Brown has had great doubt about the accuracy of the diagnosis given to his son; dual diagnosis of paranoid schizophrenia and drug addiction. "To this day, I still ... deep in my heart, I want it to be the drug," he says.

> I think it is tough. You know, I might say at this time, that I'm still not a hundred percent convinced that it is congenital mental illness. I'm wondering still if it's mental illness because of the drugs that he took for a long period of time. I'm still not a hundred percent convinced.

Pat Bryant has been seeing her son Nick's continuing relapses for years. He had been diagnosed as manic-depressive but it was many years after he began using drugs and alcohol during his teenage years. In fact, drugs and alcohol were the problems the family believed caused him to act abnormally.

> A lot of it was the interaction ... well, see I don't know how much was real mania and how much was alcohol along with the medications he was on. You know that could mess it up, too ... for whatever reason ... and this doctor said that because he would always go back to drinking that it would just deteriorate his brain further, his brain cells, and that eventually he just wouldn't be able to function at all. It was always interacting with the meds and causing this

cycle of ... anyway it is getting worse ... it's progressive in both diseases, the alcohol and the mental illness."

The Big Question: What Caused the Mental Illness?

The ultimate question family members ask themselves during the process of adjustment to the new reality is why it happened and what was the cause of mental illness. There are a number of theories relating to the causes of mental illnesses, particularly schizophrenia, including genetic and neurochemical origins, those relating to infectious and immune causes, as well as those that ascribe schizophrenia to nutritional imbalances, endocrine abnormalities, stress, sociological factors, and family interactions.[3]

For example, there has been compelling evidence for the heritability of schizophrenia. Someone with a first-degree relative with schizophrenia has an 8 to 10% risk of developing the disease, while that of the general population is about 1%. That of identical twins is said to be as high as 50%.[4] However, the fact that even twins do not have a 100% concordance rate suggests that other nongenetic factors must come into play.[5,6] The precise cause of schizophrenia and many other mental disorders has not yet been discovered. But there is a growing body of evidence that supports its biological origin, or at least that it results from a biological dysfunction. But even so-called biological causes have been speculated to manifest themselves in a number of ways.[7–9]

Some studies have suggested that complications at birth can lead to the later onset of schizophrenia. Infection in the mother during pregnancy, for example, influenza or rubella — is one complication that has been mentioned. Other possibilities include autoimmune abnormalities in brain cells and malnutrition.[10–12] One of the more popular theories of schizophrenia is based on the neurodevelopmental model. Some evidence has supported the hypothesis that during early fetal development of the brain, particularly in the second trimester, a failure can occur in the formation of the neuron network, which many years later may emerge by producing symptoms of psychosis.[13,14]

Thomas Szasz's theory of nonschizophrenia or antipsychiatry became popular in some circles in the 1970s, when he cast radical skepticism on the whole concept of modern psychiatry. He claimed that what modern psychiatry called mental illness was not based on "objective truth," but rather was related to various human "problems of living," or deviations from psychosocial, ethical, and legal standards. He even compared modern psychiatry to premodern witchcraft and demonology. According to Szasz, it was absurd and wrong to seek solutions for these nonmedical problems in a medical or even therapeutic framework, as it misleadingly prevented us from facing the real human life struggles. Therefore, he declared that mental illness did not exist, and the concept itself was a myth.[15] Although his argument is intellectually interesting, it completely lacks practical consideration for patients with severe mental illness, particularly psychotic disorders, and their families. These ideas were formed during the 1970s when biochemical science had not developed to the contemporary level. Today more sophisticated medical and scientific measures such as brain imaging are available, which can clearly present the biological transformations that accompany the development of schizophrenia, and therefore can refute much of Szasz's argument. It was also problematic to see all kinds of mental and psychological problems as belonging to the same group. However, Szasz's idea caused much confusion in the understanding of mental illness and how society should treat such patients. It is sad that even today some people still embrace this obsolete perspective.[16]

The family interaction theories created the concept of the double-bind, in which parents are considered the culprits by using a pathologically confusing communication style with their child.[17] This theory and other related theories that emphasize how family interactions with the patient can cause schizophrenia have, in fact, no statistical, scientific basis. As Torrey says, "parents are not powerful enough to cause a disease like schizophrenia simply by favoring one child over another or giving the child inconsistent messages." However, even though most psychiatrists today are aware of the absurdity of old theories such as chaotic mothering as a cause, the idea is still persistent in our society in general, even among some mental health professionals.[18]

Even in the psychiatric community, debate continues as to what exactly causes schizophrenia and many other mental disorders. The families of the mentally ill cannot reach a consensus, either. They just keep grappling with the question in their own way and come to their own conclusions. Their desperate search for the reason for their family member's mental illness brings back the classical discussion of nature versus nurture, especially the issue of genetic liability. Or they try to understand what was wrong about the patient's upbringing, the greatest "nurture" factor.

Family Environment

Many point out how dysfunctional the family of the patient was, suggesting it may be the conflict-ridden family environment that caused their family member to become sick. They also refer to parental personality and their way of raising children as possible factors that contributed to the onset of mental illness. Some also attribute a particular incident that occurred in the patient's life as the trigger of the illness. When parents themselves believe it is their pattern of raising children that caused their children's illness, naturally they are tormented by self-blame and intense guilt. Siblings also blame parents for causing their loved ones to become stressed out, which, they believe, eventually led to the illness.

Kelly Seeman sounds very certain that her adopted son Allan's problem came mainly from the irreversible act of abandonment by his biological parents. Allan was the product of a teenage relationship. Not only was the biological father out of the scene when Allan was born, his young mother was not able to take care of him, either. He has some dim memory of the first four years with his biological family, but essentially no one in the household except his grandfather wanted him. By the time he was adopted, the little boy was full of anger. Later, when Allan was ten, Kelly and her husband divorced, and her ex-husband wanted nothing to do with him, though Allan was so hungry for fatherly love. Kelly sees his illness as originating from the fact that there was "no real official treatment" in his life.

> You see, I'm not so sure. I think that — in nontechnical, medical terms — this child is so fragmented and his life has been so chaotic, I think that there is no core, there is no foundation for this child to have ever built his life out of. Because, as I've come to know now in later years, the development of a child during the first four years of their life is so crucial and this child had only chaos during the first four years of his life and continuing upheaval and chaos the next four years of his life. So, I don't see him in the sense that I see other people being described as schizophrenic and I don't know for certain. But he's never heard voices. I don't know if he is really schizophrenic, but he is just so anxious all the time and so unable to cope with life. Life is so stressful for him that he has never been able to get any kind of a hold on it. He's never been able to develop any sense of self, of security, of constancy. He has no sense of who he is. So that is my nonscientific view. What is this, a personality disorder? Maybe. Now, his behavior can be bipolar. But I think sometimes the manic behavior comes out of the anxiety. Okay, his behavior can be schizophrenic, but I'm not sure that it ever comes from what is medically determined to be schizophrenic.

Robert Kirk never forgets the bitter divorce battle with his first wife and laments that it was this terrible experience that must have severely traumatized his son Ben, who was six at the time. Although Ben eventually moved in with Kirk and his second wife when he was eight, he had already been deeply scarred. Kirk struggles with the question as to what caused his son's later illness, but he cannot help thinking that the effect of this early experience was related to it.

> Well, well, okay. You see, part of my problem is denial jumps in a lot. And I say, "Well, is he really mentally ill or is it because of such a damned awful childhood? Things didn't go right. Is it this? Is it this? Is it this?

Ruth Singer felt terribly guilty when her son's psychiatrist told her that Paul's problem was her fault. This theory that mother is mainly responsible has pretty much faded by now. But this was still in the 1970s and she believed him then.

> Yes. [I believed him.] He's the expert right? He also had at one point — I told him about the problems I was having with my son not cooperating, and you know, the way he was acting. And he had lived with me then for about four or five months. And he said that's the worst thing he could do is live with you. But I said, "Where is he going to go? In the streets?" He said that would teach him a good lesson… [but] I believed it and I kept thinking well, what did I do wrong? I raised my children as best as I could. Always with love.

Reiko Matsuoka has been blaming herself since her son Shigeru was diagnosed with schizophrenia. "I just feel sorry about him," she cries uncontrollably. "If I hadn't pushed him so hard to go to cram school, he might not have become sick…." Now she feels that she will have to take care of this child for the rest of her life because she feels responsible for his condition. When her son Mamoru was diagnosed, Shoko Inose was desperate for more information. She rushed to a bookstore and bought as many books as she could carry to learn about mental illness. "The books were so difficult, "she recalls. "I didn't understand much. But still they made me feel maybe the family causes the illness. There is the genetic factor, but in addition to that, I felt the family can be a problem." As for Naoyo Abe, she never stopped questioning herself as to what went wrong with her son Mikio, who has epilepsy and various neurotic disorders.

> The other two children of mine have no problems, they are such good children, and excellent students. They help me a lot. But Mikio, a middle child, didn't do well at school. His memory was quite good but he had the lowest grades. He was sandwiched

between the two brilliant siblings and I bet he felt inferior. He must have suffered from an inferiority complex. I think that's where the reason for his illness lies.

Marianne Schmitt also reflects on the early stage when her sister Emily claimed she heard voices.

You know, [Emily is] the youngest child, and because we came from a dysfunctional home, maybe she just … I knew the effects it had on my life and maybe it was just more intense in terms of her life. So you know, you try to find reasons, but mental illness is never the first thing, at least for me, that I would have thought of. But I think at that point I was beginning to realize that something was really terribly wrong here.

Masashi Ichikawa is critical of his father for his brother Hideo's illness. Unable to cope with the stress, Hideo quit his first job only several months after graduating from high school. He was stubborn like his father and tended to look at things in an all-or-nothing manner. Masashi thinks that his parents should have been more willing to listen to Hideo's problems and worries. They were too busy with the family business. Mieko Maruyama more bitterly and harshly criticizes her father, who was an oppressive tyrant, for creating such a suffocating home life, which produced suicide, alcoholism, and psychotic illness among five of the seven children. In her view, it was clearly one parent who made so many of her siblings lose their sanity. Junko Nomura also thinks her mother had a borderline personality, and that this greatly influenced her younger sister Chieko, who became schizophrenic. Unlike Junko, who was strong enough to eventually escape her influence by leaving home, becoming independent, and marrying, Chieko did not have the capacity to do the same and continued to live under their mother's control. Junko feels it must have a lot to do with the onset of her sister's illness.

It is harder for the spouse to know the details of a mentally ill husband's or wife's upbringing, but William Baker speculates that his wife Martha's dysfunctional home environment, where her Japanese mother attempted suicide, had given her a very difficult childhood. One teenage experience she once told him about years before she became ill stands out in his stock of information on his wife's background.

She said that, first of all, her father drank a lot — like an alcoholic — and I think that he might have molested her. Because she went through a period when she said, "I hate my father. I hate my father. If I went to his grave, I'd spit on his grave." You know, that kind of stuff. And this went on for a while, and I used to ask why she hated him. And she said one thing — she never told me that he molested her — but she told me one time she was in the shower and he came home drunk [he was her biological father]. He walked into the bathroom and just pulled the shower curtain back and said, "You're my daughter. I can look at you if I want to." That's the only thing she ever told me about that, but I have a feeling that it probably went a little deeper than that. Okay? Because that, along with the stress of her job and stuff, I think that created, you know, the problem that she has now.

The sad fact is that so many family members of patients seriously question, criticize, regret, and mourn the patient's early socialization, which cannot be changed. It is an agonizing mental struggle. This distinguishes the experience of having mental illness in the family from having other medical problems. As mentioned earlier, "in no other area of treatment for illness have families of the ill been such objects of contempt and scathing criticism by professionals as have the families of the mentally ill."[19] However, turning to the medical community for help, the families of the mentally ill have no choice but to accept and internalize the mainstream mental health ideologies of the time in which they live. The dysfunctional family as the decisive cause for the psychotic disorder is a deeply rooted belief among the general population and still among many mental health professionals.

Terkelson writes that the idea of the family having some role in the development of mental illness was first introduced in early nineteenth-century America. Although in those days the main cause for insanity was believed to be stress resulting from the radical changes in American society as a whole, families of patients in asylums were first seen as a passive, but indirect, cause of the onset of illness.[20] "If the principal cause of insanity was the disarray of American society, the family was at fault for not having shielded the patient sufficiently." It was the rise of psychoanalytic theories in the early twentieth century that marked the start of the trend of family, or rather, mother-blaming, because its central concept relied on the significance and irreversible influence of early childhood socialization. Although twin studies in the 1930s presented strong genetic possibilities for the onset of mental illness, developmental theories for psychoses were willingly accepted in the United States because the country's fundamental culture was such that it preferred environmental explanations. Soon the concept of dysfunctional family interaction was developed, leading to the formation of family therapy theories. By this time, a complete paradigm shift occurred: the family was blamed for not protecting the patient from external stress that affected the family, which in itself was seen as causing the illness.[21] In family system theories, families are sometimes criticized for perpetuating the patient's symptoms to fulfill the needs of the entire family.[22]

More recently, the concept of express emotion (EE) has been introduced, not as a causal agent of schizophrenia, but as a robust predictor of the course of the patient's symptoms at home after the patient returns from hospitalization.[23] The concept had been created through studies that identified the correlation between relapses and certain family characteristics. The patients with more relapses lived with families that tended to be highly critical, hostile, and overinvolved with the patient. The causal relations were indicated between the family's attitude and the course of the illness.[24] Therefore, the role of the family was considered not to cause the illness, but to modify the course of the illness.[25]

The concept was "uncritically accepted" by many mental health professionals[26] and was widely introduced in psychoeducational classes. Although it gave the families hope of being able to control the patient's illness, it subtly placed another burden on the families. Furthermore, various methodological problems of the EE studies have been indicated that refute its validity. In fact, compliance with medication is the most significant factor preventing relapse. Torrey says, "If half the energy devoted to educating families about high EE had been devoted instead to ensuring compliance with medications, the relapse rate of the patients would have decreased much more dramatically than anything demonstrated by EE."[27]

Thus, it seems extremely difficult to see families of the mentally ill escape explicit and implicit criticism for their influence on the development of the illness. Of course, since much of the etiology remains unknown, there is no way of determining exactly how the family plays a part. The fact is that the family is a dynamic unit in which each small part is constantly influencing every other part. However, to carelessly extend this idea to the emergence of a psychotic disorder is dangerous. For families who have endured enough burdens, it is not only demoralizing but also self-defeating. If these old ideas on families are still held by mental health professionals in any way, it deeply hurts family members. The misalliance of views between mental health professionals and the patients' families only creates a destructive environment for treating these chronic diseases.[28,29]

The Genetic Factor

Some family members were quick to connect their mentally ill children's and siblings' illness with their inescapable family heredit. Their almost fatalistic awareness mostly exempts them, however, from guilt and self-blame. Rather, they talk about it as a matter of fact. Their distress in struggling with understanding the illness was seemingly much reduced by this admission.

Maria Hafer used to meet people who implicitly accused her for failing her son's mental health. Their questions sometimes sounded to her almost as if they were asking, "What did you do wrong?" Although they were never phrased in such a direct way, they always made her ask the same question to herself. But now she has a different view. She sees it as a physical illness that can come from the genetic history. Being an adopted child, she doesn't know about her own biological family's medical history.

> Yes. And so I don't know whether there's anything in my background. In my husband's father's family there's bipolar. And we don't know, you know, what relationship there is between the different mental illnesses. Because I still say I don't know what my son has. It might be schizophrenia, but it doesn't necessarily matter, some of the medications treat one, more than one thing. I still question because a person can be psychotic just from depression. Only that he does have some strange ideas leans more toward schizophrenia.

Timothy Rosen accepted the link of his son's illness with his genetic background, which helped him ask the question constantly.

> Yeah, but I never thought in terms of mental illness. And then I found out later on that it seems that my ex-wife has several cousins that have schizophrenia. And that her grandmother committed suicide. And none of this came out until at least months — maybe a year — after my son was hit by this thing. All of these things unfolded gradually, you see.

Jane Wilson believes she grew up in a terribly dysfunctional home environment, constantly disrupted by her father's alcoholism, mental breakdowns, and abusive personality. However, Jane still thinks her sister Cathy's schizophrenia has more to do with their genetic background. "I think our family has a strong genetic tendency, yeah. I have nieces and nephews that are still quite young and that's concerned me. But it's the kind of thing you can't cover over now."

Growing up with relatives who developed mental illness, and seeing her favorite cousin gradually lose her functions because of schizophrenia, Miki Maeda was fully aware that she came from a family with a strong genetic propensity for mental illness. When her daughter Misa was diagnosed with schizophrenia, she thought, "It's my turn." Shoko Inose was extremely shocked when her only son became ill, but at the same time was reminded of what had happened to her youngest brother during his high school years.

Shoko was already married then and was living away. But she learned from her mother years later that he had some "mental problem" and was hospitalized. She also heard that one of her mother's brothers, once a child prodigy in town, had "a nervous breakdown" in his middle-age years and never recovered.

> When I heard about this uncle, and thought about my son, I intuitively sensed that there must be something genetic. My mother was very strict and demanded a lot from the children with regard to education, especially from boys like my brother. I thought I would never become like my mother, but….

Some are not as candid about their family heredity. However, despite their reluctance to face the hereditary issue, they cannot help but allude to the possibility. Kôichi Takagi, a father, says,

> You know, there is a theory that the mental illness is inherited. People with this tendency die young. You also notice few have healthy parents still living. Many of their parents have died young or at least one of them has died young. I think the mentally ill people are likely to lose one of their parents early. My wife died at fifty. It was heart disease. But she was also neurotic. I was surprised at my son's diagnosis, but then when I thought about my wife, I wondered if my son might have inherited her disposition.

When her younger brother was finally diagnosed with schizophrenia after years of bizarre behaviors at home, Yoshimi Naitô wanted to think it would be just a temporary condition. On the other hand, looking back on her family and relatives, she could not shed the thought that her family did have some propensity for "mental instability." Her maternal grandfather left his family and ran away with a geisha, leaving her mother with a miserable childhood. Her paternal grandfather committed suicide when her father was two years old. Her younger sister, who went to Manchuria before World War II to work for one year, had a manic tendency that lasted for the next ten years. Later this sister married a successful businessman and had an affluent life for about 20 years. But the failure of the family business and her son's divorce made her "neurotic" again. She is still emotionally very unstable, according to Yoshimi. Another younger sister had a tendency to be "hysterical" when she was young and received electroconvulsive treatment. When Yoshimi looks back on her own life, she remembers almost "losing her senses" when her marriage match failed due to her parents' opposition. She says, "I had to think, oh, my family has something." Honestly, I cannot say this kind of thing to others, though for all of them, the conditions had been temporary and mostly disappeared.

Spiritual Cause

Some Japanese family members occasionally touched on the Japanese cultural belief that their ancestral spirits or some karmic connection was a factor in causing the mental illness, but they mainly raised it as simply one of the possibilities. However, no one was more confident and as self-assured as Miyoko Tajima about the explanation for her son Kenji's condition, which started with severe violence at home. She became a devout member of one of the biggest new religious organizations in Japan and became convinced that the cause of his illness could be explained by this organization's teaching derived from a sect of Buddhism. There are a number of "new" religious organizations in Japan based on Buddhism or Shintoism. Some of them are controversial because their doctrines lack authenticity or their political or money-making pursuits are obvious. These new organizations are quite separate from traditional Buddhist temples and Shinto shrines. However, Miyoko decidedly and passionately talks about the cause-and-effect principle of the universe and asserts that all the unhappiness we suffer from now originated in the ancestors' wrongdoings and mistakes. To start with, she describes the strange feeling when Kenji was born.

> I could not feel love for him since he was a baby. He felt to me like someone who didn't belong to my family. When my second son was born, I loved him and cared about him so much. I realized there was a big difference. When it came to Kenji, I felt slightly detached. I couldn't explain why. This was a strange feeling.

Miyoko claims that on her parents' side, ancestors had belonged to different sects of Buddhism for many generations, which, according to her religious doctrine, were heretical schools "against the principle of the universe." This "incorrect" faith had an impact on the descendants, particularly on the first son of the family of the third or fourth generations after the heresy, and he would have to pay the price for the ancestors' grave mistakes. That's why Kenji turned out this way, according to Miyoko. He is the victim of their ancestors' mistakes.

> It comes from his past life. You know, life is eternal. The life which was floating in the universe after death chooses the womb to come

back to. It is not an accident that Kenji chose me. I used to lament why I had such a child. It's true that I had a kind of strange feeling when he was born, but I did my best to bring him up with love in this life. Why do I have to be beaten up by my own child? If I was not lucky, I could have been dead by now! But there is a reason, you know? Otherwise it is not "scientific," or doesn't make sense, does it? The reason is not found in this life but in the past life.... Something must have happened in our past life. We must have been enemies.

Other Reasons

Other possible reasons indicated by family members included the influence of cult religion. Ruth Singer learned that the possible trigger for the illness for some people who are prone to having a chemical imbalance may be environmental factors that disturb this balance. In the case of her son, Paul, who became manic-depressive, she firmly believes it was triggered by his involvement with a cult group. Maria Hafer suspects that using Phisohex soap had an impact. Her nurse had told her to use it, and it was later found to cause some nerve damage. And she still wonders: "I think I may have had the flu when he was in the uterus. You know, you question. It's not a question of self-blaming, it's a question of what happened."

Helen Hawkins also points out one traumatic experience her daughter Dorothy had when she was 13 and attending parochial school. The incident, she suspects, might have had something to do with her later illness. "I thought maybe this triggered it." Helen says. At school, one nun was unreasonably critical of Dorothy, saying that she would be a tramp, as she was popular and often around boys. The criticism and embarrassment she was exposed to in front of the class were too much for Dorothy and since then she became slightly withdrawn from her friends.

When his wife Rieko became ill and started exhibiting strange behaviors, Takashi Ishizawa looked back on their 40 years of marriage. She had always supported him as the wife of an elite and successful businessman who worked for a famous trading firm in Japan. In retrospect, he regrets that Rieko was under the heavy pressure of living abroad for many years. When her father died, they were living in India, and it was difficult in those days to return to Japan immediately. So she could not see her father on his deathbed. When Takashi had to go to Pakistan later, she stayed with their children in Japan, taking full responsibility for them even when they were seriously ill. The concern about Takashi's safety always worried her because the political situations in India and Pakistan were very dangerous at that time. She also took care of her mother when she became old and bedridden. Rieko was like a nurse to everyone. All these years of stress finally took a toll on her, Takashi thought.

Melanie Wood continues to pose the ultimate question about the ever mysterious and unpredictable onset of the mental illness. "Why did Joshua [younger brother] get sick and I didn't?"

> And yeah, of course there's now this big controversy since they've developed all this technology — I mean is it purely a biochemical disease or ... how much does environment play in it, you know. You have the purists on both sides and then you have the people who integrate it and say well, there's probably a genetic marker, yeah, but it takes stress or trauma or something.

Few are absolutely confident about the causal attribution process of their family member's mental illness. Most of them waver between different explanations and consciously or subconsciously seek and cling to the "cause" that may make the explanation easier to accept and offer them some hope. Needless to say, there is no answer. But through this mental struggle or parallel with this course of painful inquiry, many eventually reach the point where they gain an accurate understanding and accept the nature of mental illness. As Marianne Schmitt says,

> Well, I think since so many years have passed, and I've gone through so many different phases of thinking, I don't try to analyze it so much anymore. I try to accept her for who she is. I just try to love her and be a sister to her, because I know, she tells me, she loves my visits and she's the happiest when I go to see her. So I'm happy about that. At least that we ... I don't expect anything of her. I just accept the visit for what it is....[This state of mind] hasn't come easily. It's been a progressive, it's evolved because I still have in the back of my mind, did my father cause this? Or is it a genetic thing, or is it both? Maybe it had more of an impact on her. But you know I don't blame my father and he couldn't help it. I think I've come to a point where I don't analyze so much anymore, and I don't have to have answers as to why. I'm just accepting it for what it is. And just... just take her for who she is.

Notes

1. M. I. Herz and S. R. Marder, *Schizophrenia: Comprehensive Treatment and Management* (Philadelphia: Lippincott Williams & Wilkins, 2002), 255–68.
2. E. F. Torrey, *Surviving Schizophrenia* (New York: Quill, 2002), 106.
3. Ibid., 158–71.
4. Herz and Marder, *Schizuphrenia*, 3–20.

5. Ibid.
6. Torrey, *Surviving Schizophrenia*, 158–71.
7. W. R. McFarlane, *Multifamily Groups in the Treatment of Severe Psychiatric Disorders* (New York: Guilford, 2002).
8. K. T. Mueser and S. R. McGurk, "Schizophrenia," *Lancet* 363 (2004): 263–72.
9. Herz and Marder, *Schizophrenia.*
10. McFarlane, *Multifamily Groups*, 3–17.
11. Mueser and McGurk, "Schizophrenia."
12. Herz and Marder, *Schizophrenia*, 3–20.
13. McFarlane, *Multifamily Groups*, 3–17.
14. Herz and Marder, *Schizophrenia*, 3–20.
15. T. Szasz, *Ideology and Insanity* (Garden City NY: Anchor Books, 1970).
16. Torrey, 158–71; at 170.
17. M. P. Nichols, and R. C. Schwartz, *Family Therapy: Concepts and Methods*, 5th ed. (Boston: Allyn & Bacon, 2001), 27.
18. K. G. Terkelson, "A Historical Perspective on Family-Provider Relationships" in *Families as Allies in Treatment of the Mentally Ill: New Directions for Mental Health Professionals*, ed. H. P. Lefley and D. L. Johnson (Washington, D.C.: American Psychiatric Association, 1990), 9–21.
19. D. L. Johnson, "The Family's Experience of Living With Mental Illness" in Hefley and Johnson, 53.
20. Terkelson, "A Historical Perspective," 3–21; at 6.
21. Ibid.
22. Hatfield and Lefley, *Surviving Mental Illness*, 80–81.
23. L. Kuipers, J. Leff, and D. Lam, *Family Work for Schizophrenia: A Practical Guide* (London: Gaskell, 1992), 1.
24. J. Leff, J. and C. Vaughn, *Expressed Emotion in Families: Its Significance for Mental Illness* (New York: Guilford, 1985).
25. Kuipers et al., *Family Work for Schizophrenia*, 1.
26. R. H. Lamb, "Commentary to Chapter 1," in *Families as Allies in Treatment of the Mentally Ill: New Directions for Mental Health Professionals*, ed. H. P. Lefley and D. L. Johnson. (Washington, D.C.: American Psychiatric Association, 1990), 23–29.
27. Torrey, *Surviving Schizophrenia*, 340.
28. K. G. Terkelsen, "Schizophrenia and the Family: II. Adverse Effects of Family Therapy," *Family Process* 22 (1983): 191–200.
29. A. B. Hatfield, "Commentary. Therapists and Families: Worlds Apart" *Hospital & Community Psychiatry* 33, no. 7 (1982): 513.

CHAPTER 7

A Better Understanding of Chronic Mental Illness: Accepting Reality

Understanding the Chronic Nature of Mental Illness

One of the most difficult realizations about severe mental illness is its chronic nature. The illness stays with the person for a very long time, often throughout his or her lifetime. Being a psychotherapist, Anna Berger thought in the beginning that she could help her son Stan get better. So she would try all the things she had learned during her training as a clinician: she tried to be very validating for him, told him she understood how he felt, tried to be very supportive and loving toward him. However, as the years went on, she realized that this approach was not helping him. She began to learn that she was unable to make him get better. The fact she had to face was that her son has a lifelong illness.

> Well, I guess I came to know that I could not make my son well. I could care for him and try to give him what was appropriate for whatever stage of his illness he was in. And that I had to know that I had a son with a disability. I had a disabled son. And that I had to stop thinking that he was going to get well. But I never gave up hope. And I have consistently been in touch with him. I visit him wherever he is — at least … depending on whether he wants me to come or not. I have always respected his wishes. You know, I see as time goes on, more and more, even this last place that he's been

in now for the last nine months. I thought that they had a very good program and that this was a very good opportunity for him to try to move ahead. But it hasn't worked. It's too much pressure on him and he cannot do it…. I was just noticing the other day that I have said, "Well, I don't think that he's ever going to be able to work or be very functional." He lived in a board-and-care for seven years, right before he went to the hospital last July. And it was very open. He could come and go as he pleased. And he did that. He would take long walks and he would do some of his photography. And, he would be hopeful at times, but as soon as he starts to get better, it scares him because it's been so many years that he's been out of functioning. And he regresses. And that has happened over and over and over. He gets hopeful and talks about possibly going back to school or doing things, you know. And it just scares him; I guess that's what it seems like. And he regresses, so it looks like that is going to be the pattern.

Marianne Schmitt used to get depressed every time she visited her sister. But she doesn't any more.

I've come to terms. I have. I have because of the hopelessness of the situation. I think for many years I had the hope that any day, either they'll get a medication or she'll be rehabilitated enough and so as the years go by and you don't see progress, you have to begin to let go of that and just say, okay, this is who she is. I need to accept her for who she is and not expect so much because when I went in with so much expectation and she let me down, I'd be mad and angry at the situation and at her. And then I'd go in that whole thing of questioning and guilt and all that.

Many Japanese parents who were interviewed also admit that they never thought at first that the illness and hospitalization would last so long. It takes them several years, or in some cases more than ten years of relapses and repeated hospitalizations, to face the fact that their children have an incredibly persistent chronic illness. By attending the meetings of family support groups, they seriously try to study and understand the illness, but also get to know other family members who have dealt with the illness for a much longer period of time. This is shocking to some parents who want to believe that their children's problem will eventually disappear. However, not being able to see substantial improvement in their own child's condition, they realize there is no way but to face the brutal reality that there is little hope for a "cure." Tôru Yamaguchi describes that feeling.

When I joined the family support group and learned from other parents that they had been in the group for ten or fifteen years and their children had been sick all this time, I wondered to myself, "Is my daughter going to be like this?" [pause] Well, as expected, it turned out that way.

Satoko Katagiri whose son was only 15 when diagnosed as having schizophrenia, says,

In the beginning, I just believed that he would recover by twenty-five years or so. But now I feel I got bogged down and ended up being stuck. The illness wouldn't go away. I gradually began to realize that this is an incurable disease.

It was after the sixth hospitalization, that Kôichi Takagi finally realized that his son would have to cope with his illness for the rest of his life. He attended the educational classes for the patients' family members and learned about the importance of the patient staying on medication. He was also awakened to the reality of mental illness by the psychiatrist's explanation that being medicated was almost like being fettered and dragging along with heavy chains.

Well, I understand something for the first time. [pause] I used to think one gets out of the hospital because one has recovered. My son had been in and out of hospital so many times, but I still thought this way. But I realized that he left the hospital with a "disability." A disability called a mental disorder. Many parents of patients don't quite understand this point. It may be their fault. But they are seldom given the honest truth. People say, "Congratulations on getting out of the hospital!" But you know, there is nothing to be congratulated on. Your child just left the hospital with a disability. The child is already a disabled person. Parents have to accept their child back home as disabled. But many are not aware of this. I used to be just happy seeing him graduate from college and get a job. But I simply didn't know, either.

Understanding Limitations and Lowering Expectations

If the illness is deemed incurable, family members learn to adjust their expectations for the patients, which brings them down to a realistic level. "Being a parent, I had to learn to just be grateful for whatever little bit she does," says Barbara Weiss. Her daughter Jessica's mental illness was entangled with their mother–daughter relationship. But Jessica has now managed to make a life for herself at the board-and-care facility. Barbara wishes that Jessica would participate in the rehabilitation program, go to the dentist, and stay more rigorously on medication. But she also tells herself,

> You know, you get to the point where you get down to baby steps with these people that have mental illness. First, you expect greater things. But, you get to the point when they just do some simple thing, like look neat, comb their hair, take their medicine, then you're just elated over the whole thing. I mean they're doing fine because they're doing that simple thing where that was never even considered…. But expecting more, being a parent, I had to learn to just be grateful for whatever little bit she does.

Reiko Matsuoka used to have high expectations for his son as the off-spring of a highly educated family. Many relatives were graduates of prestigious universities. She now feels she doesn't need to compare him with others.

> He will do what he can do, and that's OK. It will be good if he has his own life. So as a parent, it's OK if I do my best for him. I don't want to compare him with others anymore. That's my feeling nowadays. I cannot worry about what will happen after I die. I hope he will be able to manage one way or another….

For a long time, Tetsuro Isono thought that his son's illness could be cured eventually, and as a father he would do anything for that to happen. However, having now studied the subject in depth, he has changed his view. Although currently his son's condition is stabilized, about three years ago he began to simply hope that the illness would be better "controlled" rather than being "cured."

> You know, it's like diabetes. A disease like that is a lifelong disease. It's important to live with the disease, appeasing it so that it will not get out of hand. So I began to hope that it would be OK if only he could deal with his illness like that.

After several decades of witnessing how her brother lived, Jodi Kramer has developed an interesting perspective on aging and his schizophrenia. She thinks old age will bring him an easier and less stigmatized status in society.

'Cause he's now going to be sixty-five. He's now going to be considered a senior citizen and just go into an old folk's home, I guess. Given his medication and fed breakfast, lunch, and dinner. They might even go into an old folk's home together.... Well, he's not going to go get a job and support himself and so far as being in a home, he's going to be too old for that. [But] he's going to fit into society better as an old person. He'll be a mentally ill person I feel who will sort of fit into being senile, being in an old folk's home, because a lot of people are sort of strange when they get old and feeble and so it won't be ... I mean I see he's going to have an easier .... He'll just be fitting into being old. And this was explained to me by someone in AMI and I didn't figure this out myself. Up until a year ago, I was still really frustrated about it. What my brother was going to do, and I was obsessing about it.

Separating the Illness from the Person and Developing Sympathy

One of the most essential and difficult struggles in dealing with a loved one's mental illness is that both their personality and behavior are invaded and plagued by the illness. The line between personhood and the disease is seldom clear. It is most frustrating and frightening to see a once very articulate person turning into a disoriented stranger. Many family members take it so personally that the confusion and pain are unbearable. However, separating the illness and the person seems to lead to the ultimate acceptance of the mental illness. Although they cannot stop being puzzled by the question, "Is this the illness or is he or she doing it deliberately?" or "How much is caused by the illness and how much is due to the individual's character?," they begin to see that this is the person they love but with a certain dysfunction, a chemical imbalance in the brain. They also develop true sympathy for the condition and an understanding of how the patient really feels.

Shin Okabe admits that when he was younger it was really difficult to accept his sister's schizophrenia as a disease. He was able to intellectually understand what her doctor said, but he didn't have a gut-level understanding for a number of years. But this is the key to a true understanding of the illness, he believes. "As she was repeatedly hospitalized over many years," he says, "I began to think this must be the same as other 'real' diseases. It's like when I had a stroke. It only happened to a different part of the body in her case. When I began to understand her illness, I felt much better. You can't keep worrying about hiding it."

Robert Kirk thinks he has accepted the nature of illness most of the time.

> There were times when I was in denial. [But] I've pretty much accepted it. When the logical part was in charge, then I would accept it. If I got emotional about it and I didn't want it to be that way, then I would deny it. Or, if I was mad at him, I would say, "Oh, he's just trying to manipulate me." Then maybe I would deny it. But overall, I've accepted the fact that there's something basically wrong. And, it's taken me a long time to really say, "Well, you know, maybe there is something to this chemical imbalance." You know, you say, "That's nonsense. That's the story they're giving you." And I kind of used to think that, but I don't think that anymore. I'm convinced that what Ben is suffering from is a biologically based brain disease.

Barbara Weiss admits she used to be extremely embarrassed about her daughter's condition, but now has a completely different view.

> Well, I'm not embarrassed about it anymore. I talk to anybody about it. And, she actually never did hide it. She always said, "I have a chemical imbalance." She always was right up-front.... Right, something about mental illness is like cancer. Because, you know, actually they're not crazy. It's just that their wires are not always functioning and connecting up there.

After years of guilt, confusion, and frustration, Ruth Singer has finally reached an understanding of the true nature of her son's mental illness.

> Because of the brain, because people would think, oh, they're crazy. They weren't crazy, you know. Something is wrong with him. And this reflected on me.... And I talked to him [one psychiatrist] about my son and he was one of the psychiatrists from the old school who believed that the mother was at fault. And that stayed with me a long time, until I found out maybe two years ago. No, not the mother, not the mother. Chemical imbalance.

This realization of what really happens to the inner world of the patient seems to lead many family members to ultimately understand and sympathize with the patient as a human being. Their preoccupation and frustration with the patient's inability to behave normally is shifted to the new perspective that the patient is someone who suffers from a particular symptom.

Rosanna Olmos met her twin sons' psychiatrist, who was able to clearly describe what it was really like to have schizophrenia. This man had a real knack for explaining things, according to Rosanna. It was truly an eye-opening experience for her and made her realize that the illness was not the sons' fault.

> And it [the illness] wasn't their fault. And it was just there. That softened me up a little bit and I took my husband to those same classes because I wanted him to get all straightened out. As a result, we both learned a lot. And then we were able to learn management techniques where we could deal with it better.

Helen Hawkins can empathize with her daughter's symptom of hearing voices. She thinks those voices are the real culprit for her condition. She couldn't understand why her daughter suddenly gets disturbed, but now she can put herself in her daughter's shoes.

> I don't hear them, but after a while I got to thinking, how could she concentrate if she's hearing voices in her head and you're talking and she's gotta get this conversation ... you could tell she wasn't focusing on the conversation because the voices were interrupting her.

Every time her husband became forgetful, Yoko Tomita would worry, thinking his illness had grown worse. But she has learned that the side effects of the medication can send out confusing signals that may be similar to the symptoms. She reminds herself of this and sometimes even wonders if his problem is caused by the side effects or the disease itself. In her eyes, her husband is basically the same person she married but with a mental disability, and occasionally, the influence of the medicine. And she tries to treat him as such.

> What I strongly feel these days is how important it is to respect his will. Even when he is in bad condition, not getting upset and asking what he wants is important. If I calmly wait for him and accept him.... even when he's in bad condition, he himself knows that he has a problem. I can tell he is trying so hard to regain some composure. He is trying so hard. If I say something critical to him when he is trying, it makes matters worse. So it's best to wait. When he feels better, I accept him as he is. That's best, I realized.

Facing the Reality of Social Stigma

The various new perspectives the patients' relatives eventually gain after much struggling, and the process by which they change their ways of thinking about the illness, are telling examples of the malleable human capacity to take in new information, interpret it, adjust to it, and regain a sense of control. However, the more family members deepen their understanding of mental illness through experience and education, the wider the gap they feel between their perception of the illness and the rest of society. No matter how the families learn about mental illness the existence of a social stigma is an undeniable reality. It is the factor that probably most complicates the experience. It has been this acute perception of social stigma that has aggravated their agony over the illness and isolated them from ordinary support systems that tend to shun them. After all, these families themselves were once prejudiced toward mentally ill patients and saw them in stereotypical terms. As McFarlane writes, "Self-imposed stigma and labeling change family identity and contribute to lowered self-efficacy and increased burden."[1]

Although the people I have interviewed are not mentally ill, the mere fact that they have a relative who is a mental patient stigmatizes them. Erving Goffman, in his book *Stigma*,[2] describes how social stigma is perceived and handled by various stigmatized individuals. Goffman writes that stigma can spread "from the stigmatized individual to his close connections," although the problems associated with stigma-causing attributes diminish in their intensity. Thus, because of the spillover stigma, and the family members' not-so-clearly defined position as a kind of interface between the stigmatized group and "normal" people, the latter are reluctant to have a relationship with a person who is stigmatized merely as a result of having a close relationship with a highly stigmatized individual. Robert Kirk, a father, thinks the source of stigma is "the infected feeling" people have toward mental illness. He says, "If this guy's mentally ill and he's my brother [they think] he's going to infect my children." What he means is that people irrationally fear acquiring some kind of undefined bad influence from associating with the mentally ill. It's the same feeling, he says, that parents have in not wanting their children to see people who are grossly overweight or unable to communicate in conventional terms.

This is the false conception that makes the lives of families of the mentally ill even more difficult. However, as has been reported in earlier chapters, these "second-hand" stigmatized individuals feel "they must suffer many of the standard deprivations" of the stigmatized group and are in fact "ready to carry a burden that is not really theirs."[3]

Almost all family members interviewed in the United States and Japan at once admitted they felt a social stigma toward mental illness. Some of the painful responses right after the psychiatric diagnosis only proved their acute awareness of stigma in society. Even after surviving the initial shock of diagnosis, and even though many in fact acknowledge that the social stigma has gradually decreased in recent years, its persistent presence is still felt and experienced. Some feel it intensely and as a painful experience, and others feel it less acutely and more or less learn to detach themselves from the shame and pain. However, many families both in the United States and Japan blame the mass media's descriptions of mental illness as inaccurate and distorted. Wallace Green, a father, resents the fact that even the most prestigious newspapers' reporters have little knowledge about mental illness. Marianne Schmidt thinks that it is because we form opinions early without having a lot of information, and it becomes a fixed notion until we have an opportunity to observe reality. When she started working at a retirement home, she had a stereotypical view of senior citizens as inactive and having no purpose in life, which turned out to be completely false.

As Goffman notes, the stigmatized tend to feel uncertain about how other nonstigmatized people will receive them. Therefore, when the families of the mentally ill interact with people who do not face the same circumstances, they feel they are "on," becoming "self-conscious and calculating about the impression" they make.[4] This mindset naturally makes them compartmentalize their social interactions into two categories: a group of people with whom they can talk about their mentally ill family member and the other group of people from whom they try to hide that fact. Goffman describes the stigmatized individual as "co-opting for his masquerade just those individuals who would ordinarily constitute the greatest danger." On the other hand, to the people who already know the secret of the stigmatized person, he may be willing to talk about what is currently going on with the patient.[5]

The family members interviewed both in the United States and Japan have a clear standard as to who they would and would not tell. Everyone seems to have told people who are within their close circle, such as family members and intimate friends, or sometimes neighbors. There have been cases, such as Osamu Kinoshita or Miyoko Tajima, whose sons had often caused problems with neighbors during their psychotic breakdowns (as well as screaming or violence at home). Osamu recalls that there was no choice but to tell neighbors, because he had to apologize to them after the first incident, and so he explained his son's illness to them. In the newly acquired relationships beyond this primary circle, many parents and siblings say, they do not necessarily volunteer the information, but when asked, they will not try to hide it or make up a story, either. I believe that the fact that these people were willing to participate in my interview makes the sample a group of more open-minded individuals than others. However, they, too, are selective in disclosing information about the mentally ill family member.

Frank Brown finds it quite awkward to share information about his mentally ill son with those who have no experience in mental illness. They would try to give him advice, saying Frank could do this and that as if they could solve the problem. Frank knows better than anyone that it is not that easy. He now thinks that if he brings up this topic with friends, the conversation goes in a direction that is least constructive for him. He has decided to talk about his son only in support group meetings.

Maria Hafer has noticed that there are some people who are very uncomfortable about the subject. These people used to insinuate that she did something wrong to cause her son to become mentally ill. They do not ask her any more, but she avoids talking about her son with them. Miyoko Tajima thinks that stigma can spill over particularly to the parents of the patient. She indirectly heard someone talking behind her back, saying that because her son was ill, she, the mother, must have some problems, too. Even though all her friends know about her son Nick, Pat Bryant avoids talking about him and changes the subject, focusing on her well children. Shoko Inose says she doesn't hide her son's condition from anyone. "I am very open about it," she says. All her friends and colleagues at work know. But in fact, she has never told them that her son has schizophrenia. She has told her son has *shinkei suijaku,* or "nervous breakdown," the term vaguely used by nonprofessionals for all mental problems in Japan. When she had to submit the doctor's diagnosis to her son's employer, she asked the doctor to put down the less stigmatizing label. "I express it as 'neurosis.' 'Schizophrenia' is too much. It cannot be accepted in Japan, yet. So...."

Two kinds of situations remind family members of the persistent stigma regarding mental illness: There is the overt reaction of looking strangely at the mentally ill family member, as though scared, avoiding them, and excluding them from social occasions such as weddings or other family gatherings. The other situation, which is more complex, is in the family members' own reactions to the illness, based on the views internalized over a long period of time. Among Japanese family members of the mentally ill, a particularly strong sense of stigma that originates from within themselves is perceived. Some Japanese family members interviewed even say that the people with strongest prejudice toward mental illness are the parents themselves and, without changing them first, it is difficult to do anything about the social stigma in the greater society. When his wife became ill, Takashi Ishizawa analyzed his reaction and realized for the first time his own deep sense of prejudice against mental illness.

However, as described in the earlier chapters, one of the typical responses by Japanese parents to the development of mental illness in a child was to worry about the future marriages for their other children. Some make painstaking efforts to hide the illness so that it will not jeopardize the possibility of a good match. It is true that in Japan having a mentally ill member in the family is taken very seriously in the course of decisions regarding marriage. Most young Japanese men and women today follow a Western style of courtship before deciding to marry or not, and it is based on their free choice. However, there still is a possibility that the parents may intervene and influence this process if the family background of the future son- or daughter-in-law (socioeconomic and genealogical) is deemed inappropriate. It is not uncommon for parents to hire a special investigator to make sure that their future in-laws do not have serious problems that they would otherwise not be aware of before marriage. Thus, Japanese parents feel they must censor information about a mentally ill child.

Tôru Yamaguchi, a father, seems victimized by his own internalized sense of prejudice. But it was not until he faced the utter refusal by his own brother to discuss the matter, after Tôru's daughter Yuri became ill, that Tôru realized the depth of social prejudice. If he could not even discuss it with his brother living in the same neighborhood, he thought, he had to hide it no matter what. That's why he didn't talk to anyone but his wife. He was convinced then that if anyone knew about his older daughter's illness, his younger daughter would never be able to marry. He is relieved to see her married and living a life in a city far from Tokyo. He wishes she could live closer, but in order to keep the elder daughter's illness an absolute secret from his son-in-law, he thinks it was good she moved away. He believes any illness related to the brain is regarded as "insanity" in Japanese society. It is seen as the lowest kind of disease, he says. No matter how members of support groups campaign against social prejudice, it will not go away easily.

Yoshiko Takeda, a mother, is more positive about the future of mentally ill patients and she herself is actively involved in support groups. But when it comes to her son's future, she feels she should do anything to make sure that no one, not even her relatives, know about her mentally ill daughter. She cannot hide the fact that her daughter was once hospitalized. But she never told them that she had schizophrenia. "You never know when it is time for my son to marry, who will investigate and find about it." Therefore, she says that her daughter's problem is "social phobia" or some kind of neurosis. Yoshimi Naitô also admits it is partially from her own prejudice, but she thought it necessary, as the oldest of the siblings, to protect her other healthy brothers and sisters. She did not include her younger brother in their wedding ceremonies. It was a painful decision. But Yoshimi thought it was her responsibility to make sure that her other siblings would not be embarrassed.

Junko Nomura, a sister, does not necessarily blame people with prejudice. She thinks they are not malicious in nature, but simply uneducated. And it is this lack of education that perpetuates the stereotype and prejudice about minorities and suppressed groups. Thorough education is the only way to break the vicious cycle, but it is not easy. She realized at one point that her exceptionally open attitude about her younger sister's schizophrenia was annoying other family members such as her brother and his family. Her brother, a Japanese company executive, has been devastated more than anyone else by the existence of mental illness in the family. He has refused to join support groups or confront the fact. Junko was frustrated by his obstinate denial. However, she now thinks that because social stigma exists in reality, stigmatized people also need to be protected. Like any issues of social discrimination and prejudice, people who are the victims of discrimination must be protected. "It's easy to say that we must work to change society," she says. "But I started to feel I should not make my brother suffer more than he does now. I realize that I should be careful about who I tell this to and who I don't. I will tell people who have no connection with my brother. They have to be people who, even if they know about my sister, will not hurt my brother's position." Furthermore, Junko is proud of her daughters, who are very understanding about their aunt's illness. But when Junko's second daughter, a doctor, was engaged, she and her fiancé, also a doctor, chose not to tell his parents that his future wife had a mentally ill aunt. It was the couple's decision, Junko says. These young people also thought they should not upset his parents.

These Japanese family members are torn between their new, and accurate, understanding of the mental illness, love for the patient, and conventional social mores.

Stigma and Causal Attribution in the United States and Japan

The intensity of stigma in society toward disabilities seems to be closely related to how the cause of the disability is perceived. The conception, for example, that a bad parent causes a child's schizophrenia is one of the inaccurate and misleading ideas which aggravates social stigma. The important perspective being presented by advocates today is that mental illness is like any other illness and is simply caused by a chemical imbalance in the brain. As has been described, the unscientific explanation of the cause of mental illness is often in terms of a gene or of some later acquired qualities. In the United States, it seems that defining the illness as having a genetic or other biological cause, which has little to do with one's upbringing, is regarded by family members and advocates as the way to reduce stigma. This perspective also reduces individual responsibility for the development of the disease and removes parental guilt. In the United States, whose culture strongly emphasizes self-reliance and individual autonomy, failure to be in control of one's life may be considered more shameful than in other cultures. Lefley writes that the overriding preference for an internal sense of mastery and control tend to make people reject the attribution of external causes such as "faulty genes, birth trauma, anatomic or biochemical anomalies or other discordances in human development" and "therefore must be attributed either to the afflicted persons themselves or to those who reared them."[6] No doubt spreading the explanation based on uncontrollable genes and chemical imbalance will correct the overemphasis on individual (or family member's) responsibility and self-blame. It may eventually lead to less stigma against many types of serious mental illnesses in the United States.

In Japan, the view that mental illness is a problem of chemical imbalance and is a brain disorder like a disorder of any other part of the body seems equally helpful in leading to a better understanding of the nature of mental illness. It will also help ease an accusatory view of the patient, whose problem's have been perceived as being due to a "weak" or "lazy" personality. However, it is doubtful that a strong genetic component in the explanation of mental illness will eventually solve issues stemming from the general population's stigmatizing of mental illness. In fact, it is this definition that seems to be at the core of social stigma toward mental illness in Japan. A genetic-based definition can justify the traditional view that "it runs in the family," and the negative effect can be easily extended to encompass the entire family. This results in their hypersensitivity to disclosing information about the ill family member. In a country like Japan, where the individual is not always seen as an independent agent capable of determining his or her own life, family background and its influence are sometimes taken seriously in evaluating a person. This is, of course, not expressed in conspicuous ways, but when it comes to a very personal matter such as matchmaking, negative elements, such as any family member's criminal record, debt, an extremely dissipated lifestyle, suicide, or mental illness, are seriously weighed before reaching a decision. The individual also finds it harder to separate him- or herself from the family of origin, particularly parents and siblings, when making a major life decision. A collective sense of self is much weaker in Japan when compared with other Asian and East Asian cultures. But in the United States, the contrast was clear. The intergenerational "blood" link is still considered very important in Japan. Therefore, it seems that attributing mental illness strictly to genetic makeup can leave families less able to avoid social stigma.

The model of explanation heard only from Japanese family members was the spiritual one. It is interesting, though, to be reminded that during colonial times in America, insanity was viewed as an act of God, which was inaccessible to human intervention.[7] A mother mentioned earlier, Miyoko Tajima, was exceptional in having a sense that her strong religious conviction gave her unshakable confidence in seeing her son's illness strictly in the light of her past life and principles of cause and effect. Although she was different from most Japanese parents interviewed, Japanese people in general have little resistance to accepting the view that there are many events beyond human control. The origin of this attitude lies mainly in Buddhism. Though most Japanese do not consider themselves religious, a Buddhist outlook on life is found everywhere in Japanese life. The idea that things are decided by fate, *in-nen*, or karmic causations, and therefore one has to *akirameru* (accept and resign oneself to the situation), is deeply built into the Japanese psyche even today. Even in coping with daily stress, the Japanese have been reported to attribute their successful coping to good luck and to see stress as caused by bad luck more often than do Euro-Americans.[8] However, the Japanese propensity for this traditional, fatalistic attitude may have impeded family members from taking collective action to bring a change in society's attitudes. Attributing the event to spiritual causes may be the ultimate way of eliminating individual responsibility. But it also makes it difficult to correct inaccurate views of mental illness that have existed for generations. For the Japanese, it takes a very tricky balancing act to medically understand the illness and still fight social stigma.

Nevertheless, so much is still unknown about the cause of mental illness. Even if there is a clear genetic base, how it surfaces as an illness is extremely complex. For the families of the mentally ill both in the United States and Japan, there is no question that education is the key to combating prejudice, stereotypes, and social stigma. As Gordon Collins, a husband, says,

> Very few people understand mental illness. They all think of it as something you should be able to snap out of, you know. It's mental — you should be able to deal with it on your own and fix it, you know. It's not physical. So they don't understand: if it's not physical, how come we can't deal with it? How come we can't cure it? It's a lot of education that's needed. That's absolutely necessary. A lot of education is needed for the mentally ill to be treated properly in this country.

Notes

1. E. P. Lukens, and W. MarFarlane, "Families, Social Networks, and Schizophrenia," in *Multi-family Groups in the Treatment of Severe Psychiatric Disorders*, ed. W. McFarlane (New York: Guilford, 2002), 18–35.

2. E. Goffman, *STIGMA: Notes on the Management of Spoiled Identity* (New York: Simon & Schuster, 1963).

3. Ibid., 31.

4. Ibid., 14.

5. Ibid., 95, 100.

6. H. P. Lefley, "Culture and Mental Illness: The Family Role," in *Families of the Mentally Ill: Coping and Adaptation*, ed. A. B. Hatfield and H. P. Lefley (New York: Guilford, 1987), 30–59.

7. K. G. Terkelson, "A Historical Perspective on Family-Provider Relationships," in *Families as Allies in Treatment of the Mentally Ill: New Directions for Mental Health Professionals*, ed. H. P. Lefley and D. L. Johnson (Washington, D.C.: American Psychiatric Association, 1990), 5.

8. Y. Kawanishi, "The Effects of Culture On Beliefs About Stress and Coping: Causal Attribution of Anglo-American and Japanese Persons," *Journal of Contemporary Psychotherapy* 25, no. 1 (1995): 46–49.

PART V

Living with Mental Illness:
Sources of Strength

CHAPTER 8

Becoming Active Agents: Doing Something

I think [being a sibling of a mentally ill person] challenged me. In that, I don't know if it's because of my upbringing, I've had instincts to run away from problems. And my sister has forced me to face something. It has forced me, because you can't run away from that. She's there. The problem is always there. So it's brought discipline in my life and responsibility. This is something I cannot run away from, as much as I want to sometimes. But she's my sister and I do really love her so much and I feel sorry for her and I guess it's kind of made me grow up. It's developed my character you know.... As in anything. Life can tear you down or you can turn it around. It's our reaction to it. It's our reaction. — An American sibling.

Whatever tragedy hits our home, we often must go on maintaining our basic daily routines. Our social roles and responsibilities must be fulfilled and cannot be discontinued. Even in the face of the worst disaster, we work to prevent it from destroying us completely. But how can we continue to carry such internal darkness for decades? Families of mentally ill patients interviewed have shown incredible perseverance and resilience as well as an instinct for survival. They do not remain victimized by the situation, but take the initiative in changing their situation into something that is at least tolerable. Some go far beyond the mere survival level, and, out of this disaster, create positive changes in their lives. It is in the nature of human beings to become active agents capable of observing, interpreting, evaluating, and changing a given situation, as symbolic interactionism tells us. A number of scholars have defined the concept of coping and researched its process in different situations. For example, Pearlin and Schooler define coping as "behavior that protects people from being psychologically harmed by problematic social experience, a behavior that importantly mediates the impact that societies have on their members".[1] They add that successful coping also depends on one's social resources (e.g., interpersonal networks, family, and friends) and psychological resources (personality characteristics that people draw upon to help them withstand threats, such as self-esteem and a sense of mastery as well as more specific coping responses).

What happened in emotional and cognitive terms to the families of the patients described in earlier chapters is no different from what is described in this chapter, nor do these phases take place distinctively and separately, one after another. Rather, they often occur in conjunction with each other as families make every effort to adjust to reality. But while the families more or less "reacted" to the illness in the early stage, coping orients them to more conscious, "proactive" efforts to ease their pain and distress. A variety of coping mechanisms have been indicated in the research literature: changing conditions regarding the source of distress; perceptual or cognitive manipulation of the meaning of the situation, tension management, and help-seeking behaviors, to name a few.[2–5] Likewise, family members of the mentally ill showed their resourcefulness in mobilizing and mixing various coping techniques.

The most direct way to cope with distress is to eliminate the source of the stress and resolve the problem at its root. Although it is difficult for most family members to take such a drastic action, sometimes it is the only way.

Taking Direct Action To Relieve the Source of Distress

In order to cope with the daily stress of living with his wife, who had schizophrenia, William Baker started drifting away and detaching himself from her. Although it's been nine years, what she does still makes him angry and upset, even though he has tried to tell himself, "She is sick, why are you doing this?" Since her condition has deteriorated, there has been no coherent conversation between them. When she talks, it's only she who talks and she babbles about something that he doesn't even know about. He feels that this kind of stress can easily wear him down. "I've had enough," he says.

> Oh, I'm telling you I was just so busy in trying to raise that daughter, which was extremely difficult. I just didn't have a lot of time to spend thinking about my situation. That's why now, I'm just tired. I mean, I'm tired. I just don't want to deal with it anymore.

That's why William stays out and keeps himself busy with activities outside the home as much as possible. However, it was taking a toll on him. He is planning to take the ultimate coping strategy in this case: getting a divorce. He has been thinking about it for four years and has decided to set the deadline for this action, which is their only daughter's graduation from high school. Arrangements have been made for his wife to be placed in safe accommodations where she can live on her own, and he will help her manage her money. However, it was far from an easy decision.

> Yeah, I had to deal with it. I mean, it bothered me. I mean, you think that you spend all this time with this person and then … you never thought … a divorce — yeah, you can see a divorce. Two people going in different directions. But for someone to leave you and yet you can't relate to them at all and they can't relate to you … everything is gone … all the love and trust and everything that you had with this person, you know, started dying. And you know, you just drift.

He says now "I need a peace of mind." He very frankly admitted he was looking forward to this change in his life. After all possible efforts were made to save the marriage, he has no regrets. In fact, he was hopeful for the future.

Focusing on Other Activities That They Can Control

For many family members, however, it is impossible to cut ties with the patient like this. Gordon Collins is matter-of-fact about how he lives each day with his wife, who has bipolar depression with flare-ups every two months. However, according to him, getting occupied in doing whatever he does, not thinking about the problem, staying away from it, and doing something physical as much as possible, is one way to cope with it. For example, by staying at work as long as 12 hours a day, he can avoid having to deal with it directly, he says. When he is not working, he will basically try to go out again to take refuge at neighborhood stores or keep himself busy with taking care of their baby. When his wife gets in an argumentative or accusatory mood, he just ignores it.

Many family members have turned to their own work, concentrating more on it than before so that they can forget about the illness at least during work hours or for the rewards of work, feeling that work is more controllable. Unlike the sense of helplessness about the mental illness they have to put up with at home, work has given them a sense of gratification, or at least helped them keep on going. It is a strategy of avoiding the central problem, but the other aspect of this coping is to focus on the positive aspect of their daily life activities. Although Frank Brown says there was not an hour that went by when he didn't think about his son, it was his teaching job that made it possible for him to get by each day right after the initial shock of his son's mental illness. Maria Hafer also says her job was the source of strength for her, saying, "I would go to work and the rest of the world would disappear. And I was fortunate to work with people who were very understanding and very supportive." Feeling miserable and exhausted with the never-ending demands both from his business and household work, Kôji Yamada turned to drinking in the early years. But ultimately, it was the prospect of the next day's work that gave him strength and encouragement. Working hard and seeing his daughter grow was the best coping method for him. Shin Okabe, too, was extremely busy running his business. He feels his preoccupation with making his own small company successful supported him in dealing better with his sister's illness.

As much as work becomes the central focus for attention replacement, other activities such as hobbies and exercise also help family members cope with daily stress. For example, writing a journal of her thoughts and writing poetry was a great help to Maria Hafer. William Baker thinks he has been able to keep things under control because of his rigorous running and exercising.

> That helped me a great deal. And the next thing that helps me is I run when I start thinking too much about it, maybe get depressed about it — I run. And, I exercise a lot. And, I coach track in high school and that helps me also. I can't sit down. I can't sit around. I can't sit at home too long because I can't stand to watch some of the things she does. I mean, it really kinda tears me up.

Continuing to work as a volunteer teacher of the tea ceremony has been extremely helpful to Naoyo Abe during all these years of struggle with her son's illness. She has a certificate that enables her to teach the tea ceremony, a traditional Japanese art of serving and appreciating tea. Every week she invites students to her home and offers tea ceremony lessons. When she sees her students and also occasionally organizes a large formal tea ceremony party, she feels invigorated and cheerful. This was one activity that she could concentrate on and she felt useful to others outside her home. She once seriously thought about giving it up because she felt guilty dressing up in a beautiful kimono and attending parties when her son was suffering. But she realized how important it was to continue. Now she believes that without her commitment to the tea ceremony, her life would be nothing but taking care of her husband and son.

After his wife became ill, Takashi Ishizawa reached retirement age, but continued to work for another five years, until three years ago. When he found it too hard to work and also visit the hospital frequently, he resigned his position. However, a number of activities keep him extremely social and healthy. He enjoys attending a monthly discussion group of scholars and businessmen, visiting museums, studying a Chinese fortune-telling method (like some other Japanese parents), drinking with his friends, and occasionally contributing opinion articles to business magazines. He never skips his three-mile daily walk. All these activities, he believes, help him stay healthy, which is the most important factor in successfully coping with the long battle of his wife's illness.

Haru Morimoto and her husband are the lucky couple: both love mountain hiking. Whenever they had too much stress in life, they would go up to the mountains together. They also enjoy going to Kabuki theater. But what has been most important for the reduction of their stress with regard to their son's illness has been getting away from home, doing things they both enjoy, and talking with each other at length.

Praying Ritual

Some family members in the United States find praying an important part of daily ritual and coping. Some are traditional Christians, others are members of relatively new religious faiths. Nancy Hoffman reads daily prayers in the magazine of her religious organization, follows the visualization ritual by herself, and listens to meditation tapes every evening before going to bed. Those who follow their religious activities think it is the bedrock of their coping. Some Japanese parents also mention occasionally visiting Shinto shrines, making it a habit to transcribe a Buddhist Sutra (a traditional practice by religious people to enhance their faith and to gain peace of mind), visiting places of good fortune based on "kigaku," or the Chinese philosophy of feng shui. All these activities were mentioned as something they tried at least once in the past, though there was no one who seemed to make them a daily ritual. On the other hand, those Japanese parents who professed to be members of an organized religion followed their own rituals; for example, daily chanting of Buddhist Sutras.

Seeking Help

The action that led many family members to the most successful method of coping was to seek help from others. This action seems to have had the most dramatic effect on the family members interviewed. Although many suffered from feelings of being unsupported in the beginning, they were bound to encounter someone and some group that provided them with necessary support.

For years, Kelly Seeman had struggled with her son's illness as a single mother. All she remembers is that she overcame each crisis because she just did what she had to do at that time. "I'm a survivor," she says. "I just did. I guess that's the way I get by." But without a certain personality, it would have been impossible to draw on various resources. Kelly had the intelligence and open-mindedness to take advantage of what was out there. She also seemed to have known almost instinctively how to get proper support.

> But sometimes I don't know why, but I just do. And I gravitated to an environment ... it started with AMI and then I became involved in the mental health community. And that's where I get my — and have gone in the past to get my — support.

While a substantial portion of families felt unsupported and even rejected by the system, peers, and the rest of society, many other family members also discovered places and people at a very early stage that could bring a sense of support during their difficulty. The sources of support most closely available are their own family and personal friends. Usually, it only takes one person in the family or one friend who can listen to them and understand their feelings, which is adequate in most stressful occasions.

Family and Friends   Some are lucky to be able to feel support first from their own family and a close circle of friends. Helen Hawkins remembers how close her family was and that they always stayed together as one in helping her daughter Dorothy. Miki Maeda, a Japanese mother, is a very special case. Coming from a family background where uncles, aunts, and cousins became mentally ill, Miki was also able to turn to her relatives, who were informative and understanding. There was not a sense of stigma in her the family, but only the sense of being in the same boat. Marianne Schmitt also feels blessed that she had a very close older sister she could share her feelings with about their younger sister's illness.

> And we would share our frustrations, and although we never really had any answers, at least we could talk to each other about it. And

my husband was quite supportive and helpful. So I had them to lean on.

Some can also recall having a friend who was willing to listen to them as a personal counselor or someone who was in fact in a field related to social work. They found these kind listeners' help invaluable. William Baker is still grateful to his friend who was a social worker, saying, "To this day, she's still a friend. And, she really helped me a lot to understand what is going on and some of the things I could do, who I should go to and see, things like that." Takashi Ishizawa also asked his friends and actively sought information about better hospitals and doctors, when his worry was focused on the quality of the hospital where his wife was staying.

Private Therapy Some family members sought psychotherapy for themselves. This was overwhelmingly the choice of the American family members. More than half of the American family members interviewed received individual counseling at one point in their struggle with the illness. There were only two Japanese who went into some type of counseling. But even this was not the same kind of private psychotherapy practice readily accessible in the United States. Private therapy is available in Japan, but it is not a common choice for the average person.

Therapy was a wonderful and eye-opening experience for most family members, who said it gave them a chance to open up and get things off their chests. Yoko Tomita is one of the two Japanese who received individual therapy. She went to see a counselor at her husband's hospital for only one week. Though it was a brief period, talking about her feelings to a willing listener helped calm her and gave her a chance to put her own situation in perspective. She recalls it being a very useful experience.

Glenda White has been in a therapy for many years and having a good therapist has been a major source of strength and health for her.

> It helped me in clearing things, in focusing and charting.... Or like guidance ... So I could act and do what I felt was necessary to get the help [for my daughter] and dial the numbers and not be ashamed.... And of course I'd be overwhelmed but I would always have some place to touch base with. And keep myself on track.

Being able to go through individual therapy often turns out to be a lifesaver for the siblings who grew up in the midst of family chaos and with repressed resentment for decades. However, it usually happens long after they have reached maturity. It takes some serious difficulties in other areas of their lives, such as difficulty with human relationships, to prompt them to seek therapy for the first time. Only then the unexpected, shocking realization hit them of how scarred they had been by their siblings' mental illnesses. Though painful, confronting it and releasing themselves from the long, stubborn denial of the family problem is the first step in their recovery process. They soon learn that what they had believed was a midlife crisis had another side, a deeper root, a wounded sense of self that had never been touched or healed.

Jane Wilson, sister of a patient, decided to go into therapy when she reached 40. Although she was functional in the external world, she had been feeling "dead" inside for a long time. In fact, she was very depressed to the extent that her therapist wanted to put her on antidepressants right away.

> Oh, I guess my little dog was what made me realize. He had a very bad skin disease, and instead of getting treatment, I would just sit and pick his skin. My daughters would say, mom that's so disgusting. Take him to the doctor. I had no energy to go to the doctor and I had no energy in the house. I was a wreck. I could not see anything. Now I can see brightness, I can see darkness. I can see everything. Before, it was like walking in a huge black cloud. But I functioned. I got the groceries, I went banking. I spent way too much money. But I put on the appearance of functioning. And even when my mother called, I was there.

The common problem of growing up in an extremely dysfunctional family environment is that because abnormality is the normal daily milieu, people cannot develop a healthy sense of awareness that tells them they have their own emotional needs. Jodi Kramer, a sister, who felt as though she were drowning and finally went to a psychiatrist after she was thirty, also feels it changed her life and made her strong.

Family Support Group   In the long process of seeking outside support, family members find their way to family support groups. They also attend family psychoeducation programs to learn about the illness, medications, treatment, prognosis, and ways to deal with many concerns related to the illness. Families have perceived these occasions as extremely valuable sources of coping. Although the format varies, researchers and mental health professionals also stress the efficacy of family psychoeducation programs as a critical family intervention.[6,7]

Family support groups are often affiliated with hospitals, where regular meetings are held. The National Alliance for the Mentally Ill (NAMI) is a major resource for information on mental illness and support groups. In Japan, cities and district public health centers and hospitals organize support group meetings. The way American and Japanese get in touch with support groups varies. Some family members actively sought help, but for others it was referred to them along with other information they were trying to obtain. Most of the family members interviewed were recruited through the key person in the support group network in Los Angeles and Tokyo. Many were keen supporters or enthusiastic about the function of family support groups. For many, the support group meeting was the first and only venue where they could be themselves and felt comfortable talking about their mentally ill children, siblings, and spouses.

Acceptance and Support   It is a place that provides the safe atmosphere of complete acceptance and understanding of their feelings and experiences. Wallace Green clearly says that the most helpful thing in the initial stage of coping was talking to people with similar experiences. It was effective in easing his pain over his son's diagnosis. After he found the Alliance of Families for the Mentally Ill meetings, he decided to attend a weekend seminar given for professionals. Being able to talk to psychologists was also particularly helpful. He has been attending Al-Anon meetings for those with family members who are drug or alcohol addicts, as his son's illness has been further complicated by his marijuana addiction. This group, too, has been extremely interesting and useful. Wallace feels he is getting so much out of attending the group that there isn't an evening where he doesn't walk away being touched by some little thing that he hears.

> And the beauty is, it's such a core section of life and nobody knows your last name and nobody knows what you do…. My feeling is I want to pick and choose and learn from you and that person and that person and that experience and just assimilate and integrate and pluck, you know, and distill and put it into the blender.

William Baker sees the family support group as providing valuable support.

> I was around a group of people who understood what I was talking about and could also share their experiences so that we all kind of had a bond and there was an understanding of what everyone was speaking about. Things you didn't understand — there was always someone in the group who could explain it to you. And, it was really good because I saw people come in who

couldn't deal with it — who were so emotional that they couldn't even talk about it. And, I saw, over a period of time, how they came to … to deal with the thing, you know.

Shin Okabe, a brother, thinks the greatest thing about the family support group is that one realizes one is not alone. "There are many other people in the same situation. It's like fellow sufferers sympathizing with one another." Like many Japanese parents, Kazuo Takenaka had not talked about his second daughter Shizuka's schizophrenia to anybody. He always had tried to take care of things and keep them under control all by himself. "It is my problem, so I don't need to consult with anyone," he used to think. Even he, who was the father of a patient, could not understand his daughter. "How could any stranger understand my daughter's problem?" But when Kazuo started to attend a family support group, he was surprised to see so many people with the same problem and thought to himself, "How good it is to have comrades!" It didn't take him long to find himself getting involved in the group, and now, after ten years he has become the president of a chapter in Tokyo.

"It is helpful to realize there was a place I could go and talk about my experience," was the opinion of so many family members both in the United States and Japan. In addition to learning that they are not alone, being with people who can understand them, and listening to other people's stories puts their situation in perspective. They learn to count their blessings, which also helps maintain self-esteem. Frank Brown has been attending NAMI meetings for two and a half years now.

Which was very helpful because then I could hear stories of other people and their problems and it made me realize that there's a lot, there's an awful lot of people who have the same problems and worse. I mean, many of them are worse. In some ways, that's reassuring because may be you're happy that my son isn't as bad as some of the other kids. So at least it gives you some hope that he wasn't.... So the AMI meetings were very beneficial to me, emotionally.

Yoshiko Takeda, a Japanese mother says,

The help I received from the family support group was enormous. When I joined, I was really down, though I looked fine in the eyes of other members. But I found many participants in the group were families who had been dealing with mental illness for twenty or thirty years. Then I thought to myself, I have been in this only three or four years. I cannot feel down like this! That's what I strongly felt. I also felt lucky that I had my husband. I have noticed the families of the mentally ill tend to lose a spouse or parent prematurely. They are likely to lose some member of their family. As for me, I have all my family. My husband and son are understanding and supportive of my daughter. I thought I was blessed.

Educational   The support group is very informative and educational. Ken Morris, a father, describes his encounter with psychoeducation classes and support groups as "God sent" and "The best thing that has happened to me as it relates to my son's illness."

> And, the reason I say that is because I think that probably the number one thing that a parent needs the most is education. They need to know what they're dealing with because it is so voluminous. There is so much information to know. And there is so much disinformation and there is such a huge public stigma.

The support group also provided Ruth Singer with opportunities to accurately learn about her son's illness. Various ideas and information she learned there helped her tremendously. At the hospital where her son stayed, she met a woman with a mentally ill husband who introduced her to the support group meeting for the first time.

> I went to "Share and Care" and I listened to other families. And then I started learning about the illness. Then when I was educated and understood, my entire feelings changed. That he could not help himself. That this was not my son, this was the illness doing it.… I think in my case, just understanding the illness, how it is a chemical imbalance. How medications would help. Patience. I also learned when not to yell or holler. Or disagree when they're in a certain stage.

William Baker already had a pretty good knowledge about mental illness after reading a lot and going to many lectures. Now he prefers to gain a deeper understanding and has decided to educate himself through a program called the Journey of Hope. The Journey of Hope was originally created in 1989 by the Louisiana Alliance for the Mentally Ill (LAMI) and has been sponsored by NAMI since 1995. In California the program has been active since 1996. It is a 12-week course for families of individuals with severe mental illnesses and teaches them various coping skills in specific situations as well as providing support. The courses are taught by trained AMI family member volunteers using a team teaching approach.[8] William is on the way to becoming a teacher in the program.

> I had a chance to see other people who were devastated by their problems — who hadn't gone as far as I had, you know what I mean. In their case, it was like the first time dealing with this, whereas I'd had at least a year to deal with it, and learn about it, and could share my experiences with them.

Altruism Interestingly, being involved in the family support group also brings out a new sense of altruism from some participants. As they receive emotional support and education on the illness, they experience a personal transformation from someone who was defeated and victimized by personal tragedy to someone who can provide advice and extend support to others who are still new to this problem. It is as if they are reborn with pride and a sense of new meaning in their lives. Furthermore, their consciousness of the need for social justice is stimulated and awakened. They begin to think about the larger goal of how society should treat the mentally ill, how the social system should be changed, and how their family support groups can make a difference in the greater society. MacFarlane calls it the emergence of a "mastery-based group identity."[9] He also says that it is a process in which the sense of stigma is reversed and "replaced by a kind of pride in being able, as a group, to understand and master the illness that until then has been a great burden." This may be an act of compassion for others, identification with them, mixed with other personal motives, such as getting away from one's own problem. It may be also a way to boost self-esteem by feeling appreciated. No matter where it originates, the emotional gratification is substantial. As family members become heavily involved in the group activities, some eventually become leaders or teachers for the classes. For these people, the support group becomes their raison d'être.

Helen Hawkins has been involved with a support group since her daughter Dorothy became ill. Although Dorothy's condition has stabilized and improved and the whole family doesn't feel so distressed about it anymore, she continues to attend the meetings for altruistic reasons.

> Oh, well, I've gotta be honest, I go there mostly to help others if I can, because our experience is quite a bit different than most of the stories we hear but if I can help any one of them I'm very happy to do it.... But as far as my husband, there's many times it was very depressing to him because you hear very sad stories. But on the other hand, you see somebody, give them a little advice,

and they got some good out of it ... if you helped them it makes you feel better because we've gone there since she [her daughter] had symptoms.

Shoko Inose attends a support group affiliated with her son's hospital.

I think the support group is good for letting out your worry and distress. It's also a good place to learn what kinds of problems other people are suffering from. Then I started to understand that we families should work to make a difference in society. I realized that we should not stay passive. We must take action. But in this sense, my current support group is not active enough. That's why I don't like it very much.... It is so important to send messages to the society. Older generations did nothing but hide, hide, hide, and hide. And that's what they say they did. The support group of my son's previous hospital was like that in the beginning. But after I joined, the group became vigorous and active. Now the younger members are keeping up the work.

Reiko Matsuoka is currently too busy to get involved in a support group, but she is eager to join. She was relieved and excited to find out there was a support group in the new hospital her son moved to. "As soon as I have time, I will start [to get involved] immediately! I believe my involvement in the support group will eventually lead to my son's happiness."

Shin Okabe thinks the group's activities have an educational value for the entire society.

Unless we keep this kind of organization going, the rest of the society will not even try to understand. You know the problem of this kind of disease is that it is quite elusive. Like I didn't notice my sister's illness for a long time: it is because this disease does not surface as a visible, detectable phenomenon. If there is a high fever or something, it is much easier to understand. But it's not like that. So it is difficult for the general public to see it as a disease. That's why we must send a message through our activities. Otherwise, there will be no improvement in social welfare programs.

Yoshiko Takeda has regained her energy and health ever since she became involved with the support group. She was completely down when her daughter was diagnosed with schizophrenia and hospitalized for the first time. Around the same time, Yoshiko's mother had a stroke and was hospitalized. In addition to working full-time, Yoshiko had to visit two hospitals on a regular basis, which exhausted her mentally and physically. She remembers she was always "walking with her face down in those days." After her mother passed away, she joined the support group, which unexpectedly changed her life.

> I felt invigorated immediately. I felt I had friends. It was so hard before I found the support group. I had no idea, when mental illness all of a sudden hit my daughter, about which hospital to go to. I heard many people in the group started with the local public health center at a time like this, but I didn't even know it.... I occasionally glanced through a PR newsletter from the ward office, but never took any notice of their services on mental illness. There is plenty of information about the consultation on physical handicaps, a more "decisive" disorder, you know. But never did I see information available on what to do when mental illness hits your family member. I wished they had provided such information. It would have made a big difference.... Then as I was involving myself in the support group, and as I learned to use various social resources such as a disability pension, I wanted to tell others what was useful and helpful to me. And then they started to tell me how happy they were taking my advice, which also helped them a great deal. I was so happy to know that I was helping others. I became so energetic. When I first joined, I felt my life was a living hell. I was carrying so many burdens on my shoulders. Everyone noticed how depressed I was in those days. But the family support group saved me.

Kôji Yamada says there was nothing that particularly helped him by joining the support group affiliated with the public health center in his neighborhood. But when he went to the meeting for the first time about 30 years ago, he was just surprised to see "so many old, fragile women" and wondered "how can they effectively run this group?" He was the only spouse of a mentally ill person — most of the members were parents. At that time, this support group was a part of the Tokyo metropolitan government's project on the care of the mentally ill and was one of the centers for so many family members desperately seeking help. "Is there anything I can help with?" Asking this question to himself was the beginning of his long relationship with the family support group. Today he is a president of this chapter.

Siblings and Support Groups Support groups also had an especially powerful impact on siblings. Soul searching through a one-on-one relationship with a psychotherapist in a supportive atmosphere is helpful. But the family support group gave them another kind of supportive environment, and it meant an encounter with a second "family," which they could choose to adopt.

Jane Wilson had been reluctant to go to a support group. Each time she dealt with one of her sister's crises, Jane didn't want to do anything more than that. But several years ago when she happened to be talking with someone who recommended a meeting of the local AMI, she decided to try for the first time. She still remembers the shock she had that evening, which changed her life.

> It was such an incredible experience because suddenly I was hearing the talk that I felt was right but that no one in my family was saying. [Laughter.] That was so incredible to hear people talk about medications and about acting out things openly without shame, without whispering and "don't upset anybody." It was just incredible. Just hearing about how to deal with things. I almost feel like I owe my life to this place. I feel like my healthy life, I owe to NAMI…. [What was most helpful was] the honesty and openness. The education. The information. It was from an authoritative perspective. So, when I related my own experience, people could respect it. And being able to share. Just being able to hear other people's experiences and realize that this is happening to so many people in the world….

Like Jane, Melanie Wood was in her mid-40s when she finally confronted her own emotions, which she had forced herself to suppress for several decades, relating to her brother's mental illness and her family. The support she received from the group was at once shocking and priceless, something she had never even known existed. She completely fell apart at the seams and broke down for the first time when she later listened to the lecture tapes for siblings of the mentally ill. All those years she only allowed herself to be practical and made believe that her brother's illness never affected her so much. The way she had dealt with it since adolescence was just to shut down emotionally. But she realized that it had a far more profound impact than she had imagined.

> The group leader started…. She first of all was not judgmental. She had a sense of humor. Everyone in the group had a sense of humor even though we were all kind of in the same boat, which was very, very helpful. I could talk about stuff in that group that I couldn't talk about to anyone else and they would understand.

Even when she called up the group leader between meetings, she would listen to Melanie and give her advice. She was even willing to talk to Melanie long distance. The incredible support she received from the group was truly from her own new "family of choice."

Jodi Kramer first joined Al-Anon in order to cope with her husband's drinking problem and son's drug addiction at that time. This experience of openly talking about her personal problems prepared her for the encounter with a family support group for the mentally ill. She had not previously developed any idea about or skills in talking about problems with the appropriate vocabulary to describe her feelings. Her family never allowed her to talk in that way. She says, "If I expressed a feeling, my parents would call me a bad girl. I was supposed to turn my face and not see it." This family culture taught her to shut up in the face of many things going on at home.

> [It was important to] admit that I could go and learn about mental illness and it wouldn't be painful. Before then, I had a lot of pain about other things and other issues I didn't want to face. This whole thing about mental illness in the family. I didn't like to talk about it because of the pain that I experienced when I talked about it. But I learned in Al-Anon that if you just get in there and educate yourself and get around other people that have the same problem, you learn so much and you can look at your problems differently. And there's so many different ways to handle problems that you can learn just by associating with other people.

On the other hand, there are some others who did not feel comfortable with the family support groups or were frustrated with the conventional approach. In fact, more than a few family members found the atmosphere too depressing. Naturally, it *can* be very depressing because the participants are often in the middle of a crisis — if they were not, they would not be taking part. If family members continue to feel uncomfortable, they may choose to stay away from meetings and instead find other constructive ways to turn their personal tragedies into a positive force for change.

Robert Kirk tried support group meetings for a while, but basically felt the atmosphere was too passive and not constructive. "I think some of the people at the support group meetings are really 'sad sacks,'" he says. Instead he found the Journey of Hope program much more comfortable and helpful for him. As mentioned earlier, the Journey of Hope family education program provides a structured, 12-week course for families of the mentally ill, focusing on clinical knowledge and skills needed for effective coping. The members can be trained to be volunteer facilitators and teachers. Robert Says:

> Now, I must say that it was not for an altogether altruistic reason I joined because I know "if you want to learn something, try and teach it." And I felt if I commit myself to teaching it, I'm not going to get in there unprepared and I'm going to take it and learn something. And, that's what I've been doing. And, it's paid off for me in that I know a lot more than I did and I know a lot of things I can do now.

Diane Nelson has flatly written off the support group. But that doesn't mean it is of no use for other people, she stresses. She thinks it just does not work with her personality.

> It is not something that works well with my personality and I'm afraid that I would tell people, why don't you cut out with your cheap shit and just get on with life.... I would not like a support group. First of all, I'm not somebody that can bare my heart that well, and second of all, I don't feel that I need a support group. I feel that I'm pretty strong. I recognize that support groups are very, very important for some people ... to me it would be a waste of time. Support to me is being able to get up and advocate. Support to me is the idea that maybe I can start making a bit of impact on public policy.

Faith-Based and Other Sources of Support   There are other sources that provide support. Religious organizations are another place family members can turn to for urgent help. The church Barbara Weiss attends has a 24-hour hotline with an 800 number, which Barbara has dialed many times. Being able to talk to someone anytime she wants, as long as she wishes, greatly relieves the pressure she feels.

Becoming a born-again Christian added a new dimension to Marianne Schmitt's life. The church has been a source she can go to, and it turned out to be her bedrock and foundation. She thinks "it came at a good time" as her entering into the new faith and her sister's breakdown happened about the same time.

Miyoko Tajima says that her relatives were not reliable. Her brother was trying to console her about her son's violence, but basically he was "powerless." She was even reluctant to discuss their son's problem with her husband too much, as he would come back home late every night completely exhausted. The greatest and the most powerful support came from her religious organization, which explained to her the cause of her son's illness through its karmic cosmology. This religious organization clearly has become her second family. She says, "No matter how late it was, the members came to me when I needed help."

Yoshiko Takeda also says she received solace from the counseling section of her family's religious organization. She and her family had been a member of this organization, but never did she appreciate its value so much until her daughter became ill. It helped her escape complete chaos after hearing the doctor say the word *schizophrenia*: it was a situation where she had become utterly speechless.

Although going to a private psychotherapist was a rare choice for most Japanese family members, they can recall feeling supported by people working at various types of public offices, such as the public health center. There is always a danger that these public institutions can be cold, bureaucratic, and inept places that tend to abide only by written rules. But depending on whom these family members happened to deal with, it made an enormous difference in the coping process. They never forget a Good Samaritan they have met during their difficulties.

Yoko Tomita will always remember the kindness and sympathy she received from a public health worker who was so touched by Yoko's love for her mentally ill husband. Hearing Yoko's plight, this female worker in the public health office was moved to tears. Yoko was just trying to find a pension plan for her husband. Although this health worker was not in the pension department, she went out of her way to bring Yoko's case to the people in the right department before Yoko visited the office herself.

Shoko Inose is so grateful to the people from her son's company. Big Japanese corporations usually guarantee lifetime employment for anyone who begins on the company's career track. The basic idea is that a company should be like one family and is expected to take care of employees until retirement. Nevertheless, falling ill during the first month's training period, Mamoru could easily have lost his job. However, the man from the personnel department was "unbelievably sincere," Shoko recalls. He knew that Mamoru came from a single-parent family and that he was a son with a strong sense of filial piety toward his mother. This man worked extra hard for Mamoru's case, so that he could get a long sick leave and would eventually be assigned to a simpler, stress-free work environment. Shoko Inose emphasizes she had been supported and helped by so many people including Mamoru's doctors and psychologists, hospital staff, and social workers. She was not at all shy about seeking help from all these places. "It was my policy not to carry all the burdens by myself," she says. "If I can't carry the burden, I go straight to the specialist who knows how to. I was saying to everyone, 'I am in trouble, I need help.'"

Mieko Maruyama also took full advantage of any resources available. Even now, tears flow fast when she recalls how she was helped by so many people she just happened to meet. In addition to seeing her sister's and brother's psychiatrist and social workers, she would also visit the public health center counselor for peace of mind. She has never been shy about expressing her distress and emotions. Mieko remembers how surprised and relieved she was to hear these people say, "You just do what you can do. That will be OK." They never told her to try harder as the oldest sister of seven siblings and the only one who had a normal life. For years, guilt had haunted Mieko with the thought that she selfishly moved out of her dysfunctional home by marrying. She had lived feeling crushed by the sense of responsibility and the pressure to take care of all these sick brothers and sisters. "I had always been worried about nothing but what I should do next, and next, and next," Mieko weeps. "But their words made me stop and think. Right. I can only do what I can." She also feels she was lucky to have met one extremely kind staff member in the welfare office when she went for a consultation about her brother's welfare assistance. Moved by the situation she was facing, this man also went the extra mile to investigate the best possible assistance for her brother and simplified the application procedure for her. She thinks they could not help but sympathize with and do something for her since she had no intention of keeping up appearances, but always showed honest emotions and made desperate efforts. What supported her were various words of sympathy, encouragement, and understanding from others.

> I think words are so important. Some words are painful to hear at first, but gradually become effective to relieve your pain afterwards. Good medicine tastes bitter sometimes. But you can tell if it is the honest word expressed from the bottom of someone's heart.

It seems that ultimately one is supported, invigorated, and protected by words from other human beings. These people are not simply lucky. They have a certain ability to attract others' sympathy and the unwitting capacity to move others by their genuineness, honesty, passion, and open-mindedness for any help from outside. Many Japanese family members who successfully coped with critical situations seem to express this intense sense of gratitude to others they happened to run into. There is no denying that American family members would feel a strong sense of gratitude in the same situations. But it was more distinctively expressed by the Japanese families, probably because the sense of being connected and interdependent with others is more strongly ingrained in Japanese culture. The sense of indebtedness to those people one is close to as well as to the society as a whole has been the base for Japanese traditional morality. In fact, because of the difficulties they had to endure, they seem to have become even more sensitive to human kindness.

Notes

1. L. Pearlin, and C. Schooler "The Structure of Coping" *Journal of Health and Social Behavior* 19 (1978): 2–12; at 2.
2. Ibid.
3. N. Haan, *Coping and Defending: Processes of Self-Environment Organization* (New York: Academic Press, 1977) cited by E. G. Menaghan, "Individual Coping Efforts: Moderators of the Relationship between Life Stress and Mental Health Outcomes, " in *Psychosocial Stress: Trends in Theory and Research* (New York: Academic Press, 1983).
4. T. A. Wills, "Help-Seeking as a Copng Mechanism," *Coping With Negative Life Events: Clinical and Social Psychological Perspectives,* ed. C. R. Snyder and Carol E. Ford (New York: Plenum Press, 1981), 19–50.
5. A. G. Billings, and R. H. Moos, "The Role of Coping Responses and Social Resources in Attenuating the Stress of Life Events," *Journal of Behavioral Medicine* 4, no. 2 (1981): 139–57.
6. L. Dixon et al., "Evidence-Based Practices for Services to Family Members of People with Psychiatric Disabilities," *Psychiatric Services* 52 (2001): 903–910.
7. K. T. Mueser and S. R. McGurk, "Schizophrenia," *Lancet* 363 (2004): 263–72.
8. Carlifornia Alliance for the Mentally Ill, "The Journey of Hope," 1997. Leaflet.
9. W. R. McFarlane, *Multifamily Groups in the Treatment of Severe Psychiatric Disorders* (New York: Guilford, 2002), 36–48; at 39.

CHAPTER 9

Mental Coping

In addition to taking direct action to ease their distress, family members also make many internal changes as part of coping with the situation. They try to reinterpret the meaning of their experience and to create ways to look at their situation in a different light so that they can keep going.

Personal Determination

For some family members, it was their strong personal determination that gave them the energy to survive this difficulty. Like Scarlet O'Hara in *Gone With the Wind* vowing to survive no matter what, some family members told themselves that they would not succumb to this tragedy but would overcome it in one way or another. Frank Brown realized how important the family had always been to him since his own childhood. Now that his son had developed a mental illness, he told himself,

> The family was very important. I've always had a very strong will. I'm willing myself to get through this. Not allowing myself to wobble, as we say. Also, I realize that if I'm not to get emotionally traumatized to the point where I can't react, then I can't help Don either. If I'm going to be available to help Don, I've got to be strong.

At the same time, this determination led him to willingly seek support, including psychotherapy for himself, attendance at family support groups, and educating himself about mental illness.

As described in the earlier chapter, it was extremely difficult for Ken Morris to accept that his son had schizophrenia. Like many parents, he was initially agonized and frustrated, in denial, and eager to fix his son's problem. But once he realized what it was, his usual self, a tough survivor and a successful entrepreneur, came back. He was determined to deal with this in the same way he had dealt with many other problems in life including his business enterprises. His formula for problem solving was "as soon as you have an idea, the ideas become reality."

> Without an idea, there is no possibility that you can achieve whatever it is that you want to achieve. But with an idea and a realization of what you want to achieve, then it is very simple to put together the steps that you need to and come to the goal of achieving what you want to achieve.

When friends told Maria Hafer that her son would be her life project, she said, "No." Instead she says, "He's probably going to be a responsibility for me throughout my life. But there's much more to my life than that." She has decided not to let her son's illness run her life. She refuses to be completely overwhelmed by this misfortune. Making sure that she will keep a good balance between her life as the mother of a mentally ill child and as a teacher and a writer has been an important coping mechanism. Likewise, telling herself not to get too exhausted and keep a good balance between the burden of her younger brother's illness and other aspects of her life was what Yoshiko Naitô, the eldest of 13 siblings, tried to do. "I thought the last thing I'd do was to collapse," she says.

> I had the family to protect. I had a job to do everyday. I had my own problems, but I had to think about my brothers and sisters' future marriages, rather than my own. There were so many things I had to take care of, one by one. This situation gave me strength. I thought *shinboo* [endurance and perseverance] was important.

Carrying the multiple responsibilities of getting help for his wife, raising his only daughter, and keeping his job left little time for William Baker to spend much time thinking about his situation. But he had always held a firm stance on what happens in life, and most importantly, he was determined to protect his daughter.

> Well, I think I've grown a little bit because I realize that anything can happen at any point in time. And, what you have isn't as important as life — you know, you live each day. The most

important thing is that ... to make sure that this child gets a chance in life and can exceed her capability. And not have her look back and say, "Well, I was really deprived of my life or my upbringing."

Maybe it was the accumulated stress coming from his work and the years of responsibility as head of a family of five siblings after the end of World War II, but at 37, immediately after he got married, Shin Okabe had a stroke and was hospitalized,. The right side of his body was completely paralyzed, which forced him to stay in the hospital bed for months. His chronic asthma was making his condition even worse. His sister, Yasuko, had already been placed in a psychiatric hospital. Furthermore, his wife's invalid mother was needing a lot of care at home. "Everyone must have felt this was an utterly hopeless situation," Shin says, recalling those days.

> But perhaps I am a very simple-minded man. In spite of these physical sufferings, paralysis and asthma, which were extraordinary hardships, I somehow believed that I would be OK. No matter what. I guess I was incredibly optimistic. I really believed and told myself that this disease would be cured. I couldn't move my right arm at all, you know. But I so firmly believed in my recovery.

There was a patient in the next room, a man a year younger than Shin who had also had a stroke. They were taking physical therapy together, and in a couple of months, Shin showed remarkable progress and was soon released. Later Shin heard this man's condition had suddenly deteriorated and he had died. He wondered for a moment, "Did I kill him? In a sense, we were competing with each other. But I recovered much more quickly and got way ahead of him. He must have been shocked. He had recovered enough to go though rehabilitation, but he suddenly had a relapse and died." Shin doesn't think he is a man of a particularly strong character, but he always believed he had "some vital energy for survival."

Toward Acceptance

While some people had high energy and were willing to confront and battle with catastrophe head-on, there were others whose acceptance and resignation helped them deal better with tragedy. They also were willing to change their own perspective to make it easier to accommodate the patient's plight. They tried lowering their expectations, neutralizing or finding positive meanings for having to deal with their family member's illness. They also chose to resign themselves to whatever happened, or to something they called "fate."

Anna Berger went through no less shock and agony than other parents of mentally ill children. But as a professional psychotherapist, she knew how human beings can react in situations like this.

> It wasn't a mystery to me. See, I think that people who are not in the field are still very mystified and they keep thinking they can do something to make it better, or whatever. They think they shouldn't be feeling this way or they feel guilty. But I knew that it would be very painful and that what I was feeling was appropriate because I know that. So I didn't really feel any great need to ask questions of other people and so on.

Miki Maeda came to the realization that it was her fate to take care of one of her twin daughters, Misa, throughout her life. Since childhood, Miki had been well aware that some of her relatives had mental illnesses. She had always felt there was some uncontrollable fate in her life. But she was not giving up on Misa, or giving in to the tragedy. She was simply changing her perspective drastically.

> This is my fate, I thought. My life will be with this child who will probably never marry or have her own family. Unlike most parents whose children will eventually lead independent lives, I will continue to be closely involved with her life. An unmarried daughter stays with me as I age.... That's not so bad. I used to expect her to marry and do many things like other people's children. But I decided to drop all those expectations.... Always I had felt there was some genetic issues in my family background. I had gone through so much in life by that time. [Miki had divorced, struggled as a single mother of twins, married a man 30 years older, and become a widow.] This is not my original personality, but something I learned through my experiences. I have learned to get up again quickly, even after a defeat — so many times. So maybe I know how to shift my way of thinking very quickly. I didn't want to just keep crying, you know. I thought, "I am going to live a good life with my daughter."

Fate is also the word Tôru Yamaguchi prefers to use to make peace with himself. He worked so hard to keep his store running and making everything right. Even when the business declined after his daughter Yuri became ill, he believed that as soon as she recovered, his business would thrive again. But when his grief-stricken wife got cancer and passed away, Tôru felt he lost all hope. "I thought this was my fate, after all," he said rather calmly. "There was nothing I could do. I stopped struggling and gave in to my fate." This sense of resignation, however, led him to close his business and made it possible to spend much more time with Yuri. He was also able to learn more about mental illness, including how to talk and interact with his daughter. Now he feels they have a better relationship than ever.

Kôichi Takagi was in total despair when his son became ill right after his wife died. He recalls that those days were "filled with tears." In retrospect, however, he believes that it is important to cry out your pain. If you suppress it, the pain will stay. "I think crying is good," he says.

> Shedding a lot of tears helps change one's mind eventually. So I recommend that others cry. The problem of many parents is that they don't grieve enough by crying. [Laughter.] You can go to the mountains, seaside, or anywhere and cry out loud. And then you can start rising again from there.

After hitting emotional bottom, Kôichi went on a short trip just to get away. It was also the seventh anniversary of his wife's death. He went to a place where Ryôkan, a famous eighteenth-century Japanese Zen Buddhist priest had lived. Ryôkan was a poet and master of calligraphy, born into a wealthy family. Through a series of misfortunes, he lost all his family properties and became a poor monk. He lived a simple but full life of integrity with no worldly material pursuits. While learning about Ryôkan's humble life, Kôichi began to feel that he should follow his path, at least mentally.

> He was just an impoverished monk, so to speak. But I felt I would start living again, like him. I thought I would no longer care about money and those things. You know, Japan became so materialistic. People judge others by the amount of money they have. They have been working so hard and may have accumulated some money after the defeat of the World War II, but look, Japan is not so popular in the world, is it? What's the point of being hated by others even if you have money? That's what I felt. I decided to take an early retirement and get fully involved in the family support group. My son used to accuse me of being a workaholic. Maybe it was time that I "graduated" from the company.... What's important is not to expect too much. Yes, controlling your desire is very important. First my greed needs to be controlled. Then I can tell what really satisfies me. Reducing one's desire leads to a true understanding of satisfaction.... Unless we suppress our desire,

we never know what we truly want. This way of thinking may come from Zen. But I tell others, let's work for small happiness first, and have politicians take care of big matters. So what I hope for my son is for him to be able to do what he likes to do. It is true that prejudice against mental illness exists in society. But I think in fact it is not as strong as many family members or the patients fear. It is better to be open about it, not to be too self-conscious. As long as people worry about social stigma, they will remain trapped. Like Ryôkan, I wanted to throw away my pride or vanity and to start from scratch. I'm not afraid of prejudice or being poor. I think this kind of attitude eventually will help my son's condition improve.

Learning to stop dwelling on one thing for too long and shifting her attention to another was one way Tomoko Uchimura coped with the huge pressure of her life. When her 19-year-old son Kaoru became schizophrenic, her husband suffered a stroke and became bedridden. All of a sudden, the entire family responsibility was on the shoulders of this tiny, fragile middle-aged woman who had no one to turn to. Until her husband passed away two years ago, her life centered around taking care of two ill family members. "There was nobody else but myself," was how she felt all the time. She joined a family support group, but felt envious of others in the group who could express their sorrow in tears. "I didn't even have time to cry," she says." I was under so much pressure to do so many things every day." But she came to learn to set mental limits so that she didn't think too much about something that was uncontrollable. She explains how she learned to turn off her "thinking switch."

> I think about what to do and how to do things to a certain degree. But after a certain point, I don't continue to think or worry. There are many things that cannot be solved by just dwelling upon them. I would tell myself, "No use in thinking further! Let's stop." Because there is no answer. Maybe that helped me. This was how I coped, I guess.

During the conversation with the counselor she visited for one week, Yoko Tomita realized that the reason why she was crying so much was not really for her husband, who suffered from schizophrenia. The tears were out of self-pity.

> I realized one day that I was actually angry at and sad about my situation, rather than feeling sorry for my husband's illness. I shed

so many tears because I had become so unhappy. Then I wondered, "Have I ever thought about what's good for him, from his standpoint?" I have been thinking only about how my husband's illness affected *me*, how sad I was as a wife. I don't know why my husband had to become ill, but I have no intention of divorcing him. I was sure about it. Then, I should think about what is good for him. Because, after all, I love him.

This realization changed Yoko's attitude toward her husband. Then she discovered, once she stopped being irritated by and hostile to him, he stabilized. She understood that how she interacted with him had a profound impact on his condition for better or worse. She also began letting go of some burdens and decided not to carry too much all by herself.

Before my husband became ill, I used to hate the song "Que sera, sera." It's the song that says whatever will be, will be.... One day I was watching that Hitchcock movie on TV, *The Man Who Knew Too Much*, and heard Doris Day singing the song, and it made me break down. Tears kept flowing down my face. That's right! I thought to myself, "Whatever will, be will be, no matter how sad you are...." I started to tell myself, "Whatever will be, will be...." It became my mantra.

She decided not to push herself too much and to relax more. In the beginning she simply pretended to be more relaxed, taking a nap when she got tired and expressing her emotions more openly. She would cry when she saw a sad story on TV and laugh when she was happy. In the beginning she had to force herself to be expressive. But it eventually led her to feeling more generous and relaxed. She also began to play the piano for pleasure.

Help Seeking: New Perspectives

The act of seeking help also brought various new perspectives to family members. It had been very difficult for Robert Kirk to keep a balance between wanting to help his son in any way he could and letting his son be on his own. His current wife and other relatives often accused him of not knowing how to set limits. He had problems accepting the idea of setting limits, as he always felt that it meant "You have to manipulate this person to make them do what you think they should do." However, by attending the Journey of Hope classes, Robert has learned the importance and true meaning of setting limits on what he can do. This is crucial in coping with the mental illness of a loved one. Through learning various specific skills on self-care and problem-solving strategies taught in the classes, he has come to understand that he and his son are separate individuals and that he has to take care of himself and also expect his son to do the same to the extent possible. At the same time, he acquired the ability to put himself in his son's position and tried to understand his side of the story.

> And the limits are not on him, but they are on me. The limits I set are not limits set on my son's behavior —"You can't do this." But rather I say, "Ben, this is what I can do and this is what I will do. And, I won't go beyond this…." Next is empathy. I've got to understand what he's going through. I have got to empathize with him and understand that he understands and sees things in an altered way. Therefore, I've got to be empathetic, but I've got to have certain guidelines. After I set the guidelines and I know what I want to do — but only after I know what my limits are, then I've got to be able to communicate it to Ben.

Through the exercise of "I" statements and reflective responses, Robert was able to articulate what he can do and what he cannot do. This fundamentally changed his way of approaching Ben's illness and enabled him to understand his son's feelings and emotions without making mental demands on Ben that he couldn't handle. And it resulted in a much better relationship with him.

Individual therapy can also help caretakers and other family members go beyond the immediate circumstances and more deeply explore the totality of their lives. This process eventually comes back to the present situation and helps them better deal with the situation.

Rosanna Olmos regained a sense of self-reliance years after her life was thrown into turmoil struggling with her sons' mental illnesses. She also learned to express her feelings more honestly.

> [From this therapy] well, I learned that I was an important person, that I had a right to my own feelings. That I could become independent again like when I was a kid. That my husband was not my father. That he was my husband, and it's supposed to be a partnership.

For siblings who grew up in the midst of family chaos, fending off each crisis at home, therapy as well as family support groups were life-saving experiences. New perspectives were opened up to them and a better understanding of themselves gained through therapy helped them tremendously in coping with life.

"[I learned from the therapy] that my family is nuts," Jane Wilson laughs. She had private psychotherapy after turning 40. The iron band that had suffocated her since childhood was slowly released, allowing her to admit how emotions had been suppressed at home while she was growing up. Despite the enormous problems of her father's mental illness (alcoholism) and the constant chaos and embarrassment brought on by her mentally ill sister, the family managed to live in strong denial and with psychological deception forced on all members of the household. The only emotion allowed was being happy, Jane recalls, again, with a nervous laughter:

> I'm always happy. Always happy, but really not happy. The happiness was a cover for tremendous sorrow probably. You know, the coping mechanism was always that we're a happy family. Happy, happy, happy. Everything's great! We're so happy! We love each other so much! [Laughter.] And we do everything together. Happy, happy, happy!

Individual therapy was a process of realizing what had been fundamentally missing in her life. It helped her to release all the hidden pain and rebuild her true self. This helped her to deal with basic human relationships, to cope with her life in general, and eventually gave her the foundation to better deal with her mentally ill sister.

> It's not me, it's them [who were responsible for my depression]. It's helped me in so many ways. I feel like it's given me a new lease on life. A new chance to live. To understand how few emotions I actually have and how much I have to work on feeling those emotions. [Laughter.] [I used to think] everything's so great. And I had this great job. Fantastic job. And I was a workaholic. And since then, I've been very afraid to get another job because I don't want to get into that workaholic thing. I'm learning how to structure my life so I don't get trapped into that type of pattern again. And alcohol. I learned about how alcohol played a tremendous part in my life.

Therapy also gave Melanie Wood the courage to confront what was seriously wrong with a fundamental part of her life. Growing up with excessive responsibilities for family crises caused by her mentallu ill brother, nevertheless convincing herself that this family problem did not matter, Melanie had long forgotten that she had any feelings about it at all. Accepting the dysfunctional culture of her home was the start of many changes that followed. It was the process of taking back her own life and rebuilding her true self. Although she always seemed competent and got things done, her concern was to keep up appearances and to live up to other people's expectations. This was achieved by sacrificing her own feelings. A number of support group meetings and the words from the group leader brought her to the realization that she didn't have to carry all the burden by herself. After all, she and her brother were separate individuals, a fact she came to see more clearly. The revelation instigated many changes in her life to follow. She decided to quit her teaching job, which was wearing her out at that time, although many of her old friends and her parents criticized her for leaving work she was trained for after 25 years. The leader of her family support group also helped her realize there was a completely different approach to life, one she had never had been aware of. "I just had this idea that if you work hard enough for something, you know, that you'd fix it," Melanie says.

> That's one of the things I learned — I can't fix my brother, no matter.... Can't fix my family, can't fix my brother. And I was falling apart. And once I remember she [the support group leader] said to me, if you're not getting anchored from the people and the things in your life now, then maybe you need to look elsewhere and, sort of let those anchors go. And maybe reconnect in with other people or with other situations, and she taught us one thing I remember. That the people in my life who were telling me it's your responsibility to stay in teaching, it's your responsibility, my parents, to take care of my brother, blah blah blah blah. And it didn't seem right, then maybe I should start talking to other people who were saying that you don't need to stay in teaching, if you don't feel that's right for you anymore. You don't need to take all the responsibility for your brother.

When Jodi Kramer felt like drowning for some reason she couldn't understand, she finally went to a therapist. A new way to look at her family also released her from the guilt and self-doubt that had haunted her for decades.

> Oh yes, very, very helpful. Just really changed my life and I eventually got strong again and learned to talk and express my feelings. I wasn't crazy. You know this was not crazy behavior. This was all nuts going on at my house. And it was right. I was thinking right about it. And I wasn't a bad girl for thinking it. You see, my mother always had a way of saying "Jodi, you're a bad girl when you criticize how we live here," you know.

She realized that she had to find and decide what she wanted for herself. Despite her anger and frustration about what was happening at her parents' home, she was still forcing herself to be closely involved with her family.

> [I was] too connected to them, like I was seeing my parents too much. I was going to my parents' house too much. It wasn't necessary for me to be as connected as my family wanted, for us to all be connected. That probably wasn't good for me under the circumstances. I was saying, "Oh, we're going to get together for birthday parties, and "Oh, we're going to have a family reunion, you know. And some people have family reunions every five years. But our family was having about twenty a year and every time I was going into this — having to go and see my insane brother, seeing all this dysfunction in the family. I was getting really upset about it all and it wasn't good for me and it wasn't even necessary at all.

However, the awakening achieved through private therapy sessions signals their departure from their original family. This change can bring them into further conflict with their original family members. Jane Wilson says:

> And now, it's a strange feeling because I know I may lose a lot of contact that I've had with my brothers and sisters and our family. You know, they can't accept the changes in me. But that I'm going to be much better. I've been through a lot of grieving, I've been through a lot of sadness, but actually being able to recognize the sadness rather than just thinking that I should be so happy.

Spirituality and Giving up Control

Many family members achieve a sense of personal spirituality that helps them tremendously in coping with the uncontrollable nature of mental illness. The awareness of spirituality among individuals facing acute suffering and difficulties in life has been documented.[1-3] These types of feelings came more easily for people who were already involved in a religious organization. The nature of psychological support they received from their religious faith varies, ranging from acceptance of their life in general to feeling energized and empowered. The belief that their difficulties are an assignment from a higher power who is watching over them has given them a strong feeling of being protected as well. "God" is where Marianne Schmidt turns to for strength and wisdom whenever she cannot find an answer to her life problem. This strong faith in God did not happen at once, but gradually. One of the biggest unanswered questions she had kept asking for years was what had caused her sister's schizophrenia. Was it a genetic problem, a dysfunctional family situation caused by her father's alcoholism and emotional problems, or both? She had sought any information she could get and created a family genealogy. So much time and energy had been spent contemplating the question, which was not of any help in the end. Marianne says today, "I think I've come to a point where I don't analyze so much anymore that I don't have to have answers of why. I'm just accepting it for what it is. And just ... just take her for who she is."

Marianne had also been overburdening herself with the sense of obligation and responsibility for taking care of her mentally ill sister, while her other siblings almost completely retreated from that role. Her coping is grounded in her firm belief in God. She believes that ultimately she and others will be taken care of by God, which gives her a great sense of relief and peace.

> Well, you know, as a Christian, I have pretty much placed my life in the hands of God. And knowing that he's a loving heavenly father, and that he cares about us. He cares about my sister. I've come to realize that he can take care of her. He can heal her if he chooses to do so. And by the same token, I am powerless to do anything. And so I have pretty much placed her in his hands and knowing that he can take much better care of her than I and I'll just do my role as sister and support her and love her. And I can rest in that now. I don't have to be the one that saves everybody or takes care of everybody or makes everything.... I've always been the fixer in the family. I have to fix everything. I have to take care of everybody, I have to make everything OK. But I'm not able to do that. You know, I was becoming burned out and, again, God has enabled me to see that.

It is his faith in God that keeps Gordon Collins, a Catholic, spending every day with his wife, who has bipolar disorder. He goes to church every Sunday, and religion is a central force in his coping with her illness. He sees his responsibility for his family as the mission he has to fulfill, sent from God. "Well, it's the cross you have to bear, basically," he says.

> That's what it's all about. One of the crosses that God gave me to bear is this.... That helps keep me going. You know, if I go out of my home, I just go to a quiet place, I talk to God, basically. I believe God is out there listening. Well, he is probably telling me to hang in there. That's what this is about. This is what I've given

you to do — an important job and that's what I want you to do. Your daughter needs you. Your wife needs you. You're their strength, so you have to be there.

No matter what happens, Tôru Yamaguchi believed that *Kami-sama* [God] will protect him, which kept him relatively calm even when his wife died after the battle with cancer. Following a series of tragedies (his daughter's illness and the failure of his business), he decided to join one of the new religious organizations, but says, "Basically I leave my destiny in the hands of *Kami-sama.*" Because his wife had a strong heart, doctors and nurses expected that she would suffer for a long period of time before dying. But her end was surprisingly peaceful. Tôru believes that his *Kami-sama* made it easier for his wife by causing her much less pain.

Wallace Green had never been involved with any religion. However, attending Al-Anon meetings introduced him to the importance of giving up his control to a higher and larger entity, which is basically in tune with the central theme of many kinds of spiritual faith. This is a new perspective for Wallace, who always had enormous confidence in keeping things under control and organized. Although he is greatly inspired and supported by the safe and warm atmosphere it offers, Al-Anon's first step of recognizing that one has no control is still very difficult for him to accept. He is still struggling with this idea. "I'm not quite sure what that [higher power] means," he says.

> I mean, I'm just reciting the words, just flirting with the whole concept. I'm flirting with the idea, I mean I'm doing as much as any human being can do. I have a lot going and I have all the medical services, but I'm beginning to realize that I cannot actively control my son's destiny.... I'm very controlling, you know — most physicians are. I control the universe. Everyday I get up and I control everybody under the umbrella of loving and caring — but you have a sore throat, this is what I want you to do. You have chest pain, this is what I want you to do. So in a way, I'm controlling and manipulating.... When I eventually give up control I will probably then be most effective with my son. So I'm flirting with some spirituality to turn my problem — in addition to what I'm already doing — to turn it over to a higher power. But I'm not quite sure what that means to me.

As introduced earlier, what gave Yoshiko Takeda a positive strength at the time of her early despair at the onset of her daughter's schizophrenia were the two places where she sought help. One was at the psychiatrist's office where the diagnosis was handed down. To Yoshiko, who looked obviously distraught, the doctor spoke gently, "Look, it is only my guess, but your daughter's schizophrenia may reflect the situation of your family: the whole family is not in unity. Everyone in the family may be scattered and their feelings are apart from one another. By everyone getting together again and working together on your daughter's illness, something good can come out." The doctor was in no way blaming her or her family. His remark was based on his personal belief that every phenomenon in the world was interdependent. During the conversation, the cross on his office wall also caught her attention. "Strange thing this doctor says," she thought. But it had a telling effect on Yoshiko's sense of spirituality and made her listen to his words seriously. She also went to her family's religious organization and asked for counseling. The counselor of the church told her the same thing as the psychiatrist. He said, "Let's think, and work on how we can bring something good out of this tragedy." These two incidents, which, interestingly, occurred in a very short period, gave her feelings of salvation and a sense that some larger force was at work. It convinced her that maybe this is how she should think. In the beginning, Yoshiko could not talk about her daughter's disease with her parents or siblings, but the support she was able to get from this religious consultation prevented her "from sinking too deep into depression." To this day, after all these years, Yoshiko often reminds herself of what the doctor said to her at that moment of despair. His words were the foundation for her coping with her daughter's mental illness.

> His words have always supported me. In fact, since my daughter became ill, our family has become much closer. We go on trips together. My daughter used to be very quiet, but now she is more active and more cheerful than before. We even say that the illness changed her for the better. It was in fact a blessing in disguise.

Notes

1. S. Strang and P. Strang, "Spiritual Thought, Coping and 'Sense of Coherence' in Brain Tumour Patients and Their Spouses," *Palliative Medicine* 15 (2001): 127–34.
2. L. M. Wright, "Suffering and Spirituality. The Soul of Clinical Work With Families," *Journal of Family Nursing* 3 (1997): 3–14.
3. K. I. Pargament, *The Psychology of Religion and Coping: Theory, Research, Practice* (New York: Guilford, 1997).

CHAPTER 10

How Can They Go On?

If there is successful coping, it must be a function of many factors, including successful financial management, available support resources, education, individual personality makeup, and probably luck. However, I think it is the individual's personal conception of life in general and about discrete events that enables action and utilization of social resources and ultimately makes a difference in their reality. People who were willing to participate in my interviews were mainly the primary caretakers or guardians or were acting as an agent for the patient in medical and legal settings. On the other hand, I am sure that many more family members are out there who have long chosen not to be a part of the patient's life because of their physical, financial, and various other circumstances and limitations. It may also be because they were not emotionally able to face, not to mention handle, the situations. In this sense, the people I interviewed were all survivors. All of them are not necessarily successful or happy survivors. The sense of guilt, self-doubt, regret, and profound sorrow can creep into their consciousness any time, even today. Nevertheless, they have come this far, carrying burdens that are hard for other people to comprehend. Mental illness, especially its social nature as mentioned at the beginning of this book, has produced uniquely complex situations and distinctive difficulties in the families' lives. Being families of the mentally ill has given them a certain identity, almost equivalent to that of minorities or other socially marginalized groups. It may be a small part of their self-concept, which they are not usually conscious of, but, like a land mine, when touched, it can have an impact on their entire lives. How can one live with such a heavy cross to bear? What are the sources of their strength and perseverance?

I asked all the family members at the end of the interviews what the most important thing was that had supported them and enabled them to keep going all these years, struggling with their relative's mental illness. When the question was posed, unlike some other questions, most of them had little hesitation about articulating why they had not given up or completely abandoned their involvement with the patient's life. The reasons are as varied as the number of individuals, and some raised multiple factors, but they are roughly listed as follows.

Love for the Patient

A strong sense of commitment to the patient was spontaneously expressed by some family members. When they mentioned this, the responses were quick and automatic. It could be the sense of instinctive responsibility, as many say, "Because he or she is my child/brother/sister," and it was a good enough reason for them to keep going.

The source of the strength for all these years since her twin sons became ill was "self-preservation,"

Rosanna Olmos put it decidedly.

> I guess the fact that you love the children. You know, you really love the children. So you want to help them. You have the love of your spouse. And the rest of the family. And AMI has been a tremendous support. I think all that love from all those different sources. Plus I think you get some sort of an inner strength, you know.

Ruth Singer, a mother, sees her commitment in the same way.

> What has kept me going throughout all this? The love I have for my son, the desire to learn and understand illness. The compassion that I have for other families and their mentally ill ones. The compassion I have in general for homeless people, whether they be mentally ill or not. I guess compassion for humanity. I love people. And everybody deserves to have a better life.

Diana Nelson, a sister, looks back on her life and sees things in perspective. "There is positive and there is negative," she says. Having a mentally ill brother affected her relationship with her mother, but also made her grow up to be an independent person. But she embraces her relationship with her brother despite the confusion, chaos, and pain he caused in her life. Despite the illness, he has been self-sufficient and capable of taking care of himself. She says, "And having a brother that's mentally ill was part of my life."

> He's just my brother. I don't know what else to say. [Laughter.] He could have had autism, he could have been in a wheelchair, he could have been a financial banker, he could have been the world's best lawyer — he certainly likes to argue. He's just my brother, so it didn't change my life because this is my life. You know what I mean? Any other life wouldn't have been my life.

To the question if she loved him, Diane most assuredly responded, "Oh, of course I do. Yeah, I'm proud of him."

Marianne Schmidt also emphasizes her love for her sister.

> The fact that she's my little sister, I can't turn my back on her. Sometimes I feel like it. I don't want to be involved in her life any-more. But you know, she is my sister and I can't turn my back on her and I think at times, what if it was me. What if I was the one who had to live in this situation day after day, and so that gives me a bit more perspective on it. That it could have been me. And for-tunately it was her. And I feel, if I don't, who will? So just being with her does give her some happiness and so I just cannot turn my back on her.

Timothy Rosen, a father, says at once, "It's love. It's love, because my son has a quality that makes me feel I want to do it. There's the reward." Early on, Timothy decided that if he and his son were to be together in spite of his illness and their frequent arguments, it had to be tolerable for Timothy. To make it possible, he had to have a decent and stable relation-ship with his son. He decided to take time to treat his son with respect and talk to him respectfully, not like someone who was abandoned, institu-tionalized. Naturally, it took much time for him to see his determination work in reality. He tried to find something both he and his son could do so that they can look forward to their get-togethers. They now enjoy many activities together, such as, bowling, playing tennis or billiards, eating out, and going to the movies. Spending time with his son has become the cen-tral part of Timothy's life, which causes some criticism from others, who feel that he is too easy on his son. But he thinks it important to have com-munication with his son, even though it takes time and energy. Rather than imposing rules upon his son, Timothy wants to try reasoning with him. What gives him the strength to keep going is the knowledge that he is doing the best he can for his son and having a good relationship in spite of the illness.

Kelly Seeman confesses if she had to do it all over again, she wouldn't have done it. It is apparent that when she adopted Allan 33 years ago, this was not what she expected. There were times when she tried to back away from the responsibility, but she persevered. She held on. Why?

> [After a long silence] Because no matter how bad it is — and sometimes it has gotten very bad, very, very difficult — I think I would find it impossible to live with myself if I turned my back on him. Yeah. If I turned my back on him, the turning it on him would also be turning it on part of that extended family: his wife and my grandson. I mean, if I wanted to turn my back on my son, maybe when I might have done so when he got married, but my grandson would have lived in poverty. I couldn't do that. I took one look at my grandson and I fell in love all over again.

She sees that abandoning him is like abandoning his whole family, including her grandson. Knowing better than anyone that in her son's life abandonment is the underlying dynamic that had traumatized Allan since childhood, she simply couldn't do that to him again.

What has supported Yoko Tomita most for nine years since the start of her husband's illness? Despite the pain and the lonely struggle she had to go through, she is convinced that her love for her husband has not faded one bit. She believes that this tragedy has transformed her into a better person.

> I know his illness and his personality are completely different things. It's his personality I like. That's why I could live with him. I think it important to respect his personality and his will. So whatever I do, like buying a condominium, I always consult with him. I have tried not to make a decision by myself. This is the life for both of us.... What I like about him is he doesn't discriminate against people. My husband never looks down upon others. He is not a calculating person. Some may say that's because he doesn't have to deal with real life problems. But I think he has been always like this since he was a child. To me this is an ideal way of living. Of course I have to live a life with realistic concerns. But he doesn't have to, and that's OK. I am content with it. Being with him, it's like he is satisfying a part of my deep wish. That is why being together with him is meaningful to me. So I am very

grateful for his presence even though he became ill. I am originally a self-centered person. I used to get irritated and angry very
easily if things didn't go as I wished. But his illness made me
much more considerate of other people's feelings. It really
changed me. People now come to me for advice. I was sometimes
consulted before, but now I am more careful than before about
what to tell them. I am willing to talk to them as much as time
allows. If there is anything I can do for them, I like to. I only wish
I had more knowledge to help more people…

In her darkest moment, Shoko Inose wished she had "disappeared like
smoke in the sky." But it was her son, after all, the only child she had raised
by herself after she lost her husband. To the question of what has supported her in dealing with her son's mental illness, she says,

I have decided to protect him to the end … [pause] because he is
dear to me. People say that I am overprotective and he is a
mommy's boy. But I don't care. I am determined to see him stand
on his own someday. I may have failed for the first twenty-five years.
Then it may take another twenty-five years. But I am determined.

The onset of illness in his wife of 40 years has reminded Takashi
Ishizawa of how precious she is in his life.

It makes me happy if my wife gets better even a little. My strong
wish to see her in better condition keeps me going. I think it's
important for me to stay healthy, so I walk every day for exercise.
When I am walking, I get ideas and new perspectives about
things, like how important it is that I am in good health to help
her get better. The most important is my wife's health, and the
second is mine. Unless I am healthy, I cannot take care of her. We
are like two wheels of one car. I also think I should have done this
and that for my wife when I last saw her. I keep walking sometimes thinking what she likes and what makes her happy. Maybe
I'll go to her favorite store and buy something for her. It may be
just a small thing. I think about my daughters' birthday, what
I will give them, thinking about these things keeps me going and
makes my life worthwhile.

Family Support

Some believe that solidarity with other family members was the major
source of their strength. Having an understanding spouse, other healthy

children, and siblings to whom they can talk and help each other has been priceless, as Ken Morris says confidently, "Yeah, I don't think there's anybody else that's supported me all these years — just my wife."

Haru Morimoto, a mother, calls her life with her husband a "three-legged race." In this race, it is crucial that two people run in harmony, or they fall. She believes it is her close relationship with him that has kept her going all these years. "If I had to do it all by myself, I might have been hospitalized with my son," says Haru.

Jane Wilson says a sense of humor is important, but "picking the right man" brought the most success in her coping with her sister's illness. There were times when she turned to drugs and alcohol, but ultimately her husband was a tremendous support and the bedrock in her life.

Their Own Upbringing

Many family members responded with a strong conviction that the source of their strength was the home environment where they spent their childhood and grew up. The reference point they go back to is their parents. It doesn't matter how old the person is. I heard them describing their parents as the source of their personal pride, too. A mother in her 70s recalled how strong her mother was, and the memory of her mother's strength guided her way through difficult times. Linda Katz says, "I've been looking back upon it. I think I have great inner strength and I had a mother who had that, too. I think her influence was very strong." It is interesting to hear them go back several decades to where they originally came from and discover that what they experienced and learned then still has a profound influence on how they cope with their lives today. It is not surprising to see that what we acquired in our early socialization period has a lasting influence on our life. But it seems that the belief, knowledge, and wisdom they developed then is particularly crucial in dealing with life problems later in adulthood.

Frank Brown was born and raised in California. He also had no hesitation in attributing his strength to his upbringing

> [The source of my strength is] my upbringing. From my stick-to-itiveness. To stick to a problem. And not to run away. I don't run away from a problem — I guess I'm too stubborn to — I could run away, you know, from it. And get lost. But that's not the way. My family brought me up [this way].... Not only my parents, but my coping power I learned in the thirties. We didn't have money, you know. Great Depression. And you had to survive. You had to

be a survivor and that's just the way I am. And I imagine there are a lot of other people like that too.

Robert Kirk believes it is the "gene" he received from his parents that has kept him going, despite all the despair and ups and downs about his son's illness. Particularly, the personality he inherited from his mother, who lived to 91, has made him basically a hopeful person who can look on the bright side of things. His personal strength is clearly anchored on this perspective of life.

I say, "Just do the best you can. Keep a good outlook. Look at the half-full part of the glass. And, don't berate yourself. Don't berate yourself. Don't give yourself a hard time by saying, 'Oh, I shouldn't have done that. Oh, it was a mistake to do that.'"

For Rosanna Olmos, her inner strength came from the family tradition she grew up with. Her parental family was descended from pioneers who had lived in California since the seventeenth century. "I think there's just those kind of people who survive. You know," she says proudly.

Yeah, the origins of the family, some sort of a strength and dig your teeth in and — keep going. You know, we weren't supposed to be quitters. And it's easy to give up and force your spouse, and run off and do something else.

Maria Hafer was an adopted child and her adoptive mother set a good example of how to be strong in times of family crisis. When her adoptive father had periods of severe depression, how her mother handled the situation and maintained her professional and her personal life was what Maria always returned to in order to regain her strength.

Pride and confidence as a completely self-made businessman gave Ken Morris the continuous strength needed to tackle his son's illness. His father's death when Ken was 13 forced him to learn to take care of himself, and the years of hard work and success taught him that he could achieve anything once he put his mind to.

William Baker remembers how his mother and father were always together, which gave him a sense of rootedness to grow from. "It's like a tree," he says. "It gives you a stability when you come from a strong tree." Furthermore, being an African-American man growing up in the South in the 1940s made him "stronger than most people." But what kept him going and gave him hope was his strong wish to see his daughter graduate and go to college. Knowing how to draw a line between getting himself involved and the decision not to let his wife's illness destroy his entire life has made it possible for him to keep his own sanity.

Philosophy of Life and Self-Definition

Clearly, early socialization is the foundation for the belief system we develop later. But the family members also referred to a certain philosophy of life they acquired through later life experiences and their own education. Furthermore, defining oneself as a human being who is intrinsically strong and capable of handling situations seems to have provided a base for their strength and guided them through tough times. This is a testament to the fact that a human being constantly creates meanings and beliefs throughout life. Solid assumptions about one's self have a powerful impact on coping processes. As Lagrand and Rand discuss, the beliefs about one's self as well as about how best to cope are extremely important in the successful adaptation to changes in life, particularly those relating to loss.[1]

Glenda White, a Mexican-American, raised as a Catholic, married a Jewish man, and converted to Judaism. "Nobody likes a Mexican-Indian Jew," she laughs." If you can survive that, you can survive anything." Having had a borderline personality disorder herself, nothing came easy for her, but she always knew how to survive. She says she believes in God, one god that is universal regardless of the differences on the surface, as any god is ultimately the same all over the world. She also made it her philosophy that she should never be ashamed of seeking help when needed. If she keeps trying to find help, she feels she will eventually find the right help.

> If you stay right here, you'll just never know what's out there. And that's to me, I know there's a lot of beauty out there. And I want all I can get and if I don't take any risks, then I'm not going to get it.... When I've been in pain, I've always asked for help. I was never ashamed. When I was in school, going to junior college I went for the counseling service. I mean, it was very painful, but in the meantime, I didn't want to stay like that and I think that one of my bad characteristics of being a borderline is I'll bite the bullet.

Miki Maeda has similar perspectives on how to cope with life. She lost her parents at age ten, moving from one relative to another in different towns during her childhood, got married, and then divorced. Her life had been full of adversity. She has a strong sense that something like "destiny" has guided her. This upbringing also gave her the subconscious preparedness for life tragedies and the clear awareness that anything could happen in life. At the same time, it also taught her how to survive hard times by getting proper help. Her survival skill meant that that she is never shy about asking for help from others.

> Probably because of my experiences from childhood, I knew it was impossible to support myself all alone. So I learned to find people who could understand me as soon as possible. [Laughter.] For that, I involve other people in my business. For example, when I happen to see someone in the neighborhood with the same problem, I go and tell them about my experience. You know, I take action, I initiate contact from my side. When they are interested, I talk more openly about my situation. Most families have someone with some kind of disability — always, always. It could be their child or one of their relatives.... Because I am so willing to talk so candidly, they feel like talking about their problem, too, and they ask me for advice. You know, no human being is perfect. Everyone has got something, but they cannot keep hiding.

After the divorce, Miki took a job as a housemaid for an American family living on a military base in Japan. She thought at first that she would not be able to communicate, speaking little English. Besides, she thought, Americans would not be interested in other people's business, anyway. However, her American employer was the one who took an interest in her life situation first and asked her a number of questions. "Do you have children?" "How are they doing when you are working?" With a combination of a limited English vocabulary and gestures, she tried to explain that she was a single mother of twins. To her complete surprise, the American couple was willing to offer an arrangement for Miki so that she could be with her daughters while baby-sitting their children. She was encouraged by this incident. She says,

> I learned this survival skill from Americans, I can almost say. Even if I couldn't speak English, if you are willing to be open about yourself, you can communicate. So they sympathized with me and helped me. I have learned from this experience that if you are open, there is always someone out there who will understand and help. The important thing is not to hide. This is something many Japanese cannot do.

Leland Miller remembers that since his school days as an art major he had been impressed with various Oriental philosophies, including Buddhism. The thoughts that always seemed to help him were "The only true self is no self" and "By being selfless we could reach some kind of enlightenment."

> And if I did something that I was so involved in that all my attention went into this thing, this was almost like a revelation to me. This was like enlightenment. And so, you lose all the trappings and the problems because you become completely involved in this immediate experience and therefore you lose the self. And in losing the self, you really find the self. You really find yourself. And, I really don't know how to explain it beyond that. So when I've had things come along, I just try to thoroughly involve myself in what's happening at that moment.

What Leland implies is that, despite all the devastating events, it is important for him to throw himself into the middle of the matter in question and just work on it with no regard for anything else, totally concentrating and focusing on the problem. This approach helped him get through a number of crises.

The experience of running his own company as well as reading books on military strategies written by Chinese and Western philosophers such as Sunzi, Confucius, and Mencius gave Osamu Kinoshita a great deal of wisdom that he found useful in dealing with many life problems. He knows life is uncertain, with many ups and downs. Human beings are not stable creatures, either. Things are constantly moving and changing. "Who knows what tomorrow will bring?" he says.

> Of course no one wants to suffer, but you never know, a difficult time may turn out to be a good one in a second. There are times in life when you look back later on the incident which made you feel despair once, but in fact, you realize that it ended up bringing something positive.

Since he was inspired by the life of the Japanese Zen Buddhist priest, Ryôkan, Kôichi Takagi's biggest support was his philosophy, which drastically transformed his workaholic lifestyle. He learned that it was important to control one's greed and stay satisfied with what one has, to be patient and relaxed, for the sake of both his own life and that of his son. Furthermore, not to be disturbed by worldly competition for material wealth has become the goal he has tried to emulate. But he also created his own slogan, which he reminds himself of from time to time. One volunteer worker at the hospital said to him once, "It is OK to be slow, relaxed, and clumsy." "This word impressed me very much." he says.

It took me some time to really understand what it meant. In order to understand, one has to change one's values by 180 degrees. It's important not to panic [*aseru*]. The Kanji character for *aseru* is written as the mind gets rough, right? Anyone who learns for the first time that illness has occurred in their family member gets panicky. And then, after a while, they become impatient. But if one goes through these stages, he eventually learns to take things easy little by little.... [So I tell myself] "be slow, relaxed, and being clumsy is fine." We all change with time, gradually. For example, when new family members come to see me in panic right after the diagnosis [of mental illness], I first listen to them. When their sick children are getting out of the hospital, then they start to have a lot of expectations for the children, like "I want my child to get a job and...." When they begin to realize that it is not so easy, then they are brought to the awareness that being relaxed about this is the only way to cope with it....

Both Shoko Inose, a mother, and Junko Nomura, sister of a mentally ill patient, say that they are not at all religious, but each expresses the similar idea that all human beings are equal before some larger entity and that everyone deserves respect. This conviction has kept them believing that despite the socially stigmatized handicap, their mentally ill family members deserve justice, respect, and to be treated with integrity.

Defining oneself as someone capable of surviving the tragedy becomes an unshakable support for their self-image, and consequently the source of their strength.

Good health and a stable income to support her family were the backbone of her life, says Yoshimi Naitô, the oldest of 13 siblings. She never married or had her own family. Her life seems to have been spent on financially taking care of her big family after their father died, particularly her sick brother. Yoshimi confesses that there were times she wanted to be freed from the family responsibility. On the other hand, she also feels that even if she had married and had her own family, she might have worried about her brothers and sisters even more. "Probably I would always stop and look back on how my brothers and sisters were doing, which would be more difficult," she says. She sees herself as a kind of person who cannot ignore others in distress. She has been actively involved with a family support group and other activities for the mentally ill as a volunteer. Her friends say that she should not be so busy with work and enjoy herself sometimes. But Yoshimi cannot help it when she is needed, not only by her family, but everyone she knows.

Takashi Ishizawa defines himself as a survivor with nine lives. When he was assigned to work in India and Pakistan, he suffered from many local diseases including dengue fever, malaria, and dysentery. He doesn't even remember how many times he got sick, but he recovered each time. However, nothing was more scary, he recalls, than the intensive air raids during the Indo-Pakistan war. He would run between endless bombs falling from the sky. The German Embassy in his neighborhood was blown up. "I was lucky," he says. But this experience has given him confidence that he will be the strong one in the family in order to make his wife better. He doesn't want his married daughters to be too concerned with their mother. His favorite saying is from a Chinese poem on military tactics, which means "One leader's patience can support the courage of one hundred people." If the top leader is strong enough, the situation can be controlled no matter how many bad things happen. He has been repeating these words to himself whenever he has been in trouble since he lived in Pakistan. The "patience" in this expression, he says, implies "perseverance, prudence, and self-control."

When hitting bottom, there were times when Kay Yamamoto wished she could end her life. She thought she and her son might be better off dead together. But today she feels she was in fact an optimist deep down. She survived the Great Tokyo earthquake in 1923 and the biggest air raid, which annihilated Tokyo during World War II. "But everyone in those days had the same hardship," she says. "I was loved by my parents. I married my husband, and life was good. My son's illness is probably the only worry in my life. Other than that, I have had a happy life. I don't think I was particularly unhappy. I am optimistic."

Faith in a Higher Power

As noted in earlier chapters, some of the interviewees clearly expressed a very strong sense of faith in their religion that was effective in their day-to-day coping. There is no question that their faith has been the greatest source of their strength in years of or even lifelong struggles with their family members' mental illnesses as well. Whichever "God" it may be, the sense of being watched over, tested, and ultimately protected becomes another anchor for the family members to hold onto in their lives during their struggles.

As described earlier, Marianne Schmidt has seen her God as the infinite source of her energy, support, and comfort in dealing with her sister's illness. It enables her to take it a day at a time when things are difficult and get her down.

As much as you want to depend on your husband or your family, your friends, they're only human beings too, and really they are powerless, as I am, in the face of change, whatever it might be. But I have found He has wisdom far beyond mine. He sees the whole situation. He is there with my sister and that brings peace in knowing that He is taking care of her and I don't have to. So that is my source.

For some Christian family members, mental illness is perceived as a test of their faith and strength. Again, it is this definition of their problem that enables them to endure the burden. Gordon Collins says that his marriage was not what he thought it would be in the beginning. He wanted a partnership with his wife, but these days he is overwhelmed by the feeling that he is the one doing it all. But despite the unexpected difficulties in his life with a wife who suffers from bipolar disorder, he believes that God has a plan for him.

Well, God has a grand plan. [We're] not always privy to the grand plan. And he sees me doing what he needs me to do and this is one of the things he needs me to do. He needs me to take care of my little baby and take care of my wife. Without me, they wouldn't be taken care of. They would probably be dead, basically…basically, that's what it is. So, that's what I'm here for. And that's what He says I need to be doing and He's going to help me do it. He talks in subtle ways and I talk directly with Him.

Masashi Ishikawa became a Protestant during his college years. The Christian faith supported him in facing his brother's schizophrenia and dealing with his other family problems. He believes that God would not have presented him with this difficult situation unless he had the capacity to handle it. Therefore, it is his responsibility not to run away from God's assignment and to do his best to take care of the problem. Though the pressure makes him unbearably distressed at times, he hopes to grow as a person and do better for his brother.

Ichizô Ohira also became a Protestant at age 23 when he came down with pleurisy. He thought it was tuberculosis, an incurable disease at the time, before antibiotics were available. His regular prayers to God, as well as the passing of several decades since the beginning of his daughter's illness, have gradually helped ease his pain. "There must be a reason for God to create this situation," Ichizô says gently — he is over 80 years old. He has come to "appreciate everything God has given" him, including the mental illness of his daughter.

Barbara Weiss grew up as an orphan. When she was little and her father died, her mother fell apart and also died of cancer. She was raised in foster care, being separated from her sister. In spite of her terribly deprived early upbringing, Barbara had developed a belief that God and she were one. "I would never have made it, except that I had this relationship with God," she says enthusiastically. "God" for her is Christian, unitary, and nonsectarian. When she was living in a series of foster homes, she became by turns Protestant, Catholic, and Jewish, depending on the foster home she was assigned to. She definitely has her own personal understanding of and her own version of "God." But it doesn't seem to be important, no matter which "God" it is, as it has worked for her all these years. Since she was little she has talked to her God in her mind, has written a note to God just like having a conversation with a secret, imaginary friend in her heart. Barbara made God her best friend, and she was never alone. She also developed a view about death as only a transition for a soul to walk through. There is much more to this life than what we see and it is the same for her mentally ill daughter, Jessica, according to her.

> But, I think that it's impossible that this little soul — this precious, little soul — is only going to have one chance at this thing they call "Life." And, this body could screw it up. You know, I mean, I made a lot of mistakes. I mean, I'd hate to think that this is all there is. You know, there's more than this. So, I mean, I think it's reassuring. And, you know, when I look at my daughter, I think, "It's only one time, Jessica. If this is what your little soul shows your body to make this journey…"

The feeling that we're not alone, but existing with some force beyond our knowledge, is also expressed by many, and they agree that it has consoled them tremendously. Even if they do not belong to a particular religious organization, or cannot articulate their specific faith, many family members interviewed have referred to some spiritual force that they only vaguely feel created this situation and that always watches and protects them in both good and bad times. Most importantly, they have referred to a kind of mysterious feeling that there is some meaning behind what they go through. Although many American family members had been attending church at one point of their lives, this "force" they are now describing is not the God of their church. In fact, many of them even became skeptical of the traditional concept of God in their cultures, especially after their loved one became ill. Instead some simply call it a higher power, sometimes with an eclectic perspective, as Jodi Kramer, a sister, says.

Well, I had this faith in the higher power that there's purpose to life and meaning. There's purpose and meaning. It isn't just all a bunch of junk. There's purpose and meaning and that you each have to find a purpose and meaning. No matter who we are, we're important.

As ambiguous as it may sound, Melanie Wood also feels that some spiritual forces and the awareness of these forces have helped her go through her life as the sister of a mentally ill patient.

I feel that there's more out there perhaps than we can perceive, you know, with our limited perception. Scientists and engineer types and educated people, a lot of times they get very indignant about anything like that, but.... And I was that way before, but there have been plenty of experiences and so much that happened that I can't dismiss something. But then on the other hand, I think, well, why the crazy things happen. So right now, I have a faith and I'm not sure what it's in but I've met so many people and experienced so much. They are wonderful people.

"Fate" or "destiny" was again mentioned by some as a consequence of their spiritual awareness. Kelly Seeman looks back on her stormy life with her adopted son and sometimes thinks "It was just too hard." If she had to do it all over again, she knows she wouldn't take him as her child. Yet, there are times when she feels that there's a quality that it was meant to be.

Maybe I'm fatalistic. Maybe this was ... this was what my life was intended to be about. No, that's not entirely true because being fatalistic implies that you don't have any control over your life. And, I think I allow my emotions to take precedent over a more practical approach to life.

There is no question that, for Haru Morimoto, the existence of her husband was the most precious source of support for dealing with her son's illness. As noted in earlier chapters, quite a few parents of mentally ill patients in Japan turned to new organized religions for comfort. As for Haru, she never liked the idea of joining a formal religion. However, she feels there has been something beyond her control and she was meant to have this son with schizophrenia.

I have had this feeling since I was a child. The feeling that there is something larger than our human existence. I don't know if

I should call it *Kami-sama* [God] or Buddha. But it's something we cannot control. I don't know why I felt this way as a kid, but I still have the same feeling, which might have supported me. I don't like the word *fate* very much, but still I feel I was destined to live this way. There may be something I cannot see and someone who does it. Eventually it boils down to this feeling: I cannot escape from it. So being with my husband and struggling with our son together may have been a part of it, too. Maybe this kind of outlook has helped me. That's why I have come so far no matter how much I cried. Of course, when I was busy crying I couldn't think this way. But once I calmed down later, I always came back to this feeling eventually.

The uncontrollable nature of mental illness has led many to a kind of spiritual awakening. It has also evoked their imagination to construct a different version of reality through transforming the commonplace interpretation of the disaster of mental illness into something uniquely personal and profound. There may be different ways to psychologically analyze why this state of mind can happen to families of the mentally ill. Some may call it a defense mechanism by people who have had too much pain to accommodate within their system. The term *defense mechanism* here implies that religious perspectives only serve as tension reduction, as a form of denial, or are simply passive and avoidant reactions.[2] However, such analysis basically seems futile. In fact, it doesn't seem to matter much as long as such spiritual awakening and creation of personal meanings work to help family members cope with their life better.

Victor E. Frankl, a survivor of the Holocaust, and the founding father of logotherapy, believes that all men have an innate will to search for meaning and it is this "will to meaning" that makes them able to live through even the most dire circumstances.[3] This mental endeavor may add further inner tension to the already existing distress, but it eventually brings us to the awareness that there is a meaning to one's existence. And it is precisely this mechanism that enables the person "to survive even the worst conditions." Frankl declares in *Man's Search for Meaning* that "life is potentially meaningful under any conditions, even those which are most miserable. And this in turn presupposes the human capacity to creatively turn life's negative aspects into something positive or constructive."[4]

Frankl's formulation of this concept is also intimately connected with a deep sense of spirituality. A scene in a concentration camp is poignantly described when he talked to his fellow inmates who were exhausted and on the verge of entirely losing hope and the energy to go on.

Then I spoke of the many opportunities of giving life a meaning. I told my comrades (who lay motionless, although occasionally a sign could be heard) that human life, under any circumstances, never ceases to have a meaning, and that this infinite meaning of life includes suffering and dying, privation and death. I asked the poor creatures who listened to me attentively in the darkness of the hut to face up to the seriousness of our position. They must not lose hope but should keep their courage in the certainty that the hopelessness of our struggle did not detract from its dignity and its meaning. I said that someone looks down on each of us in difficult hours — a friend, a wife, somebody alive or dead, or a God — and he would not expect us to disappoint him. He would hope to find us suffering proudly — not miserably — knowing how to die.[5]

"Someone looks down on each of us in difficult hours" interestingly resonates with the feeling that many family members of the mentally ill come to have through their struggles.

Hope

Finally, what has supported the families is hope. They vaguely anticipate that something good will eventually come out of their struggles. The conviction that their pain, efforts, and hard work will not be wasted. While interviewing, I have heard stories of this terrifying experience of having mental illness in the family forging "the latent, untapped strengths of individuals and families."[6] There is no question that his son's illness provoked Wallace Green to reflect on things that never mattered to him before. It may be tied in with the fact that he is getting older, he says. At times an acute sense of despair attacks him and maybe there is a chronic despair that functions subliminally since he, as a medical doctor himself, knows all about the disease and the prognosis. However, referring to a symbol in the Chinese language for "crisis" as expressed with a character "opportunity," he believes even when a door closes and you're wounded, if you allow it to happen, something else opens. His son's illness changed a lot of his perception on life. "As a result of my son's illness I think I'm becoming a better person," Wallace says. He used to see life as controllable, or was never interested in religion before. But he has been awakened to a sense of spirituality for the first time in his life. He still does not feel completely comfortable with the concept of giving up his control to the higher power, or praying that his son gets stronger, either. But, at the same time, he is vaguely aware that this is the direction in which he is moving. He says,

"It's, I think, a vehicle for me to feel somewhat more peaceful and hopeful about his terrible problem." But when asked what has supported him most, he quickly responded, "[What keeps me going is] hope. Hope that he would get somewhat better. Hope that there will be new medication coming on board that will be cleaner and more refined than the current medication, with less side effects." He truly believes that hope for a better treatment is a realistic future, and, in the meantime, he is determined to give his son as much love and support as he can.

Neither does Maria Hafer consider herself as a particularly religious person. Rather, it was a lot of reading and therapy that gave her insights into life and a rock to hold onto, as well as hope. The hope is not necessarily about her son's illness getting better, but the hope for life itself. The therapy also helped Maria's healthy daughter to cope with life with a mentally ill sibling. What supported Maria through these years is crystallized in her observation about her daughter's change.

> This experience that you're going through can devastate you, it can really mess up your life if you let it. Or you can learn from it, you can become a stronger person. And you can learn to handle all kinds of things from this. And I think that my daughter remembers that and she says that that really helped her. And indeed she may have grown this way anyhow, but she was a shy kid. Not too sure of herself. And she grew to be a real leader.

Masashi Ishikawa believes that at the very end of the hardship, there is hope. He doesn't know what kind of hope it is, but if one sees everything simply as a fate, there is no room for hope, he says. It is difficult for him to link the simple acceptance of fate with strength for coping. His own spiritual faith makes him believe that everything assigned by God eventually leads to his personal growth.

Finally, the hope for someday making her "unfinished business" complete keeps Naoyo Abe going. The "unfinished business" is her son's illness. She wants to see him better and capable of standing on his own. Like most parents of the mentally ill, she is happy to do anything it takes to make that happen. At the same time she knows better than anyone else that there is no real end to her efforts. Nevertheless, she doesn't want to give up this marathon without a goal in sight. "I am still challenging his illness and many other things" she says. "I think everyone in the same situation feels this way. This is what it is like to be the parent of a mentally ill child."

Notes

1. L. E. Lagrand, and T. A. Rand, *Changing Patterns of Human Existence: Assumptions, Beliefs, and Coping with Stress of Change* (Springfield, IL: Charles C. Thomas, 1988).
2. P. I. Kenneth, *The Psychology of Religion and Coping: Theory, Research, Practice* (New York: Guilford, 1997), 163–97.
3. V. E. Frankl, *Man's Search for Meaning* (New York: Washington Square Press, 1984), 126.
4. Ibid., 161.
5. Ibid., 104.
6. H. Gravits, "The Binds That Tie — And Heal: How Families Cope with Mental Illness" in *Annual Editions: The Family 04/05*, ed. K. R. Gilbert (Guilford, CT: McGraw-Hill/Dushkin, 2004), 161.

Epilogue

I launched this project with the intention of describing the sufferings of families in a socially stigmatized condition. Also, as a sociologist interested in cross-cultural comparison, I was particularly anticipating significant cultural differences in the family's experiences in the United States and Japan. There have been, of course, a number of interesting contrasts, which can be attributed to the sociocultural background of these two countries.

For example, Japanese parents, especially mothers, seem to have a stronger propensity to identify themselves with their child's problem and to carry the whole burden themselves. At the time of their deepest despair, they often said they wanted to kill themselves. In addition to the cultural tolerance toward suicide in Japan as explained in an earlier chapter, it may be also understood from the perspective that the social and cultural expectations of being a mother in Japan leave them no choice but to be a selfless, devoted parent when a child has a grave problem. As for the family interaction, there seems to be much less open and direct communication among members of Japanese families, especially between parents and healthy children. As I have presented, the healthy children also need to be protected, strongly supported, and educated about their siblings' illnesses. I am personally doubtful if this secretive approach within the home is in family members' best interests. Japanese culture tends to emphasize nonverbal communication and intuitive understanding of others' feelings. It is often assumed that if people are close, like family members, they do not need to clearly verbalize their wants or needs. However, such an assumption is not helpful in families that are coping with mental illness. With so much confusion and so many unknown factors in dealing with mental illness, husband and wife, parents and children, and brothers and sisters all need more than ever to have more open and honest communication. Furthermore, with regard to the social support that society can provide to families, I find easily available psychological counseling is seriously lacking in Japan. Although in recent years therapy and counseling have drawn more attention, the concepts are unfamiliar to most Japanese, and when faced with unmanageable distress, those who are willing to seek help beyond their primary group opt for spiritual, if not formal religious, counseling. And indeed, many of these services are genuinely helpful. But it is also true that many others have only commercial motives rather than a sincere intention to help others. There were many Japanese family members that I thought would benefit greatly from some kind of psychological counseling, if not necessarily American style individual or group therapy.

Having said this, I would like to point out that my initial curiosity and attempts to find significant cultural differences mostly failed. Despite some differences, which can be attributable to cultural background, the experiences, emotional responses, and consequences of serious mental illness cause the patient's family members to have very similar experiences in both the United States and in Japan. They are confused in the beginning, shocked by the diagnosis, worry about and suffer from various implications and consequences, and are terrified by social stigma in the same ways. I heard families in both countries say that having a mentally ill patient in the family had once made them feel it was absolutely the worst thing in the world. I also heard them say they went through "a living hell" at least once with the patient. They all try to cope in many different ways, and, interestingly, many have touched their sense of faith in something larger than themselves. In fact, I was overwhelmed by the commonality rather than the differences in the families' struggles with mental illness in two countries.

The family is a mysterious entity. Its permanent influence has no equivalent with any other human ties. Still, unlike most relationships, one cannot choose one's family of origin. Once born into a family, one can never cease to live as a member of the family. Of course, as the family passes through different phases, each individual member will develop his or her life apart from the original home. But the awareness of originally being a member of a certain family is never erased from one's consciousness. Having a child with a mental illness is no parent's choice, either. But when it happens, no matter how the parent decides to deal with it (including the decision to have nothing to do with the child), they will always live with the fact that they have a mentally ill son or daughter. The spouses' sufferings cannot be underestimated, either, although they seem to have freer choices than parents or siblings regarding the relationship with the patient. The family they had created was meant to be permanent. If a child arrives, their connection with the mentally ill spouse will be particularly complicated, which makes it extremely difficult to sever the knot. Family members are like a crew sharing a boat and sharing its destiny. Many things can happen to this boat, but mental illness is definitely one of the most profoundly influential matters from which no one on the boat can escape.

From this perspective, I have been especially touched by the stories of the patients' siblings who were often deprived of an ordered home and who have struggled with emotional difficulties for a long time, often quite unaware of the source. Of the people I interviewed, only one case involved the child of a mentally ill patient. Setsuko Kitano, 45, is a Japanese woman whose mother has suffered from schizophrenia for as long as she can remember. Setsuko's childhood was in fact one of the most painful stories I heard. Her mother had constant breakdowns at home, and the stigma was openly and ruthlessly expressed to Setsuko by others, effectively destroying her childhood and adolescence, and even her young adult years, when her engagement was broken off due to the opposition of her fiancé's family. Despite this cross that she had to bear, Setsuko has turned out to be an extremely strong, self-reliant, and capable individual. She has been able to draw necessary help from many people she met in life. But the wounds she suffered are still too evident to be put behind her. I could not help but see the trauma and burdens that she carries are deeply affecting her life today.

These are the hidden or silent voices of the most vulnerable victims of the mental illness in the home. Any discussion of mental illness must include family experiences, and support and psychological care for the families' sufferings must be a part of the picture. These are so badly needed, as mental illness at home is truly a highly "contagious" disease.

Family Members Who Participated in Interviews

The family members interviewed for this study were recruited from respected family support networks in Southern California and Tokyo. The leader/organizer of the network was first contacted and asked to cooperate. The leader/organizer gave the group members the author's letter asking them to participate in the interview. The author also visited several support group meetings and asked for member participation. Many interview participants introduced other family members who they personally knew and thought were appropriate for the study. Therefore, the author does not claim that she interviewed "average" or "typical" families of the mentally ill or that a sample was randomly selected. All the names of participants were changed, and very minor changes with details of their backgrounds were made to conceal their identities. This list contains:

Name used in the book (age at the time of interview)
Patient's name used in the book (age) and relation to the family member
Diagnosis reported by the interviewees
(Approximate number of years since the diagnosis)
Patient's early symptoms noticed by family members

From the United States

Name (age) Family member/patient	Diagnosis (years)	Early symptoms
1. Ken Morris (55)/ Charles (27), son	Schizophrenia (7 years)	College dropout, depression, unable to concentrate, persecutory delusions
2. Wallace Green (63)/ Mike (30), son	Schizophrenia (5 years)	College dropout, delusions (broke TV)
3. Frank Brown (66)/ Don (35), son	Schizophrenia (5 years)	Vocational program dropout, unable to retain jobs, drug addiction
4. Robert Kirk (71)/ Ben (37), son	Schizophrenia (16 years)	Bizarre behaviors, delusions, drug habit, unable to retain jobs
5. Timothy Rosen (74)/ Bruce (35), son	Schizoaffective disorder (17 years)	Drug habit, involved in cult, hallucinations
6. Linda Katz (72)/Rick (49), son	Schizophrenia (29 years)	Volunteered to see a psychiatrist
7. Glenda White (56)/ Shelly (24), daughter	Borderline personality disorder (12 years)	Stealing, school dropout, runaway, self-mutilation
8. Maria Hafer (61)/Jeff (34), son	Schizophrenia (20 years)	Irritability, obsessive-compulsive behavior, unable to eat or talk
9. Kelly Seeman (72)/ Allan (37), son, adopted	Schizophrenia (time of diagnosis unclear)	Various psychological problems since early childhood. High anxiety, hyperactivity, disruptive nature
10. Pat Bryant (57)/Nick (29), son, adopted	Manic depressive (7 years)	Hyperactive as child, drug addiction
11. Nancy Hoffman (70)/Barry (47), son	Schizophrenia (20 years)	Headaches, dizziness, craving for sweets, depression, suicide attempt
12. Rosana Olmos (64)/ Raymond and Andy (both 36), twin sons	Schizophrenia (19 years)	Unable to think clearly. Delusions (microphone in teeth sending messages)

13. Anna Berger (73)/   Schizophrenia (24 years)   Unable to organize.
Stan (43), son   Volunteered to see a
                                                                     psychiatrist

14. Barbara Weiss (75)/   Schizophrenia (22 years)   Drug addiction,
Jessica (48),   hallucinations
daughter

15. Helen Hawkins (71)/   Schizophrenia (20 years)   Persecutory delusions
Dorothy (48),
daughter

16. Ruth Singer (68)/   Manic depressive   Involvement in a cult,
Paul (36), son   (8 years)   unable to work

17. Leland Miller (54)/   Schizophrenia (30 years)   Extremely tense.
Rosalyn (49), sister   Disappearing from
                                                          home

18. Diane Nelson (48)/   Schizophrenia (time of   Anger, drug habit,
Warren (53), brother   diagnosis unclear)   grandiose delusions,
                                                        persecutory delusions

19. Melanie Wood (56)/   Schizophrenia (38 years)   Bizarre behaviors,
Joshua (52), brother   hallucations, paranoia

20. Jane Wilson (45)/   Schizophrenia (more   Aggressive, sexually
Cathy (50), sister   than 25 years)   extravert behaviors,
                                                 Often disappearing from
                                                 home

21. Marianne Schmidt   Schizophrenia   Ran away to other states,
(43)/Emily (40),   (approximately   hallucinations (voices
sister   20 years)   telling her to cut her
                                                        wrists)

22. Jodi Kramer (59)/   Schizophrenia (36 years)   Delusions (TV talking to
Doug (65), brother   him), hostility

23. Gordon Collins   Bipolar II   Unable to work, mood
(50)/Andrea (43),   swings
wife

24. William Baker (58)/   Schizophrenia (9 years)   Bizarre behavior, interest
Martha (45), wife   in a cult, hostile
                                                        language

From Japan

Name (age) Family member/patient	Diagnosis (years)	Early symptoms
1. Osamu Kinoshita (64)/ Noboru (27), son	Schizophrenia (10 years)	School refusal, somatic complaints, avolition, disorganized behaviors, violence at home
2. Kôichi Takagi (61)/ Tamotsu (31), son	Schizophrenia (6 years)	Persecutory delusions, volunteered to see a psychiatrist
3. Tôru Yamaguchi (72)/ Yuri (42), daughter	Manic depression (23 years)	Reluctant to attend college, depression
4. Ichizô Ohira (82)/ Megumi (53), daughter	Schizophrenia (30 years)	Persecutory delusions
5. Kazuo Takenaka (77)/ Shizuka (40), daughter	Schizophrenia (22 years)	Reluctant to go outdoors, persecutory delusions, laughing and crying while alone
6. Tetsuro Isono (68)/ Teru (33), son	Schizophrenia (9 years)	Unable to work, bizarre laugh
7. Yoshiko Takeda (55)/ Emiko (27), daughter	Schizophrenia (5 years)	Bizarre behaviors (following a stranger)
8. Reiko Matsuoka (56)/ Shigeru (22), son	Schizophrenia (6 years)	School refusal, violence at home
9. Kay Yamamoto (81)/ Hiroki (51), son	Schiphrenia (30 years)	Withdrawn, angry, violence at home
10. Miyoko Tajima (65)/ Kenji (40), son	Obsessive-compulsive disorder (20 years)	Violence at home
11. Miki Maeda (65)/ Misa (42), daughter	Obsessive-compulsive disorder	childishness, depression, somatic complaints, school refusal, unable to eat or sleep
12. Satoko Katagiri (58)/ Yosiki (36), son	Schizophrenia (18 years)	Bizarre, impulsive behavior, falling school grades

13. Shoko Inose (62)/ Mamoru (33), son — Schizophrenia (10 years) — Persecutory delusions

14. Nobu Shimada (76)/ Akira (47), Toshio (44), sons — Schizophrenia (both; more than 25 years) — Violence at home, withdrawn

15. Haru Morimoto (74)/ Hitoshi (48), son — Schizophrenia (12 years) — College dropout, unable to work, persecutory delusions (TV reporting about him)

16. Naoyo Abe (77)/ Mikio(47), son — Epilepsy and various neuroses (23 years) — Loses consciousness during seizures

17. Tomoko Uchimura (57)/Kaoru (29), son — Schizophrenia (9 years) — Quit job, headaches and other somatic symptoms

18. Mieko Maruyama (65)/ Yumiko (50), sister, Yôsuke (61), brother — Schizophrenia (both; approximately 25–30 years; caretaker can't recall exact diagnosis or early symptoms because she was living away from home)

19. Junko Nomura (56)/ Chieko (54), sister — Schizophrenia (24 years) — Flattening of emotions, verbal abuse, delusions

20. Yoshimi Naitô (78)/ Mitsuhiro (60), brother — Schizophrenia (33 years) — Bizarre behaviors, uanble to work, runaway

21. Shin Okabe (70)/ Yasuko (64), sister — Schizophrenia (34 years) — Very tense, wandering, verbal hostility

22. Masashi Ichikawa (55)/ Hideo (47), brother — Schizophrenia (approximately 25 years) — The interviewee can't recall early symptoms because he was living away from home

23. Yoko Tomita (43)/ Eiji (42), husband — Schizophrenia (8 years) — Very tense, compulsive hand washing

24. Takashi Ishizawa (66)/ Rieko (64), wife — Schizophrenia (5 years) — Verbally hostile, talks only to herself, unable to take care of herself or do household chores

25. Kôji Yamada (73)/   Schizophrenia (30 years)   Persecutory delusions
    Hitomi (68), wife

26. Setsuko Kitano (45)/   Schizophrenia (more   Since caretaker's early
    Makiko (64), mother   than 40 years)   childhood, mother
                                                       was unable to care for
                                                       her. Mother often did
                                                       not sleep or eat,
                                                       talked to herself

Bibliography

Allpsych online. http://allpsych.com/disorders/mood/index.html

American Psychiatric Association. *Diagnostic and Statistical Manual of Mental Disorders,* 4th ed. rev. Washington, D.C.: American Psychiatric Association, 2000.

Antonovsky, A. *Health, Stress, and Coping.* San Francisco: Jossey-Bass, 1979.

Bella, R. N., R. Madsen, W. M. Sullivan, A. Swidler, and S. M. Tipton. *Habits of the Heart: Individualism and Commitment in American Life.* Berkeley: University of California Press, 1985.

Billings, A. G., and R. H. Moos. "The Role of Coping Responses and Social Resources in Attenuating the Stress of Life Events." *Journal of Behavioral Medicine* 4, no. 2(1981): 139–57.

Black, C. *Changing Course: Healing from Loss, Abandonment, and Fear.* Center City, MN: Hazelden, 1999.

California Association for the Mentally Ill. *The Journey of Hope,* 1997. Leaflet.

Dearth, N., B. J. Labenski, E. M. Mott, and L. M. Pellegrini. Families Helping Families: Living with Schizophrenia. New York: Norton, 1986.

Dixon, L. et al. "Evidence-Based Practices for Services to Family Members of People with Psychiatric Disabilities." Psychiatric Services, 52(2001): 903–10.

Doll, W. "Family Coping with the Mentally Ill: An Unanticipated Problem of Deinstitutionalization." *Hospital and Community Psychiatry,* 27, no. 3(1976): 183–85.

Frankl, V. E. Man's Search for Meaning. New York: Washington Square Press, 1984.

Goffman, E. STIGMA: Notes on the Management of Spoiled Identity. New York: Simon & Schuster, 1963.

Gravits, H. "The Binds That Tie — And Heal: How Families Cope with Mental Illness." In Annual Editions: The Family 04/05, edited by K. R. Gilbert. Guilford, CT: McGraw-Hill/Dushkin, 2004. First published 2001 by Psychology Today, March/April.

Haan, N. Coping and Defending: Processes of Self-Environment Organization. New York: Academic Press; cited by E. G. Menaghan "Individual Coping Efforts: Moderators of the Relationship Between Life Stress and Mental Health Outcomes." In Psychosocial Stress: Trends in Theory and Research., edited by H. Kaplan, 157–191. New York: Academic Press, 1977.

Hatfield, A. B. "Commentary. Therapists and Families: Worlds Apart." *Hospital and Community Psychiatry* 33, no. 7(1982): 513.

——— "Coping and Adaptation: A Conceptual Framework for Understanding." In *Families of the Mentally Ill: Coping and Adaptation,* edited by A. B. Hatfield and H. P. Lefley, 60–84. New York: Guilford, 1987.

——— "Family as Caregivers: Historical Perspective." In *Families of the Mentally Ill: Coping and Adaptation,* edited by A. B. Hatfield and H. P. Lefley, 3–29. New York: Guilford, 1987.

——— H. P. Lefley. *Surviving Mental Illness: Stress, Coping, and Adaptation.* New York: Guilford, 1993.

Hawley, D. R., and L. DeHaan. "Toward a Definition of Family Resilience, Integrating Life-Span and Family Perspectives."*Family Process,* 35(1996): 283–98.

Herz, M. I., and S. R. Marder. *Schizophrenia: Comprehensive Treatment and Management.* Philadelphia: Lippincott Williams & Wilkins, 2002.

Ito, Y. Director of "Harakara no Ie" Welfare Association. Public Lecture given at Tokyo Health Center, February 6, 2004.

Johnson, D. L. "The Family's Experience of Living with Mental Illness." In *Families as Allies in Treatment of the Mentally Ill: New Directions for Mental Health Professionals,* edited by H. P. Lefley and D. L. Johnson, 31–63. Washington, D.C.: American Psychiatric Association, 1990.

Johnson, J. T. *Hidden Victims, Hidden Healers.* Edina, MN: PEMA, 1994.

Kawanishi, Y. "The Effects of Culture on Beliefs about Stress and Coping: Causal Attribution of Anglo-American and Japanese Persons." *Journal of Contemporary Psychotherapy,* 25, no. 1(1995): 49–60.

Kobasa, S. C., S. R. Maddi, and S. Courington. "Personality and Constitution as Mediators in the Stress-Illness Relationship." *Journal of Health and Social Behavior,* 22(1981): 368–78.

Kuipers, L., J. Leff, and D. Lam. *Family Work for Schizophrenia: A Practical Guide.* London: Gaskell, 1992.

Lagrand, L. E., and T. A. Rand. *Changing Patterns of Human Existence: Assumptions, Beliefs, and Coping with Stress of Change.* Springfield, IL: Charles C. Thomas, 1988.

Lamb, R. H. "Commentary to Chapter 1." In *Families as Allies inTreatment of the Mentally Ill: New Directions for Mental Health Professionals,* edited by H. P. Lefley and D. L. Johnson, 23–29. Washington, D.C.: American Psychiatric Association, 1990.

Lefley, H. P. "Culture and Mental Illness: The Family Role." In *Families of the Mentally Ill: Coping and Adaptation,* edited by A. B. Hatfield and H. P. Lefley, 30–59. New York: Guilford, 1987.

Leff, J., and C. Vaughn. *Expressed Emotion in Families: Its Significance for Mental Illness.* New York: Guilford, 1985.

Lukens, E. P., and W. MacFarlane. "Families, Social Networks, and Schizophrenia." In *Multifamily Groups in the Treatment of Severe Psychiatric Disorders,* edited by W. McFarlane, 18–35. New York: Guilford, 2000.

Mainichi Shimbun (Mainichi Newspaper). "Futookoo Saita 139,000 (School Non-Attendance Record High, 139,000)," August 10, 2000.

McFarlane, W. R. *Multifamily Groups in the Treatment of Severe Psychiatric Disorders.* New York: Guilford, 2002.

Mueser, K. T., and S. R. McGurk. "Schizophrenia." *Lancet,* 363(2004): 263–72.

National Alliance for the Mentally Ill (NAMI). California website http://www.namicalifornia.org/

Nichols, M. P., and R. C. Schwartz. *Family Therapy; Concepts and Methods.* 5th ed. Boston: Allyn & Bacon, 2001.

Oshima, I., and K. Nakai. "The Japanese Mental Health System and Family Movement: History, Present Status, and Research Findings." In *Innovations in Japanese Mental Health Services,* edited by J. M. Mandiberg, 13–23. San Francisco: Jossey-Bass, 1993.

Pargament, K. I. *The Psychology of Religion and Coping: Theory, Research, Practice.* New York: Guilford, 1997.

Pearlin, L. "The Sociological Study of Stress." *Journal of Health and Social Behavior,* 30(1989): 241–50.

Pearlin, L., and C. Schooler. "The Structure of Coping." *Journal of Health and Social Behavior,* 19(1978): 2–12.

Strang, S., and P. Strang. "Spiritual Thought, Coping and 'Sense of Coherence' in Brain Tumour Patients and Their Spouses." *Palliative Medicine* 15(2001): 127–34.

Szasz, T. *Ideology and Insanity.* Garden City, NY: Anchor Books, 1970.

Takizawa, T. *Kokoro no yamai to kazoku no kokoro* (in Japanese; Mental Illness and the Psychology of the Family). Tokyo: Chuo Hoki, 1993.

Terkelsen, K. G. "Schizophrenia and the Family: II. Adverse Effects of Family Therapy." *Family Process,* 22(1983): 191–200.

———. "The Evolution of Family Responses to Mental Illness through Time." In *Families of the Mentally Ill: Coping and Adaptation,* edited by A. B. Hatfield and H. P. Lefley, 151–66. New York: Guilford, 1987.

———— "Chapter 1. A Historical Perspective on Family-Provider Relationships." In *Families as Allies in Treatment of the Mentally Ill: New Directions for Mental Health Professionals*, edited by H. P. Lefley and D. L. Johnson, 9–21. Washington, D.C.: American Psychiatric Association, 1990.

Torrey, E. F. *Surviving Schizophrenia*. New York: Quill, 2001.

Weiss, L. G., and L. E. Lonnquist. *Sociology of Health, Healing, and Illness*. Saddle River, NJ: Prentice-Hall, 1994.

White, J. M., and D. Klein. *Family Theories*. Thousand Oaks, CA: Sage, 2002.

Wills, T. A. "Help-Seeking as a Coping Mechanism." In *Coping with Negative Life Events: Clinical and Social Psychological Perspectives*, edited by C. R. Snyder and Carol E. Ford, 19–50. New York: Plenum Press, 1981.

Winton, C. A. *Frameworks for Studying Families*. Guilford, CT: Dushkin, 1995.

Wright, L. M. "Suffering and Spirituality. The Soul of Clinical Work with Families." *Journal of Family Nursing*, 3(1997): 3–14.

Index

A

Abrupt onset of mental illness, perceptions of, 28–30

Acceptance of mental illness. *See also* Stigmatization of mental illness
as coping mechanism, 163–165, 175, 177–181
by family members, 61–65
in Japan, 7–12
in United States, 3–6, 61–65

Adjustment problems of mentally ill patients, parents' perceptions of, 22–26

Adopted children, mental illness in, abandonment seen as factor, 125–129

Aging, schizophrenia and role of, 140–141

Al-Anon, as family support network, 163, 170, 187

Alternative techniques, families' attraction to, 45–46

Altruism, as coping mechanism, 166–168

Anger of family members
during hospitalization of patient, 50–51
as response to mental illness, 40–43
siblings' resentment of parents, 63–65

Antipsychiatry theory, 123–124

Antipsychotics, for schizophrenia, 59–65

Attention replacement, as coping strategy for family members, 158–159

Audio perception, in schizophrenia, 21–22

Autoimmune disease, schizophrenia linked to, 123

Avolition, in schizophrenia, 120–121

B

Behavioral patterns
enabling behaviors of parents, 103–110
protective behaviors of siblings, 98–110
separation of, from patients' personalities, 141–143
as sign of illness, 26–28

Belief systems about mental illness. *See also* Cultural attitudes toward mental illness; Spirituality
daily impressions of family members and construction of, 116–121
as survival of mechanism, 196–200

Biological causes of mental illness, 123

Bipolar disorders, diagnosis of, 47–48

Birth complications, schizophrenia linked to, 123

Black, Claudia, 96

Borderline personality disorder
diagnosis of, 46–47
of marital partners, 73–75

Buddhism
rituals of, as coping strategy, 159
spiritual causes of mental illness linked to, 132–133, 150
survival skills rooted in, 197–200, 204–205

C

Caregivers
active/inactive roles, for spouses, 79–81
extended family members as, 94–95